A Taste of Ohio History

John F. Blair, Publisher

Winston-Salem, North Carolina

A TASTE OF
OHIO HISTORY

A Guide to
Historic Eateries
and Their Recipes

DEBBIE NUNLEY & KAREN JANE ELLIOTT

Published by John F. Blair, Publisher

*The paper in this book meets the guidelines
for permanence and durability of the
Committee on Production Guidelines for
Book Longevity of the Council on Library Resources.*

ON THE FRONT COVER, CLOCKWISE FROM THE TOP—
*The Clifton Mill in Clifton, Peerless Mill Inn in Miamisburg,
and The Precinct in Cincinnati*

Library of Congress Cataloging-in-Publication Data

Nunley, Debbie.
A taste of Ohio history : a guide to historic eateries and their
recipes / Debbie Nunley & Karen Jane Elliott.
p.   cm.
Includes indexes.
ISBN 0-89587-245-5 (alk. paper)
1. Cookery. 2. Restaurants—Ohio—Guidebooks. 3. Historic
buildings—Ohio. I. Elliott, Karen Jane, 1958– II. Title.

TX714.N84 2001
647.95771—dc21
2001043473

Design by Debra Long Hampton

To my daughter, Dori, whose infinite support, patience,
and understanding far exceed her years
Debbie

To my parents, John and Ann Lidiard, who taught me to be a strong,
independent woman, and who have been telling me to "write a book" for years
Karen

Contents

1. Clay Haus
2. Main Street Bistro
3. Rossilli's GreenTree Tavern
4. Casa Capelli Restaurant & Lounge
5. The Hammel House Inn
6. The Brass Pig Eatery
7. Sojourner Café
8. Pufferbelly Ltd.
9. Iron Horse Inn
10. The Dennison Depot Canteen Restaurant at The Dennison Railroad Depot Museum
11. The Pufferbelly Restaurant
12. Schmidt's Restaurant und Sausage Haus
13. Clementine's
14. Hoster Brewing Co.
15. Willoughby Brewing Co.
16. Mancy's Steaks
17. That Place on Bellflower
18. Club Isabella
19. Benders Tavern
20. Court Street Grill
21. The Heritage Restaurant
22. Arnold's Bar & Grill
23. Mecklenburg Gardens
24. Grand Finale
25. The Zoar Tavern & Inn
26. Great Lakes Brewing Co.
27. The Clifton Mill
28. Stockport Mill Country Inn
29. Jay's Restaurant
30. Peerless Mill Inn
31. Goshen's Mill Street Tavern
32. Old Mill Winery
33. Pioneer Mill of Tiffin
34. The Refectory
35. Engine House No. 5
36. Olde Jaol Brewing Company
37. The Precinct
38. Teller's of Hyde Park
39. The Phoenix
40. Clough Crossings
41. The Schoolhouse Restaurant
42. Smedlap's Smithy Restaurant
43. Old Warehouse Restaurant at Roscoe Village
44. The Levee House Café
45. Elevator Brewery and Draught Haus
46. Coldwater Café
47. La Canard Fortunato
48. The Brown Jug Restaurant
49. Schlegel's Coffee House
50. Biddie's Coach House
51. Angel of the Garden Tearoom
52. Twin Creek Tea Room
53. Olde World B & B and Tea Room
54. Swan House
55. His Majesty's Tea Room
56. Tapestry & Tales
57. The Morgan House Restaurant
58. The Inn at Cedar Falls
59. The Cabin
60. Cowger House #9
61. The Cabin Restaurant at Mario's International Spa & Hotel
62. Lake White Club
63. Ye Olde Trail Tavern
64. Klosterman's Derr Road Inn
65. Bellfair Country Store
66. Bluebird Farm Restaurant
67. The Granary at Pine Tree Barn
68. Homestead Inn Restaurant
69. The Sawyer House
70. Murphin Ridge Iinn
71. Barn Restaurant at Historic Sauder Village
72. The Barn at Walden
73. Spread Eagle Tavern
74. Emmitt House
75. The Old Tavern
76. Rider's 1812 Inn
77. Don's Pomeroy House
78. Dante's Pizza & Pasta House
79. Brandywine Inn
80. Chester's Road House
81. Seven Stars at the Worthington Inn
82. The Buxton Inn
83. The Forum Grill at The Vernon Manor Hotel
84. The Golden Lamb
85. Columbian House
86. GunRoom Restaurant at The Lafayette
87. Shaw's Restaurant & Inn
88. Hotel Millersburg
89. Maumee Bay Brewing Co.
90. The Howard House Restaurant
91. English Ivy Restaurant
92. Great Expectations
93. The Candlelight on Center Street
94. The Davenport House
95. Lenhardt's
96. Java Supreme
97. The Garden Restaurant
98. Allisten Manor
99. The Oaks Lodge

Restaurants Featured in *A Taste of Ohio History*

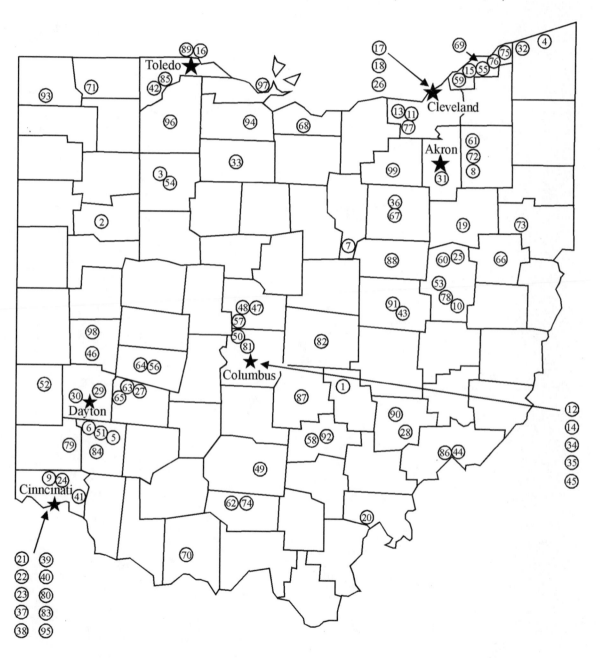

Preface

Our love of historic restaurants began who knows when. From earliest childhood memories, we both recall being fascinated by them. We began sharing the experience in 1993, shortly after we both moved to the northern suburbs of Pittsburgh. Going to historic restaurants was a method of getting to know yet another new area, after a series of moves. We were active volunteers at the elementary school our children attended, and word quickly got out that we had these wonderful luncheon adventures. Soon, we had a group of ladies who shared the joy of discovering wonderful relics. Over lunch, in an atmosphere steeped in history, these women became some of our dearest friends.

The restaurants that are of the most inter-est to us really fit into two categories. The first are longstanding inns, taverns, and the like that have been in business in the same locale for a significant period of time. In these, we look for historical integrity inside and out. In other words, we want them to look as if George Washington, Abe Lincoln, or some other famous personage might walk in any minute. The second type includes restaurants housed in historic buildings such as schools, churches, barns, and train stations. In these locales, the portion of the building that is old or original varies, as conversions from one use to another have necessitated some changes, and modern building codes have dictated others. The exteriors have changed very little, so each is quite recognizable as what it once was. Buildings that once served as stores have probably changed the most inside, although the long, narrow rooms are unmistakable. Since stores are defined more by the wares they've carried than their architectural features, this isn't surprising.

Our focus is on buildings that are more than one hundred years old, although on occasion we consider locations slightly younger than that if the history is of particular significance to the area. As we compile our initial list for consideration, we read absolutely everything we can. Typically, this starts with an Internet search for restaurants with their own web sites. Frequently, it also involves going through the yellow pages town by town, county by county, looking for names of restaurants that "sound historic." Because we try to represent each state thoroughly, we contact convention and visitors' bureaus and chambers of commerce for any literature they might have. This usually gives us additional information, as well as confirming our Internet resources. As we begin our travels, the gathering of information continues, as we pick up local fliers, seek personal recommendations, and drive the back roads in search of a "find."

As we compiled a list of close to five hundred Ohio restaurants, we knew from experience that some of them wouldn't have maintained their historical features. Others would want to participate but would never quite get around to it. A few would think that sending us the recipes and history just wasn't worth the effort. The very few that choose not to participate for this reason always sadden us, because invariably they're fabulous places full of interesting facts that we wish we could share.

Alas, in about three hundred pages, we can't begin to include every eatery anyway. Our goal is to be as thorough as possible in representing cuisine, price points, types of establishments, and historical information, while comprehensively and appropriately representing the cities and counties across the state. In more ways than one, our books truly are *A Taste of . . .*

Our favorite part of the research continues to be meeting and talking to the people involved with the restaurants. Their stories are intricately woven into the fascinating history of each locale. As always, there were certain aspects of local history we expected to learn, such as those involving prominent families and their lovely homes. We were thrilled to find Underground Railroad locations and to learn how significant Ohio was to the cause. Other stories took us quite by surprise, and we hope you find them equally enlightening.

As in our previous book, we organized the restaurants into chapters based on what they have in common. The cohesive thread in each reflects a slice of Americana that still exists throughout the state. Thriving Main Streets, farmsteads, and log cabins all provided inspiration for chapters, as did the Underground Railroad. We've started the book with a chapter called "Main Street, USA," because in small towns across the heartland, what could be more appropriate? In this chapter, you'll find an establishment from the Underground Railroad. Helping slaves to freedom was so pervasive within this town that it was mainstream on Main Street!

Within each chapter, we have listed the eateries in the order visited. The one exception is the travel chapter, "How Do I Get There from Here?" where we've arranged them by mode of conveyance, and within each mode by the order in which we visited. We've used pen-and-ink drawings to introduce each chapter. Each restaurant is represented by its own logo, giving the write-up its own unique heading.

Now that our second book is completed, we continue to be amazed and thankful that so much history has been saved. Sometimes as we travel, we have difficulty telling exactly where we are as we drive past one megastore and chain establishment after another. While we accept that they serve a purpose and have a place in our economy and our lives, we lament the stories, history, and culture lost as independent businesses struggle to survive. We salute the warm, wonderful people throughout Ohio whom we've gotten to know, and hope that their stories, and this book, will in some way encourage others to take on the challenges and rewards of maintaining their local history.

Acknowledgments

We would like to thank the many, many people at the chambers of commerce, the convention and visitors' bureaus, and other local agencies throughout Ohio. Special recognition goes to Catherine Howard, Amy Rutledge, Melissa Childs, Karin Johnson, Theresa Carper, Pat Ellis, Gail Renfro, Karen Lenehan, Mindy Feikert, Melissa Reuther, Linda Basye, Christina Thrasher, Cathy McPommel, and Alan Raney for their guidance and their enthusiasm. They all went above and beyond the call of duty in helping us feature their individual areas. A big thank-you also goes to all those people who called us to make suggestions, especially Dorothy Crabtree and Tom Watson, and to the editors of the *Logan Daily News*, who searched their archives for information.

I would like to extend my personal gratitude to the Hillenbrand, Seltz, Boretzky, Mapel, and Casey families for their help and support throughout this book. Without their generosity, completion of this project would not have been possible. I hope they all know how much I appreciate their opening their homes to Dori, and how truly grateful I am for their friendship.

Debbie

I will be forever grateful to my husband, Gordon, and my children, Singen and Cherith, for their support, help, and unflagging devotion, especially during those weeks I was not at home to be friend, mother, taxi driver, and chief cook and bottle washer, when they all had to make do or do without!

Karen

CHAPTER 1

Main Street, USA

The Hammel House Inn

Long the center of commerce and community activity throughout
America, Main Street is not just a location but a term that has become
synonymous with a down-home atmosphere. As society has changed,
many Main Streets have struggled to survive. This chapter celebrates those
establishments, and those cities, for which Main Street is still going strong!

Clay Haus

123 WEST MAIN STREET
SOMERSET, OH 43783
740-743-1326

Owner Betty Snider is a direct descendant of one of the voyagers on the *Mayflower*. Maybe that kind of lineage explains her love of history, artifacts, and old implements. She and her husband, Carl, opened Clay Haus in 1979 at Betty's insistence. Today, her son, Scott, and one of her grandsons are actively involved in the business. The restaurant was named for her father, Irwin Clay Priest. The spelling of *Haus* honors this area of German settlement and her husband's Pennsylvania Dutch heritage.

As we browsed the old pictures along the walls, including many of family ancestors, we were particularly drawn to the one of the statue dedication in the town square. Ladies in their long dresses and fanciest hats and gentlemen in their best attire had gathered en masse for this civic celebration. Today, this area of Somerset, with a large flag flying over the likeness of Civil War general Philip Sheridan, still looks almost identical to what is in that photo.

That square, just a block down the street from Clay Haus, used to be the hunting area for George Jackson. Clay Haus sits along what was once Zane Trace, the first major roadway through Ohio. At the time Jackson owned the building, the downstairs Keeping Room was at street level, but resurfacing through the years has raised the roadbed about five feet. It was in this room that George Jackson enjoyed a meal of venison and wild turkey that he'd caught while hunting with his cousin, President Andrew Jackson.

We were seated by the fireplace in the upstairs dining room. It was a treat after driving through the sleet on a January day. The cozy room had antique pictures and farm implements adorning the walls. Original random plank flooring, lace curtains, and a wedding-ring quilt all enhanced the quaint atmosphere.

The food was as comforting as the atmosphere. Lunch choices included a BLT and a Barbecue Beef Sandwich. Side dishes such as German Potato Salad, Three Bean Salad, and Marinated Carrot Salad are all popular choices. Debbie chose a traditional plate lunch of Meat Loaf, Mashed Potatoes, and Green Beans, which really hit the spot. The Meat Loaf was a full inch thick, reminiscent of Grandma's. Karen also went traditional, enjoying a bowl of Bean Soup with a Pennsylvania Dutch flair—dumplings. It came with a large wedge of Cornbread that had just been cooked in a large cast-iron skillet. With heartland cooking like this, we certainly weren't going to skip dessert, particularly after we discovered that Betty does the baking herself. Karen's Cream Puff was full of whipped cream and topped with Chocolate Sauce. Debbie's Walnut Pie was a delicious kin to Pecan Pie.

We truly enjoyed chatting with Betty and Scott Snider and learning about their life with the restaurant. We heard lots about their ghost, Mariah, whom Scott once saw waving at the kitchen door and Betty once mistook for one of her employees. Male ghosts have also been spotted, particularly on the stairs. As usual, we left without meeting any of them. Maybe next time.

GERMAN POTATO SALAD

6 large potatoes
½ pound (8 to 10 slices) bacon
½ cup onions, chopped
1 cup vinegar
2 cups water
1 tablespoon salt
1 teaspoon pepper
1 cup brown sugar
1 to 2 tablespoons flour, if needed

Peel and slice potatoes. Boil in a large pot of water until soft but not mushy. Drain. Brown bacon and onions in skillet until bacon is crisp. (Don't worry if bacon gets dark; this enhances the flavor.) Combine vinegar and water and add to skillet. Add salt, pepper, and brown sugar. Bring to a boil to thicken. If you need to thicken the liquid further, combine flour with about 1 tablespoon water and stir into skillet. Put potato slices in a large bowl.

Toss with salt and pepper if desired. Add hot dressing from skillet, stirring gently. Serve warm. Serves 8 to 10.

SAUERBRATEN

3- to 4-pound chuck roast
½ cup pearl onions
¾ cup celery, chunked
¾ cup carrots, chunked
½ cup vinegar
1 cup red wine
1 cup water
½ cup brown sugar
½ cup gingersnaps, crushed
1 tablespoon salt
1 tablespoon peppercorns
½ tablespoon allspice
1 bay leaf
½ to 1 cup sour cream, as desired

Place chuck roast in a roasting pan. Put all remaining ingredients except sour cream in roaster with the roast. Cook at 350 degrees about 2 to 3 hours until roast is tender. Remove from oven. Take roast and vegetables out of broth. Stir in sour cream. If mixture is too thin, stir in additional crushed gingersnaps to thicken to a gravy consistency. Slice roast. Serve on a large platter with vegetables. Drizzle gravy over top; serve remaining gravy in a gravy boat. Serves 8 to 10.

213-217 SOUTH MAIN STREET
LIMA, OH 45801
419-224-0473

No one is exactly sure when the first building was erected on lot 93 at 213 South Main Street. It is estimated that a modest house was constructed here between 1837 and 1847. By 1887, the Sanborn Fire Insurance maps showed a small dwelling. In 1888, Dr. Charles Metzger occupied the building. He had been a first lieutenant for the 125th Ohio Volunteer Infantry Regiment, which saw action in the Civil War. Now a successful physician and surgeon, he lived in 213 and set up his practice in 215. It was during his tenure that the building took its present form.

In 1907, Charles Metzger's wife, Clara, sold the property—which now consisted of 213, 215, and 217—to The Lima Home Baking Company. One of the new owners, a Mr. Frank Colucci, was a very successful businessman. An Italian immigrant, Colucci had started his career in the employment of the Baltimore & Ohio Railroad Company. He had moved progressively upward on a succession of railroad construction projects across the country. He was reputed to have an "excellent business ca-

pacity and judgement." Indeed, by the time he purchased the building outright in 1912, he was a stockholder and director of the American Bank of Lima. He also owned a real-estate company, which he operated out of his Main Street property.

Over the next seventy years, the three addresses that comprise the Main Street Bistro housed a hatchery, a music instrument store, a furniture store, a bar, apartments, and a used clothing store. The property looks much the same today as it did during the 1800s, a beautiful two-story brick building with a small turret at the center and tall sash windows on the second floor, surmounted by wrought-iron balustrades.

The inside of this Victorian building has been restored to much of its original splendor. The current owners have built archways into the exposed-brick walls to connect the three rooms on the first floor. The original plank floors are still there, as is the tiled entranceway to the bar area. Victorian chandeliers and wall sconces enhance the ambiance. The two dining rooms have a definite bistro flavor, with brown paper laid over white linen tablecloths. An interesting collection of cartoons about the food served here hangs on the walls. In the bar area, we were delighted by the collection of black-and-white photographs of many of the oldest buildings in Lima.

On the day we visited, executive chef Alisa McPheron Kujawa had prepared a selection of dishes for us to sample. We began with the Chicken Gumbo, which was spicy and delicious. The Crawfish Cakes were equally good, served with a side of Tomato Corn Relish. Debbie particularly enjoyed the Crispelli, a stuffed-crepe creation served with Roasted Red Pepper Cream Sauce. We also sampled Gambari, which consisted of Pan-Roasted Prosciutto-Wrapped Shrimp together with Balsamic Caramelized Onions, and the Jumbo Deep-Fried Cheese Ravioli, both of which were good. Dessert is always Karen's favorite. Although the Tiramisu was wonderful, the Chocolate Truffle Cake won the day. Not too rich, it was definitely melt-in-the-mouth good.

CRAWFISH CAKES

1 small red onion, diced fine
½ green pepper, diced fine
½ yellow pepper, diced fine
1 pound crawfish tail meat, cooked and diced
¼ cup thick mayonnaise
1 small egg, beaten
1 tablespoon Old Bay seasoning
2 to 3 cups breadcrumbs
2 tablespoons vegetable oil
½ cup Lemon Cream Sauce (see next column)

In a medium skillet over medium heat, cook onions and peppers until onions are translucent. Place in a large bowl and set aside to cool. When cool, add crawfish, mayonnaise, and beaten egg and combine thoroughly. Add seasoning and half the breadcrumbs and combine. Slowly add enough breadcrumbs to bind mixture together. Separate mixture into 8 equal balls. Form each into a patty and roll in remaining breadcrumbs to coat. Place patties in the refrigerator and chill for at least 30 minutes.

Heat oil in a skillet over medium heat. Sear patties and cook for 2 to 3 minutes on each side. Serve hot with Lemon Cream Sauce. Serves 4.

LEMON CREAM SAUCE

3 cups heavy cream
pinch of salt
pinch of pepper
2 teaspoons lemon zest
juice of ½ lemon
1 tablespoon fresh parsley, chopped

Heat cream in a saucepan on high. Add salt, pepper, lemon zest, and juice. Cook until thickened. Finish with chopped parsley. Yields 2 cups.

GreenTree
~Tavern~

201 SOUTH MAIN STREET
FINDLAY, OH 45840
419-423-5050

When we first started writing, neither of us was particularly fond of Crème Brûlée. Gradually, we developed a taste for this dessert, until suddenly, one evening, we tasted the Crème Brûlée at the GreenTree Tavern. Pure and simple, it was the best either of us had ever eaten. Chef Gary Rossilli also sent out a square of Tiramisu, one of Karen's all-time favorites, which we thoroughly enjoyed.

Gary was very generous in letting us sample, and the people at the table nearby were somewhat affronted when three wait staff laden with plates and platters descended on us. We started with the Crab and Spinach Cannelloni in Lemon-Dill Sauce, which was fabulous. That was quickly followed by tasty portions of Smoked Chicken Ravioli, Focaccia, Homemade Italian Sausage, Blackened Meat Loaf, and Wild Mushroom Pesto Bruschetta with fresh mozzarella. Talk about gastronomic delights! The Italian Sausage is still made from a family recipe, which Gary's dad developed and sold in his Cleveland grocery store. He used to travel to the restaurant to make it for Gary but finally decided that Gary was accomplished enough in the kitchen to make it for himself. The Meat Loaf, served with Garlic Mashed Potatoes and topped with Sherry Molasses Sauce, is the most popular item on the menu, and we could certainly see why.

Gary, his wife, Meg, and Meg's brother, Mike, own the restaurant. They're an enthusiastic bunch who were all doing very different things in 1994 when they decided to get into the restaurant business. Mike was in Florida working at a chain restaurant, Gary was a plumber, and Meg was working for a locksmith. They'd grown up in the building's heyday, knowing that when their parents went out for the evening, they were going to "The Fort"—The Fort Findlay Motor Inn, a very popular hotel, bar, and restaurant during the 1960s, 1970s, and 1980s, when Marathon Oil had its headquarters here in Findlay. Constructed in 1840 as the GreenTree Inn, the building originally served as overnight accommodations for stagecoach travelers on the route between Cincinnati and Detroit. In 1880, it became the Sherman House, a name that Emil Petti revived when he purchased the property in 1987. It was from him that the Rossilli clan took over.

At the back of the main dining room is a lovely antique piece left by Mr. Petti. It was once used in the movie *The Unsinkable Molly Brown*. The porcelain inserts, woodwork beading, and other Victorian details are lovely. We rushed home, rented the movie, and, sure enough, there it was. Considering the terrific items on the menu and the friendliness of the Rossillis, we think they're unsinkable, too.

ROASTED RED PEPPER VINAIGRETTE

3 large red peppers, roasted, peeled, and seeded
1 cup rice wine vinegar
1 tablespoon Dijon mustard
1 teaspoon dry mustard
2 cups olive oil
salt and freshly ground pepper to taste

In a blender, combine peppers, vinegar, and mustards. Purée. Put mixture into a bowl and slowly whisk in olive oil until mixture is emulsified. Add salt and pepper. Yields approximately 4 cups.

FLORENTINE MASHED POTATOES

5 pounds Yukon Gold or red-skin potatoes, skin on
16-ounce box frozen chopped spinach, thawed
1½ cups mozzarella cheese, shredded
½ cup Parmesan, grated
4 sticks butter, cubed
1/3 cup heavy cream
salt and pepper to taste

Dice potatoes into medium-sized cubes. Place potatoes in a large pot and cover with at least 4 inches of cold water. Bring to a boil and cook until potatoes are tender but not falling apart. Drain and place in a mixing bowl. While potatoes are cooking, thoroughly squeeze all of the liquid from the spinach. Add ½ of the spinach to the potatoes, along with ½ of the cheeses, ½ of the butter, all of the cream, and salt and pepper. Combine using an electric mixer. Add remaining spinach, butter, and cheese. Blend mixture until thoroughly combined. Yields 10 to 12 generous servings.

CALAMATA OLIVE SPREAD

1 cup garlic cloves, peeled
1 tablespoon olive oil
2 cups calamata olives, pitted
¾ cup extravirgin olive oil
½ cup sun-dried tomatoes, chopped coarse

Preheat oven to 350 degrees. Place garlic cloves on a piece of foil and drizzle with 1 tablespoon olive oil. Ball up foil and bake for 15 minutes until garlic is soft and golden. In a food processor, combine garlic and olives; continue to process while drizzling in extravirgin olive oil. Remove mixture from processor, place in a small bowl, and stir in sun-dried tomatoes. Yields 3 cups.

CASA CAPELLI

GREAT FOOD
CHOICES
&
SPIRITS

4641 MAIN AVENUE
ASHTABULA, OH 44004
440-992-3700

In 1847, a petition was filed with the Ohio General Assembly at Columbus requesting authority to form a bank in Ashtabula. In due time, the petition was granted, and The Farmer's Bank of Ashtabula opened. The original offices were located above George Hubbard's hardware store, on the second floor of the wooden building directly across the street from the present bank. It's easy to imagine the excitement in the village when four horses pulling a huge coach along the dirt roads arrived with the first shipment of silver and gold bullion and bank notes. The Farmer's Bank operated as a state bank until the end of the Civil War. The shareholders petitioned for and were issued a national-bank charter in 1865.

The bank occupied several other buildings in town until 1904, when it moved to 4641 Main Avenue. Constructed just one year earlier, the building was an elegant home for the rapidly expanding bank. Ornate Corinthian columns stood on both sides of the main lobby, surmounted by a barrel ceiling with a gorgeous arched stained-glass skylight. Over the ensuing decades, the bank and its shareholders stood at the forefront of convenience and comfort for both staff and customer alike. There are many newspaper articles about the comfort of the staff's chairs and the new Formica counters, reputed to be the finest of their kind. The two vaults featured the most up-to-date safety measures. Each required the pouring of sixty-one cubic yards of concrete, since the walls were to be eighteen inches thick and re-inforced with steel bars. Each vault door was more than a foot wide, stood seven feet high, and weighed more than fourteen thousand pounds. As an added safety precaution, the bank directors insisted that a vault ventilation system be installed.

Today, visitors will discover that few changes have taken place. The walls are now painted a delicate lavender and are paneled with green marble, but the columns and barrel ceiling still exist. There are four enormous crystal-and-brass chandeliers overhead, two of which rotate. Guests may actually dine inside one of the bank vaults. Here and there amongst the profusion of fig trees and hanging plants are relics of the building's history. There are old deposit bags, checks, and even photographs and newspaper clippings to examine.

Oscar and Alexandra Tomasio are delightful. They encouraged us to sample many of the delicious items on the Italian-Mexican menu. The salad dressings and salsas are all home-made here. We tried the Mild Salsa with fresh-baked Tortilla Chips. It was very good indeed.

Our families echoed this when we brought a couple of jars home with us. We also sampled the Langostinos Alexandra, the Marinara Calamari, and the Pollo de la Casa, all of which were tasty and beautifully presented. Karen, a huge Tiramisu fan, was very tempted by the Tiramisu with Kahlua but was persuaded to try the Apple Chimichanga instead. Served with a scoop of Vanilla Ice Cream and Caramel Syrup, it was fabulous. As the menu states, *"Mi Casa es su Casa."* Casa Capelli is most definitely a home away from home!

LANGOSTINOS ALEXANDRA

1 pound angel hair pasta
1 cup butter, melted
1 cup lemon juice
3 tablespoons Parmesan, grated
1 tablespoon fresh garlic, chopped
¼ teaspoon salt
$^1/_8$ teaspoon white pepper
24 ounces frozen langostinos
½ cup tomatoes, diced
4 teaspoons parsley
1 green onion, chopped
4 lemon wedges

Prepare pasta according to package directions. While pasta is cooking, place next 6 ingredients into a sealed container and shake well. Pour sauce into a large sauté pan and heat to medium. Add langostinos and bring to a simmer. Simmer about 5 minutes. Add tomatoes and parsley. Mix well. Serve immediately over pasta. Garnish with green onions and a lemon wedge. Serves 4.

APPLE CHIMICHANGAS

4 12-inch flour tortillas
2 cups Apple Filling (see below)
4 scoops vanilla ice cream
6 tablespoons caramel sauce
1 to 2 tablespoons powdered sugar

In the center of each tortilla, place ½ cup Apple Filling. Fold one end in, then both sides; roll tightly. Deep-fry rolled tortillas 1 to 3 minutes until golden brown. Remove from oil. Serve with a scoop of ice cream. Decorate with caramel sauce and powdered sugar. Serves 4.

APPLE FILLING

2¼ pounds apple slices, frozen
½ cup butter
1½ cups sugar
1 tablespoon cinnamon
1 tablespoon lemon juice
¼ cup cold water
¼ cup flour

Place apples, butter, sugar, cinnamon, and lemon juice into a large pot and bring to a rolling boil. In a small container, combine water and flour to make a slurry. Add slurry to apples and stir until thick. Lower heat and cover pot. Allow to simmer for 5 to 8 minutes until apples are tender. Remove from heat and allow to cool. Yields 7 to 8 cups.

THE HAMMEL HOUSE

121 SOUTH MAIN STREET
WAYNESVILLE, OH 45068
513-897-2333

Travelers to Waynesville in 1844 alighted at The Hammel House Inn, since it was the local office for the People's Stage Lines. At that time, the fare from Cincinnati to Waynesville was just $1.25. The inn's owner, Enoch Hammel, was popular with the locals, and this house of entertainment prospered under his tenure.

Hospitality has been a byword at this location since the original James Jennings Log Tavern was built on the site in 1799. The log structure was replaced in 1817 by the present frame part of the building. A brick addition was completed in 1822. There are many stories about famous people who stayed at the inn. President Martin Van Buren honored the inn with a visit, as did Vice President Richard Johnson in the 1820s.

We enjoyed the story about William Mummer, a less distinguished visitor who came to the inn in 1866 and set up his photography business here. Mummer was a self-proclaimed "spirit photographer," who claimed to be able to photograph spirits lurking on the premises. Business was brisk that summer until the day he developed a portrait of an elderly gentle-

man and a ghostly hand appeared on the gentleman's shoulder. Every photograph he took thereafter contained the ghostly hand. William was reputed to be so frightened by these apparitions that he fled the inn, never to return.

In 1901, William and Ollie Casey Gustin renovated the inn. They gave this country hotel an air of gentility and refinement. Advertising its "inviting and restful atmosphere," they created a reputation that continues today under the ownership of John and Mary Jo Purdum. The main entrance with its harlequin-painted wooden floor and the shady porch that extends the full length of the building invite visitors to stay awhile and relax. There are no televisions or telephones here—just delightful guest rooms, each with a cozy four-poster bed, stenciled walls, and plank floors.

We enjoyed the colonial feel of the dining room. Plain white walls and candle sconces complemented the exposed bricks and the large fireplace. The hunter-green swags at the windows were echoed in the leaf motif running around the top of the room. The Hammel House Inn is well known for its homemade soups and desserts, so we opted to each try a piece of the Coconut Cream Pie. Debbie has devoted a great many calories over the years to finding the perfect Coconut Cream Pie, and she declared that this was the very best she'd tasted in a long time!

On display at the inn is a little poem about hospitality and The Hammel House Inn. We assumed it was of recent composition until

Mary Jo explained to us that she had found the poem way before she ever heard of this inn, or indeed of Waynesville. It was a fine example of serendipity at work in this lovely historic building.

QUICHE

2 cups Swiss cheese, shredded
9-inch unbaked pie shell
1 cup cheddar cheese, shredded
1 cup cooked chicken (may substitute broccoli or
    other ingredient of choice)
4 eggs, beaten
2 cups half-and-half
¼ teaspoon salt
¼ teaspoon white pepper
¼ teaspoon paprika
¼ teaspoon nutmeg

Preheat oven to 375 degrees. Place ½ of Swiss cheese in pie shell. Add cheddar, followed by rest of Swiss cheese. Place cooked chicken or other ingredient of choice on top and spread evenly. In a medium bowl, combine eggs, half-and-half, and seasonings. Pour egg mixture into pie shell. Bake for 1 hour. Serve warm. Serves 8.

SHIRLEY'S DILL TARTAR SAUCE

4 cups mayonnaise
½ cup dill relish
3 tablespoons onion, grated fine
¼ teaspoon garlic powder

Combine ingredients thoroughly and place in a sealed container in the refrigerator until needed. Yields 4½ cups.

The Brass Pig Eatery
245 SOUTH MAIN STREET
SPRINGBORO, OH 45066
513-748-2546

The Brass Pig Eatery was bustling the day we stopped in for lunch. The building was constructed by Jonathan Wright, founder of Springboro, in 1835 as M & J Wright General Merchandise. Today's open dining room—with plenty of space across the wooden floor for displaying merchandise—reflects this use. Green wallpaper festooned with mauve and white cabbage roses now decorates the walls where shelves once held wares. An old peg rail still runs around the perimeter of the room.

Wright's sons, Mahlon and Josiah, operated the store from 1835 until sometime between 1885 and 1895. Dry goods were sold on the northern side of the store, while grocery transactions took place in the southern half. Eggs and butter were frequently bartered for other items. The Wrights offered excellent service, frequently traveling east by horseback or wagon to obtain special items for customers. One of the most interesting things they procured was for Mahlon's daughter, Mary. Women supposedly came from miles around to see the first sewing machine in Warren County and to marvel at the clothing she made with it.

The village of Springboro was reported to be the most active stop on the Underground Railroad. Records indicate that no runaways were ever captured while in the care of Springboro families. As a matter of fact, local history says that bounty men were once forced to turn back when practically the entire town came out to block their path and keep them from their appointed mission.

In the late 1800s, the Wrights sold the building to the Siegfrieds, who operated the store until 1930. After that, the Springboro Grange bought the building and used it for meetings until 1989. From that point until today, the old M & J has been used as an antique store, a gift shop, and a restaurant.

We sat at a table in what was once the grocery. Near the wide front windows, which were attractively outfitted with lace curtains and a single candle, we gazed in amazement at the tiny white house across the street. Historical placards said that it and the larger home next door date to 1835. Much of historic Springboro—including The Brass Pig and these two homes—still stands.

We sipped Pink Lemonade as we scanned the menu. Karen quickly decided on the daily quiche selection, which was Quiche Lorraine. She vowed that it was quite good, particularly the crust. Debbie practically had to do eenie, meenie, minie, moe to choose between the Cashew Chicken Sandwich, which the restaurant recommended on wheat, and the Herbed Egg Salad Sandwich. Eventually, the Egg Salad won out, and it was delicious in its simplicity.

Sometimes, you're just hungry for something reminiscent of childhood days on the family farm.

The dinner menu boasts Pork Loin Medallions, Rotisserie Chicken, and Ribs, all of which are served with a special Raspberry Barbecue Sauce. Debbie, a barbecue fan, is anxious to try one of these choices on another occasion.

FRENCH BUTTER CRUST CHEESE QUICHE

French Butter Crust

2 sticks unsalted butter, frozen
5 tablespoons vegetable shortening
3 cups all-purpose flour
pinch of salt
pinch of sugar
3 tablespoons ice water

In a mixing bowl, grate the butter. Add next 4 ingredients. Using a fork or a pastry blender, combine until crumbly. Add ice water gradually, just until mixture comes together. Chill while preparing Egg Filling.

Egg Filling

4 eggs
2 cups half-and-half
¼ cup milk
pinch of salt
pinch of pepper

pinch of cayenne pepper
2 cups grated cheese (Swiss, cheddar, Colby, or other favorite)

Combine eggs, half-and-half, milk, salt, pepper, and cayenne until well blended.

Evenly divide French Butter Crust into 2 sections. Press each section into a quiche pan. Sprinkle cheese over each. Pour filling equally into quiche pans.

Bake at 425 degrees for 15 minutes. Reduce heat to 350 degrees and bake another 30 minutes. Serves 12.

Note: One cup diced ham, ½ cup chopped and steamed broccoli, and ¼ cup chopped mushrooms may be added to above filling. Another option is to add 1 cup crabmeat and 1 cup chopped spinach. These additional ingredients may be used together or individually, according to taste.

267 WEST MAIN STREET
LOUDONVILLE, OH 44842
419-994-0079

The Sojourner Café is a casual restaurant that is serious about its food. Owner John Barker describes the eatery as having "big-city food in quaint downtown Loudonville." I'd have to say that I agree. Karen was back in Pittsburgh the day I made my trek to this village of twenty-eight hundred people. The population swells to about ten thousand from May through the beautiful fall-foliage season. The area proudly proclaims itself to be the biggest and best canoeing site in the state, with at least eight canoe liveries in operation. Camping and other outdoor activities bring throngs, so the café is aptly named.

The foundation of the building may be traced back to the early part of the 1800s, when Sapp's Dry Goods Store operated here. That structure burned in 1847. Around the same time, Chapter 240 of the International Order of Odd Fellows was founded. The precise date is not known, but since the chapters are numbered chronologically, the inception date of this particular group was between 1838 and 1859.

The Odd Fellows bought the old dry-goods building in 1860 to use as a meeting hall. At that time, the Odd Fellows had a specific architectural style for their lodges, so they added details to the Loudonville structure accordingly. Another fire in 1903 forced the building to undergo renovation and reconstruction again. Not all was destroyed, though. Some Odd Fellow memorabilia, including a jacket, was later found in the attic rafters.

Eventually, the building became a saloon and tavern. It has operated as such pretty much from that time until now, excluding a short stint as a tire store during the 1930s. Depending on the year, local residents could get a bite to eat at The Owl, The Corner Restaurant, or, as John put it, "The Brass Plate something." It seems that as the owners changed, the name varied slightly, from The Loudonville Brass Plate to The Brass Plate Café to other variations on the theme. Today, with a different name and an unusual menu, Sojourner Café stands on its own.

I had the special of the day, Ham and Bacon over Honey Raisin Walnut Bread, topped with eggs and Hollandaise Sauce. It was an unusual twist on Eggs Benedict. The salad that preceded my entrée was a beautiful assortment of spring greens, red cabbage, sliced mushrooms, cucumbers, tomatoes, baby corn, and slivered almonds, topped with tasty, homemade, sugar-free Poppy Seed Dressing. The Battered Salmon Sticks, served with Petal Sauce and Cole Slaw, also caught my eye. The Pea Salad, made with baby peas and fresh spinach, is a popular summer selection, as is the Fresh Watercress Salad, served with homemade Citrus Dressing, fresh strawberries, mandarin oranges, walnuts, and almonds. For dinner, the restaurant is proud of its Black Angus Steaks. The Seafood Trio of salmon, halibut, and swordfish, served with a side of Mango Salsa, sounded interesting, but I'm sure I'd have headed to the Shrimp Wellington and Coconut Shrimp combination plate, had I been there later in the day.

RASPBERRY VINAIGRETTE

4 cups raspberries
2 cups salad oil
½ cup honey
½ cup white vinegar
³/₈ cup lemon juice

Cook raspberries until soft. Place them in a blender and purée. Strain if desired. Add remaining ingredients and whisk together. Chill and serve. Yields approximately 3 cups.

STROGANOFF

1½ quarts boiling water
1 tablespoon beef base
8 ounces mushrooms, sliced
5 shallots, sliced
½ cup butter
2 tablespoons garlic, minced
3 pounds stew meat
1 cup Cabernet Sauvignon
1 cup roux
2 tablespoons Hungarian paprika
1½ cups sour cream
16-ounce package egg noodles, cooked according
   to package directions

Place water and beef base in a large pot. Bring to a boil. Sauté mushrooms and shallots in butter and garlic until tender. Set vegetables aside. In same skillet, sauté beef. Stir in wine. When beef is browned, add vegetables and meat to boiling water. Pour into a large container. Stir in roux to thicken. Stir in paprika. Let mixture cool slightly. Stir in sour cream. Serve over noodles. Serves 8 to 10.

CHAPTER 2

How Do I Get There from Here?

Schmidt's Restaurant und Sausage Haus

Transportation during the early years of this country proved a great
challenge. Many long and arduous journeys took place on foot, on horseback, or in some type of rough conveyance. Each of the restaurants featured
in the following pages had some part in getting people from one place to
another. Livery stables, trolley repair depots, train stations—all played a part
in making the task of getting from here to there just a little bit easier.

FRANKLIN AVENUE AND WEST MAIN STREET
KENT, OH 44240
330-673-1771

Interestingly enough, there are several Pufferbellys in the area, including a fire station in Erie, Pennsylvania, and another train station in the Cleveland area. At one time, all were owned by the same individual; the Cleveland station changed hands just prior to the publication of this book.

There is no mistaking this brick building for anything other than a train station. Built in 1875, it has an interesting story to tell. It seems that during the time George Hinds was stationmaster, a circus was in town. Now, this wasn't uncommon, nor was it rare for circus personnel to try to finagle lower fares or free rides to their next destination. One day, the circus master, unsuccessful in his negotiations with Mr. Hinds, absconded with the ticket money, leaving his performers stranded. It was in this circumstance that the stationmaster came across a shivering boy dressed in a flamboyant shirt, puffing on a stogie. "My good man," the boy began, "I'll give you eight dol-

lars for my fare to New York now and pay the rest after the show." Mr. Hinds declined, stating that the circus master had already been turned down. But seeing how pitiful the boy was, Hinds's generosity eventually got the better of him, and he gave the boy the rest of the fare, along with an additional ten dollars. The boy shed tears of joy and promised to return the loan. It was some years later when Mr. Hinds received an envelope addressed to him that contained tickets to a local traveling show. Upon arriving, he was ushered backstage, where he recognized a more mature version of the boy he'd helped. "Why, Whitey Dunkenfield!" Mr. Hinds exclaimed. "I don't go by Whitey anymore," the young man replied. "I'm known as W. C. Fields. Here's the ten dollars you loaned me and ten dollars more for interest."

We thoroughly enjoyed the story, as well as the décor. Framed telegrams told the stories of people who missed trains and caught wrong trains, which brought us visions of comic situations, the stuff of which early motion pictures were made. Also framed and displayed along the walls were many, many photographs and pictures related to rail history. A full-sized carriage that may once have conveyed a local citizen to the station hung above one section of the restaurant, and an old luggage cart laden with baggage was suspended nearby.

Since our visit was on a Sunday, we took advantage of the buffet, which included salads, quiche, omelets, waffles, several entrées, and many dessert choices. Debbie enjoyed the

Chive Potato Salad and the Barbecued Beef. Karen's favorite was the Sweet and Sour Chicken. The regular menu features sandwiches such as a Spicy Black Bean Burger and a Cashew Chicken Croissant. Thin Crust Pizzas are quite popular, as are the Barbecued Jamaican Shrimp and the Thai Shrimp Pasta.

It is said that W. C. Fields delighted in telling of his experience at the Kent station. The tale has even been credited with starting the tradition of traveling performers honoring the harried stationmasters of this world. Today, in Kent, it's hats off to chef and general manager Kevin Long and his staff as they welcome travelers from near and far.

HERB-CRUSTED SALMON

¼ cup dried basil
2 tablespoons dried thyme
2 tablespoons dried oregano
1 teaspoon rosemary, crumbled
½ teaspoon pepper, ground coarse
½ cup flour
1¼ teaspoons salt
5 8-ounce salmon fillets
2 tablespoons olive oil, divided

Preheat oven to 375 degrees. With a mortar and pestle, blend all ingredients except salmon and olive oil until mixture is very fine. Dredge salmon on both sides in herb mixture. Coat a baking pan with 1 tablespoon of the olive oil. Place salmon in pan. Brush top of each fillet lightly with remaining olive oil. Bake in oven for 8 to 10 minutes until salmon is cooked through but not overdone. Serves 5.

MARGARITA PIE

1 stick margarine
1¼ cups salted pretzels, crushed fine
½ cup granulated sugar
14-ounce can sweetened condensed milk
2 tablespoons lime juice
2 tablespoons tequila
2 tablespoons triple sec
1 drop green food coloring
2 cups whipping cream

Generously grease a 9-inch metal pie pan. In a medium saucepan, melt margarine over low heat. Remove from heat and stir in pretzels and sugar until well blended. Press mixture firmly over bottom and up sides of pie pan, forming a rim above edge of pan. Place in freezer to firm while making filling.

Mix sweetened condensed milk, lime juice, tequila, triple sec, and food coloring, being careful to measure accurately, as too much liquid will keep the filling from becoming firm. In another bowl, beat whipping cream with an electric mixer until peaks form when beaters are lifted. Gradually fold condensed-milk mixture into whipped cream, mixing gently but well. Pour into crust.

Freeze uncovered at least 8 hours. Wrap airtight and return to freezer until ready to serve. Serves 6 to 8.

Iron Horse Inn
Restaurant

40 VILLAGE SQUARE
GLENDALE, OH 45246
513-771-4787
WWW.IRONHORSEINN.NET

The hamlet that became Historic Glendale started in the 1840s as a railroad labor camp. The settlement was clustered on property deeded to John C. Symmes in 1792 and was situated around the Cincinnati, Hamilton & Dayton Railroad right of way. George Crawford and Henry Clark had a different vision for the property. In 1851, they purchased six hundred acres for residential development, establishing the first known planned subdivision community in America.

In 1853, Bracker Tavern was constructed for community refreshment. When Prohibition came to pass in 1918, the tavern became more of a restaurant, although slot machines and liquor, conveniently hidden in the foundation, were available in the back room of the wood-frame structure. Not being able to openly serve liquor wasn't all bad for this establishment. During this same time, it also supplied food for inmates at the local jail. Its reputation for good food became so widely known that hobos frequently chose to be locked up rather than to move along, just so they could have a meal prepared by the tavern.

As Glendale developed into a true suburb of Cincinnati, many professional men and their families moved to the area. Many of these gentlemen were Proctor and Gamble executives who would catch the train to work; that train departed just outside the tavern. The rail line ran right past the Ivorydale Plant, where Ivory Soap was made, making these men some of the first local commuters. The lovely Victorian homes just down the street speak to their success.

Eventually, a daughter of the Bracker family and her husband, Robert Heine, took over the saloon. They installed a soda fountain and sold ice cream and penny candy—quite a change from the back-room Prohibition days! They also served hot soup and sandwiches. In 1962, Bracker Tavern was purchased by a group of investors, who changed the name to the Iron Horse Inn to honor the 1856 steam engine. The restaurant was sold again in 1971 and again in 1984. The latter transaction brought the Iron Horse Inn to Dewey and Betty Huff, who established a tradition of having nationally known jazz artists perform during Sunday brunch. The jazz continues today, with live music four nights a week.

Current owners Edward, William, Robert, and Henry Sawyer are brothers with a long family tradition in Glendale. In June 1994, they purchased the inn and began its restoration and renovation. Today, the downstairs dining room is painted a rich red, aptly reflecting the bold creations of chef Ron Wise. Starters such as Duck Sausage in Cabernet Demi-Glace and Limoncello Smoked Salmon with Fennel Slaw are among his creations. And Sassafras Barbecued Porkchops and Filet Mignon topped with Smoked Duck Breast and Gorgonzola cheese are sure to attract diners' notice.

One customer recently paid the proprietors quite a compliment, as a northbound train slowed to a stop on the tracks just outside the inn. The engineer climbed down and went inside, demonstrating that he didn't want to miss an opportunity to dine at the Iron Horse Inn.

TASSO-ESCOLAR STEW

1 cup onions, diced
½ cup celery, diced
½ cup carrots, diced
¼ cup olive oil
1 cup tasso ham, diced
2 cups potatoes, diced
1 cup canned tomatoes, diced
1 bay leaf
4 cups fish stock
1 pound escolar (mackerel)
pinch of cayenne
salt and pepper to taste
lemon slices or wedges, if desired
chopped Italian parsley, if desired

In a large pot, sauté onions, celery, and carrots in olive oil. Add ham, potatoes, and tomatoes. Add bay leaf and stock. Simmer until potatoes are tender. Add escolar, cayenne, and salt and pepper. Garnish with lemon and parsley and serve immediately. Serves 6 as an appetizer or 3 as an entrée.

SHRIMP GRITS

8 cups water, salted
2 cups instant grits
fresh cracked black pepper to taste
2 cups small shrimp, peeled and deveined
¼ cup butter
1 cup cheddar cheese, shredded

Bring water to a boil. Stir in grits and pepper. Cover and reduce heat to simmer. Cook 3 to 4 minutes. Add shrimp and butter. Cook about 4 minutes until shrimp are done. Garnish with cheddar. Serves 12.

LAVENDER SYRUP

1 tablespoon lavender blossom
½ cup sugar
½ cup water
1 teaspoon light rum
½ cup Parfait Amore liqueur
1 tablespoon lemon juice

Put all ingredients in a small saucepan and reduce by ½; this will take about 3 minutes. Strain and let cool. Yields approximately ¾ cup. Syrup may be enjoyed over ice cream or pound cake. Or it may be mixed with vanilla ice cream for an interesting shake, or added to sugar cookie mix to make Lavender Cookies.

THE DENNISON DEPOT CANTEEN
RESTAURANT AT

Dennison Railroad Depot Museum

400 CENTER STREET
DENNISON, OH 44621
740-922-6776
WWW.DENNISONDEPOT.ORG

"Fly Boy Chicken Dinners," "Chow Time Sandwiches," "Submarine Seafood," "B-17 Boneless Chicken Breasts," and "Victory Garden Salads" are the menu categories at The Dennison Depot Canteen Restaurant.

This location was once a Salvation Army canteen that served 13 percent of American military personnel during World War II, operating from March 1942 to April 1946. This made the Dennison Depot the third-largest canteen in the United States. Coming from eight counties, working day and night, 3,957 women volunteered here during this time, passing out approximately 2 million sandwiches, 1.5 million cookies, and similar quantities of milk, coffee, and other selections. Pictures of the volunteers and of men lining up for meals are proudly displayed on the wall. A quote from an unknown soldier reads, "When you are headed to war, homesick, afraid, you have no money, and are very hungry—receiving free food from friendly people in a hometown that is very much like your home you left—it was like a dream come true." Soldiers traveling through Dennison on the National Defense Railway Route were so appreciative of this effort that they fondly nicknamed the town Dreamville.

Today, guests are seated at tables covered with blue cloths with charming white antimacassars in the center. As they choose among the Two Breast Chicken Dinner, the Shredded Steak Sandwich, the Taco Salad, and other items, they can enjoy the memorabilia displayed throughout. Murals of railroad scenes featuring people from workmen to wealthy travelers have been painted on one wall. Framed sheet music of the World War II era decorates the walls, as do railroad-crossing signs and railroad insignias. Many other knick-knacks are collected here and there.

The train station was built of brick and sandstone in 1873. At one time, it housed the Western Union telegraph office and saw as many as twenty-two trains per day pass by. Situated halfway between Pittsburgh and Columbus, the depot was once a stopover point for trains called the Spirit of St. Louis and the Jeffersonian. Doris Day, Dwight Eisenhower, Glenn Miller, and Harry Truman are but a few of the famous people who passed through this terminal.

As we walked around the exterior, we admired the decorative stained-glass upper windows. Karen smiled, saying that it reminded

her very much of the English stations she'd used as a child.

Scheduled for demolition, the building was saved by local citizens in the early 1980s. Today, the depot is again a vital part of the community, closely linked to many events in town. In addition to the restaurant, it houses a gift shop and a railroad museum. Excursion trains follow the historic Panhandle Route of the Pennsylvania Railroad, now called the Columbus & Ohio River Railroad. Fall-foliage trips, a murder-mystery evening, a holiday train ride, or a simple dinner at the old canteen may prove just your ticket.

MEATBALLS

5 pounds ground beef
¼ cup garlic, chopped
¼ cup parsley flakes
1 cup breadcrumbs
¾ teaspoon salt
¾ teaspoon pepper
3 eggs

Combine all ingredients in a large mixing bowl. Knead with hands until thoroughly mixed. Using an ice cream scoop, form into 3-inch balls and place in a jelly roll pan. Bake in a 350-degree oven for 12 to 15 minutes until firm and well browned. Drain. Yields approximately 3 dozen of this size or 5 dozen 1-inch meatballs.

SPAGHETTI SAUCE

60-ounce can California Red tomatoes, whole
60-ounce can prepared spaghetti sauce of choice
2 tablespoons sugar
2 tablespoons parsley
¼ teaspoon garlic salt
1 teaspoon paprika
2 tablespoons Parmesan

In a large saucepan, combine all ingredients except cheese. Bring to a boil, then simmer over low heat for 1 hour. Add Parmesan and stir to combine. Yields 12 cups.

30 DEPOT STREET
BEREA, OH 44017
440-234-1144

When the depot that now houses The Pufferbelly Restaurant was built in 1876, it replaced a dingy, dilapidated building that was an eyesore to the community and a disappointment to passengers. Conversely, the new building—made of local stone, roofed with slate, and adorned with a twelve-foot-wide veranda—was a great source of pride. A forty-five-foot tower and flagstaff and a platform extending two hundred feet in either direction along the rails ornamented the front of the building. The interior saw to the creature comforts that the previous building had overlooked. The oak moldings were designed to create an attractive contrast to the tinted pine walls and ceiling. Today, both the interior and the exterior are remarkably similar to the days of old.

We enjoyed looking at the memorabilia displayed on the wall. A valise and old suitcases are artfully arranged in the dining room to the left of the entrance. A piece of wood signed by several men hangs in the bar area. Dated 1876, it was found during recent reno-

vations. A framed copy of an old telegraph is just around the corner. Several collages of tickets to Elyria, Cincinnati, Medina, Delaware, and other destinations can be found throughout the restaurant. The framed obituary of railroad man Casey Jones also makes interesting reading. Just outside the restaurant is the Berea Pullman, a restored 1927 Pullman dining car outfitted for private dining for parties of up to twenty-seven.

It was quite chilly the day we visited, so Karen ordered the Chicken Gumbo, while Debbie selected the Beef Noodle Soup. Both were served piping hot and full of delicious morsels. The Quiche, served with a Popover fresh out of the oven, looked scrumptious as it was delivered to a table nearby. Another menu item that appealed to our palate was the Turkey Pita Grill, consisting of turkey, bacon, and Monterey Jack cheese grilled on pita bread, then topped with Horseradish-Sour Cream Sauce. We also eyed the San Francisco Beef Sandwich, served open-faced on pumpernickel bread and topped with Mushroom Wine Sauce and colby cheese. In a mood for beef, we discussed the Steak Madagascar, a six-ounce fillet served with mushrooms and Green Peppercorn Sauce.

Save room for dessert, as The Pufferbelly has selections ranging from Fruit Crumble to Bananas Foster. The Boule de Neige is a dark-chocolate creation laced with Grand Marnier and topped with whipped cream. Yum. The Black Forest Coupe—a scoop of Black Cherry Ice Cream nestled in a Chocolate Cup, then surrounded by Raspberry Sauce and whipped cream—was a temptation hard to pass up.

The restaurant was busy during our lunchtime visit. Just as we were finishing our meal, we heard an unmistakable rumbling just outside, reminding us that although freight and passenger trains no longer stop here, The Pufferbelly Restaurant keeps the hustle and bustle of this depot alive.

 THE MIKADO

3 pounds boneless pork loin or pork tenderloin
3 eggs
2 tablespoons soy sauce
½ teaspoon garlic powder
½ teaspoon poultry seasoning
1 teaspoon salt
½ teaspoon pepper
1½ cups breadcrumbs
½ cup sesame seeds, toasted
1 teaspoon seasoned salt
12 English muffins, split
2½ cups applesauce
½ cup honey
1 teaspoon ginger
24 slices muenster cheese

Roast pork approximately 1½ hours until just done. Cool. Slice pork at an angle to achieve 24 three-inch-by-three-inch slices about ¼ inch thick. Combine eggs, soy sauce, garlic powder, poultry seasoning, salt, and pepper in a shallow bowl. In a separate bowl, combine breadcrumbs, sesame seeds, and seasoned salt.

Dip pork slices in egg mixture, then coat with breadcrumb mixture. Place slices in a skillet and brown on each side. Toast English muffins. Place a breaded pork slice on top of each muffin half. Combine applesauce, honey, and ginger in a small bowl. Spoon ¼ cup of applesauce mixture over each muffin half. Top with a slice of cheese. Place under broiler to heat and melt cheese. Serve open-faced. Serves 12.

SEA SCALLOPS SCANDINAVIAN

½ cup flour
½ teaspoon white pepper
½ teaspoon paprika
¼ cup butter
10 ounces bay scallops
¼ cup Chablis
½ cup hollandaise sauce
½ teaspoon dill
1 tablespoon Dijon mustard
rice pilaf
stir-fry vegetables

Combine flour, white pepper, and paprika in a shallow container. Melt butter in a sauté pan. Dredge scallops in flour mixture, shaking off excess. Sauté in butter until opaque and crusted, stirring gently so as not to break up scallops. *Do not overcook.* As scallops finish cooking, pour Chablis into pan. In another bowl, combine hollandaise, dill, and Dijon.

To serve, place scallops on a bed of rice pilaf. Pour hollandaise mixture over scallops and garnish with stir-fry vegetables. Serves 2.

SCHMIDT'S RESTAURANT
UND SAUSAGE HAUS
240 EAST KOSSUTH STREET
COLUMBUS, OH 43206
614-444-6808

Family is important to Geoff Schmidt, as was obvious when he showed us the family portraits and other memorabilia hanging on the wall. He is most proud of his father's paintings that grace the walls alongside works of local German Village artists. The family has run the business since 1886. Geoff's brothers and sisters are all still involved in some aspect of the operation. The founder, John Fred Schmidt, left Germany at the age of seventeen and settled in Columbus. In partnership with several others, he formed the Columbus Meat Packing Company. After several years, J. Fred Schmidt sold his share and formed a new partnership, establishing another meat-packing house on East Kossuth Street, in the area known today as German Village. The business grew until the 1960s, when the influx of chain grocery stores and large packing operations forced the Schmidts to close shop. It was either that or sacrifice the quality of their product.

As a business alternative, the family decided in 1967 to open a small retail meat store in an old livery stable built in the 1890s. They processed and packed the meat in the back and offered sandwiches and cold drinks to the customers while their orders were being filled. After only two weeks, the restaurant was already in need of expansion, as customers came in just to eat. The heavy wooden door speaks to the family's heritage—a large wooden lard paddle has been used as the door handle! Inside, smooth wood floors, stall-like booths, and old brick walls tell of the building's past, as do the bright red stable doors in the room that houses the daily buffet.

Rather than spend our calorie allotment for the day at the German Autobahn Buffet, we opted for the Chicken and Spatzel Salad for Debbie and the German-Style Meat Loaf for Karen. Both were yummy. Unable to completely behave when such excellent German desserts were available, we decided to share a German Cream Puff filled with Mocha-Almond Cream. It was light and delicious—a lovely way to end an enjoyable meal.

Many of the recipes on Schmidt's menu today are courtesy of the original waitresses, who still wear traditional German costumes. Longevity is common here. Several of the wait staff have been working at the restaurant for more than thirty years!

Fortunately, a fire in 1983 that burned the entire upstairs of the restaurant did not destroy the structure. Undaunted, the Schmidt family immediately began restoration—and tried to figure out how to keep the restaurant open during the reconstruction. Fortunately, it was late spring and early summer, and the Schmidts were able to set up a big tent outside, creating a *biergarten* atmosphere. Once the business details were attended to, the family turned its attention to creating something positive out of a difficult situation. Realizing that others had suffered more than they had as the result of fires, the family donated the first proceeds of the tent restaurant to the Children's Burn Unit in Columbus. We think that pretty well sums up what the Schmidts and their restaurant are all about—service to the community.

SCHMIDT'S SWEETKRAUT

20-ounce can sauerkraut
¼ cup canola oil
¼ cup apple cider vinegar
½ cup sugar
1½ cups celery, chopped fine
1 cup onion, chopped fine
⅓ cup green pepper, chopped fine

Drain sauerkraut and set aside. In a separate bowl, combine oil, vinegar, and sugar. Mix well with a wire whisk until uniform in color. Add celery, onions, and peppers to mixture. Continue to whisk until liquid becomes a light green. Add sauerkraut and mix well by hand. Refrigerate overnight. Serve chilled. Yields 6 cups.

 PEACH PIE

2 egg yolks
⅔ cup sugar
1½ tablespoons milk
2 sticks margarine, softened
3 cups flour
30-ounce can peach halves, drained
1 tablespoon tapioca
¼ teaspoon cinnamon
¼ cup sugar

In a medium bowl, mix egg yolks, sugar, and milk until blended. Add margarine and mix until blended. Add flour and mix slowly until all flour is moistened. Refrigerate dough for at least 4 hours; refrigerating overnight works best.

Preheat oven to 375 degrees. Divide dough into 5 equal parts. Using 3 parts of the dough, roll out to ⅛-inch thickness and lay in a 9-inch pie pan. Press dough into bottom and around edges. Remove excess dough. Poke holes in the bottom with a fork. Bake crust 10 to 12 minutes until light brown.

Dice peaches and place in a large bowl. In a small bowl, mix tapioca, cinnamon, and sugar. Add mixture to peaches and blend by hand. Place peach filling in piecrust. Roll out remaining 2 parts of dough to ⅛-inch thickness and cut into 1-inch strips. Lay strips across the top, evenly spaced in a crisscross pattern. Bake for 50 minutes until crust is golden brown. Set aside to cool. Cut and serve. Serves 8.

8092 COLUMBIA ROAD
OLMSTED FALLS, OH 44233
440-235-1223

Clementine's is owned and run by two very enterprising women, Anne Shier Klintworth and Doris Rundle. They began by managing their own wholesale bakery, creating a large number of cakes and pastries for local hotels and restaurants. However, they wanted to sell their wares directly to the general public and thought that a Victorian tearoom would be ideal. Started as a place that served soup and bread, high tea, and a selection of wonderful teas and coffees, Clementine's was very soon a great success. Gradually, the menu was expanded to include sandwiches and salads, and a Victorian restaurant emerged.

Today, Clementine's is located in the very center of Grand Pacific Junction. This small area is filled with beautiful historic buildings and interesting shops, all linked by brick walkways. The buildings have been lovingly restored by Clint Williams, who owns the local realty company. The largest building is the Grand Pacific Hotel, built in the 1830s. Constructed as a girls'

seminary, it was moved across the river to its current location in 1858 and is rumored to have been a stop on the Underground Railroad. Clementine's is located in a late-1800s building that was at one time a livery stable for visitors to the Grand Pacific Hotel.

We sat in the back parlor, known as "the Garden Room." This charming room has its original wide-plank floors and an overhanging hayloft above the sliding livery door. It is attractively decorated with tables and chairs and hanging plants. Small rugs and just a hint or two of lace at the windows and on the mantels give the room a warm, cozy feel. The tall loft ladder set against the wall in one corner of the room reminds guests of the original use of the building.

We talked with Doris about her love for this old building as we sipped our choice of teas—traditional Earl Grey Tea with just a hint of bergamot oil for Karen and a refreshing Berry Jubilee Tea for Debbie. Several soups and a large number of salads and sandwiches are on the menu. Debbie enjoyed her Broccoli Quiche, made with Clementine's Hash Brown Potato Crust and served with a large helping of seasonal fresh fruit. Karen chose the Roasted Eggplant Sandwich, which was made with roasted red peppers and basil aioli and served with creamy Macaroni Salad. The list of desserts was enormous. We had considerable difficulty in choosing just one to sample. Eventually, we got up from our table and wandered out to the cake case in the shop to see this marvelous selection for ourselves. Finally selecting a Lemon Tart to share, we were not disappointed. The pastry was crumbly, and the lemon filling was tangy and mouth-wateringly good.

There is plenty to see here. Guests enjoy not only the fabulous pastries they can purchase and take home to share, but also the shelves and tables upstairs stocked with fine china and Victoriana. The large glass-fronted case at the bottom of the staircase contains the most delectable homemade chocolates. We bet you won't be able to resist one!

GRANDMA'S STUFFED CABBAGE SOUP

2 cups onions, diced
1½ pounds ground beef
3 tablespoons olive oil
½ cup brown sugar
1 small head cabbage, diced
2 14 ½-ounce cans diced tomatoes
4 cups beef broth
2 28-ounce cans tomato sauce
1 tablespoon lemon juice
2 cups cooked white rice
salt and freshly ground black pepper to taste
Croutons for garnish

In a large soup pot, sauté onion and ground beef in oil until meat is browned. Do not drain. Add sugar and cabbage and mix well. Add next 4 ingredients and bring to a boil. Reduce heat and simmer for 1 to 1½ hours. Add rice and simmer 10 more minutes. Season with salt and

pepper and garnish with croutons. Serves 12.

SAUSAGE AND FENNEL SOUP WITH PASTA

1 pound sweet Italian sausage
1 bulb fennel
¾ cup onions, diced
1½ teaspoons garlic, minced
3 tablespoons olive oil
14½-ounce can diced tomatoes
14½-ounce can crushed tomatoes
4 cups chicken broth
¾ cup orzo
2 cups fresh spinach, stemmed and torn into small pieces
salt and freshly ground black pepper to taste
Asiago cheese for garnish

In a large skillet, sauté sausage until well browned, breaking into small pieces. Drain sausage and set aside. Cut off top of fennel. Wash and dice white part of bulb. Sauté fennel, onions, and garlic in olive oil until onions are soft and translucent. Add diced tomatoes, crushed tomatoes, and chicken broth. Bring to a boil, then reduce heat and simmer for 25 minutes. Add sausage and orzo and cook until orzo is just done. Add spinach and cook another 3 minutes. Season with salt and pepper and garnish with Asiago cheese. Serves 12.

HOSTER BREWING CO.
550 SOUTH HIGH STREET
COLUMBUS, OH 43215
614-228-6066

I was slightly under the weather on the cold January day that I visited Hoster's. Karen was elsewhere in Columbus, so it was up to me to make the most of this visit. Fortunately, the chef took pity on me, bringing me a sampler of the three soups available that day. One of them was sure to make me feel better. I started with the Broccoli Cheese Soup, which was truly as good as my own. That's a compliment I don't hand out very often! Broccoli Soup is one of my daughter's favorite foods, and has been since her early childhood, so I've become something of a connoisseur, as she's ordered and rejected many bowls that didn't taste like mine! The Vegetarian Chili, served with a dollop of sour cream, was excellent, with just the right spiciness. My brother-in-law, Todd, an attorney in the area, had told me how good the Beer Cheese Soup was, but it surpassed even my highest expectations. It was simply the best of its kind in my Beer Cheese Soup experience.

Just inside the entrance to the restaurant is a large poster highlighting Columbus beer making. It's a tradition credited primarily to German immigrants, whose population in this area was quite large. The Hoster Brewing Co. was named in honor of the area's first and perhaps best-known brewery. The name, purchased from the Hoster family years after the original brewery was no longer operational, rekindled the brewing tradition.

The beer recipes used here are in keeping with the dark ales and lagers that the early German settlers made. The beers are brewed in the front of the restaurant and fermented either downstairs or down the hall from the dining room. The large brew tanks are visible through the expansive front windows, piquing the interest of passersby. The tanks are located at what used to be the entrance of this trolley repair house. The trolleys were rolled from High Street into the cavernous garage-like area that now houses the main dining room. It's obvious from the size that there was room for several cars to be worked on at one time. Once repairs were completed, the cars were rolled out the back and put into service once again.

In the spacious main dining room, items of the period decorate nooks and crannies, as well as the original brick walls. A bar area has been placed in the center, giving the restaurant a casual, very social feel.

On a previous visit to Columbus, before I ever thought of writing a book, Hoster's had caught my eye. I'd intended to visit, but an ice storm that shut down the city foiled my plans.

This time, although it was chilly, the streets were clear, so I finally got my wish.

APPLE CHUTNEY

3 Granny Smith apples
juice of ½ lemon
2 teaspoons olive oil
¼ yellow onion, diced fine
¼ teaspoon fresh ginger, minced
²/₃ cup sugar
²/₃ cup water
½ tablespoon cinnamon
pinch of allspice
pinch of nutmeg

Peel and dice apples and place in a large bowl of water mixed with lemon juice. In a medium skillet, warm oil and sauté onions and ginger until tender. Remove from heat and set aside. In a medium saucepan, combine sugar with ²/₃ cup water, cinnamon, allspice, and nutmeg. Bring to a boil. Drain apples and add them to spice mix. Add onions and ginger. Cook on low until thickened; do not overcook. Remove from heat and refrigerate immediately in a sealed container. Yields 2 cups.

TEXAS BBQ SAUCE

1 tablespoon plus 1½ teaspoons butter
2¼ cups onions, minced
2 generous tablespoons granulated garlic
2¼ cups mustard
2 generous tablespoons dry mustard
2¼ cups chili sauce
1¾ cups granulated sugar
¾ cup Worcestershire sauce
1 generous teaspoon white pepper
1 generous teaspoon black pepper
1 tablespoon cayenne pepper
9 cups water, divided
9 ounces demi-glaze base
½ cup honey, scant

In a medium skillet, melt butter over medium heat. Sauté onions and garlic until tender. Set aside. Place mustards, chili sauce, sugar, Worcestershire, and all 3 peppers in 8 cups of the water. Simmer. Mix remaining water with demi-glaze base, making a smooth paste. Add onion and garlic. Add mixture to kettle and bring to a boil. Reduce heat and add honey. Sauce may be kept in refrigerator for up to 3 weeks. Yields 10 to 12 cups.

4057 ERIE STREET
WILLOUGHBY, OH 44094
440-975-0202
WWW.WILLOUGHBYBREWING.COM

This enormous red-brick building was originally a railway-car repair depot for the Cleveland-to-Ashtabula interurban rail line. Now over a hundred years old, it also holds a claim to fame as Lake County's first brewpub since Prohibition. The only obvious additions to the carefully preserved structure are the huge Palladian windows along the length of the building. Inside, the warehouse-like quality of the building has been retained. Visitors can still look up and see the large steel beams that once held the overhead cranes necessary for the repair shop.

A great deal of care has been taken with the décor of this beautiful building. Overhead are large, dangling light fixtures that help to draw the eye to the small train track that circles the central area of the dining room. Beer advertisements from days gone by have been carefully painted onto the interior brickwork. The brewery proudly displays a photograph of its founder, T. J. Reagan, with Bob Taft during the governor's visit to the brewery in 1998. Other equally historic pictures of the surround-

ing area can be found around the room, including an aerial view of the old street that clearly shows how little has changed in the past hundred years.

The brewery operations are clearly visible behind the bar at one end of the building. The shiny stainless-steel and copper tanks add a charm of their own. Watching the staff at work creates a definite need to taste the various brews created here. Karen was interested to note that, of the six samples of beer in the Brewhouse Sampler, two are of English heritage. The Lost Nation Pale Ale is a sharp beer rich in hops that was originally brewed to survive the long voyage from Britain to India for Her Majesty's troops. Visitors interested in unusual beers should try the Railway Razz, made with red and black raspberries. It was the Silver Medal winner at the 1999 Great American Beer Festival.

Like the beer, the food is excellent. We started with a sampling of the three soups on the menu that day. The Potato and Cheddar Ale, the New England Chowder, and the French Onion Soup were all piping hot and garnished with homemade croutons. We found the menu choices to be unusual and creative, particularly the Three Cheese Beer Fondue. We sampled the Swiss, Gruyère, and Gouda cheeses—baked with Willoughby Pale Ale—by dipping a large selection of fresh vegetables and breads. Karen's favorite dish was the Southwestern Pub Pizza, which consisted of grilled chicken, black beans, Roasted Corn Salsa, cheddar and Asadero cheeses, tasso ham, and Sweet

Chile Sauce. It was absolutely yummy. The service was prompt and attentive, even during that very crowded Wednesday lunchtime.

Don't forget to save room for the Grand Finale, a Special Reserve Root Beer float. The old-fashioned root beer is created on the premises, brewed with honey and root extracts. The float also features rich Vanilla Ice Cream and a Chocolate Cigar. You're going to love it!

CHARDONNAY MUSSELS TOMATO

2 pound mussels
¼ cup pesto
½ cup white wine
1 cup cream
salt and pepper to taste
2 lemon wedges for garnish
freshly chopped parsley for garnish
6 crostini

Cook mussels, pesto, and wine in a skillet over medium heat. Cover to allow mussels to open. When mussels open, remove from skillet and place equally on 2 serving plates. Add cream to skillet and reduce until slightly thickened. Pour over mussels. Season with salt and pepper and garnish with lemon and parsley. Serve with 3 crostini per plate. Serves 2 as an appetizer.

SPINACH CON QUESO

2 tablespoons margarine
½ cup onion, diced
2 tablespoons jalapeño pepper, diced
¾ cup white sauce
¾ cup heavy cream
2 teaspoons scallions
¾ teaspoon Worcestershire sauce
⅓ teaspoon Tabasco sauce
salt and pepper to taste
1¼ pounds Pepper Jack cheese, grated coarse
½ pound frozen spinach, drained and chopped

Melt margarine in a skillet. Sauté onions and jalapeños for 3 minutes until onions are translucent. Add white sauce and cream and bring to a simmer. Add remaining ingredients and stir well until cheese is melted. Transfer to a serving dish. Serve with tortilla chips or crostini. Serves 6 to 8 as an appetizer.

953 PHILLIPS AVENUE
TOLEDO, OH 43612
419-476-4154

It was a raw, wet day when I visited, so it didn't take me long to decide on my order. I needed to warm up, so I opted for the New England Clam Chowder, positively recommended by one of Mancy's staff members. She did not steer me wrong. I also enjoyed the Spinach Salad with Button Mushrooms, topped with roasted pecans and warm Bacon Dressing. The two items made a nice luncheon combination.

As its name suggests, Mancy's is well known for its steaks. Strip, Filet, Porterhouse, T-Bone, and Rib-Eye cuts all appear on the menu. Any of the steaks may be ordered with Cajun spice, cracked black peppercorns, or fresh garlic. Bearnaise, Hollandaise, or Bordelaise Sauces may be added, as may sautéed mushrooms or sweet onions. The Tournedos Oscar is considered one of the house specialties, but the New York Strip with Toasted Walnut Blue Cheese Sauce also caught my eye.

Gus Mancy and his cousin Nicholas Graham founded the Ideal Restaurant in 1921. They converted an old Oldsmobile carriage dealership on Phillips Avenue into an eatery. Located at the end of the trolley line, it was a convenient spot for customers, and business grew. As its popularity expanded, the restaurant became known for its Tiffany lamps, chandeliers, and stained and leaded glass, as well as its quality menu.

Then, in 1973, the original Mancy's suffered a devastating fire. The only thing that remained was the scorched wooden statue of a clown. Still smiling, he stands repainted in the entryway of Mancy's today.

In rebuilding from the ashes, the owners paid great attention to re-creating and preserving the memory and feel of the restaurant. Much of the glass throughout the restaurant once graced elegant homes, offices, and churches in the area. The entrance was garnered from a Historic West End residence on Collingwood Boulevard that at one time was home to the Toledo Art Club. Other glass panels from the same stately home were used as dividers in one corner of the dining room. Astounding examples of beveled and leaded glass rescued from old Toledo homes have been incorporated in other areas of the restaurant.

The fourteen stained-glass panels were discovered by someone whose hobby was decorative window glass. They came from a small church in Michigan and now form the foyer ceiling at Mancy's. The old Penn Central railroad station in downtown Detroit provided the railroad benches from which the dining booths were crafted. Although both bars in the restaurant were made around 1900 by a firm located in Toledo, they were obtained from very different locales—one came from West Virginia and one from Michigan. The stained-glass depiction of Rip Van Winkle came from an even more unlikely source, a Chicago speakeasy once owned by Al Capone. Karen wasn't with me to experience all these interesting finds, and trying to describe them over the phone was just impossible. It's one of those places you just have to see for yourself.

OYSTERS ROCKEFELLER

1 cup spinach, rinsed and drained
¼ medium red onion
5 strips bacon, fried crisp
⅜ teaspoon white pepper
½ teaspoon Tabasco
¾ cup heavy cream
2 egg yolks
1 cup breadcrumbs
3 tablespoons white wine
1 tablespoon lemon juice
⅜ teaspoon cayenne pepper
½ teaspoon garlic, minced
36 oysters
¾ cup hollandaise sauce

In a food processor, finely chop spinach, onion, and bacon. Combine with next 9 ingredients in a large bowl. Place 1 tablespoon of mixture on top of each oyster. Brown approximately 4 minutes. Spoon 1 teaspoon of hollandaise over each oyster. Brown 30 seconds and serve. Serves 6 as an appetizer.

FRENCH ONION SOUP

2 tablespoons beef base or 8 bouillon cubes
8 cups water
1 tablespoon brown sugar
1½ teaspoons white wine
1 large onion
2 tablespoons butter
16 large croutons
16 slices mozzarella cheese
1½ cups Parmesan

Combine first 4 ingredients in a large pot and bring to a boil. Sauté onion in butter until a light golden brown. Combine onion with soup mixture. Place 2 croutons in bottom of each of 8 cups or soup bowls. Ladle soup into cups. Top each with 2 slices of mozzarella and sprinkle with Parmesan. Brown under a broiler until bubbly. Serves 8.

11401 BELLFLOWER ROAD
CLEVELAND, OH 44106
216-231-4469

Lobster Bisque or the Chilled Raspberry Soup? That is the question. Such are the choices that guests have to make when dining at That Place on Bellflower. Choosing among entrées like Roasted Duckling, Chicken Champagne, and the house specialty, Veal Sweetbreads, is just as difficult. Karen vowed that the Veal and Leek Strudel would have been her choice. Debbie might have chosen the Crispy Parsley Trout Hunan. Since we were there about two in the afternoon, we opted for a dessert. Because we couldn't decide among Cheesecake, Torta Ciccolata, Sweet Potato Pie, and the four Ice Cream Truffle selections, we asked our server, Marko, for his recommendation. He emphatically replied, "Torta Ciccolata!" Our arms don't need to be twisted too hard to order a chocolate-and-raspberry combination, so we quickly placed one order. We then asked him to recommend a second dessert, and he replied, "Torta Ciccolata!" We'd found a fellow chocoholic. In the end, we ordered the Piña Colada Truffle, a refreshing combination of vanilla ice cream, coconut, and Pineapple Sauce.

The restaurant can best be described as cozy. It was once the stable and carriage house of a large estate. Original brick floors, posts, and beams further enhance the ambiance. We were seated at a small table overlooking the lovely courtyard. During warm-weather months, it's a popular place to grab a late bite to eat after nearby cultural activities. Our favorite room is at one end of the restaurant. It encompasses the original fireplace and really gives a feel for the building's past use.

The modern artwork displayed throughout is in such stark contrast to the structure and its past that it works perfectly. The majority of the paintings are in black and white; most are contemporary nudes. Many of these are the work of Joseph Glasco, a Texas artist whose work current owners Isabella and David Chesler collect.

This carriage house made the transition to restaurant during the original hippie days of the late sixties and early seventies. However, the chef did not serve up granola and tofu. At one time, this was a hamburger joint, then a pizza parlor, until Isabella Chesler and her son, David, purchased it. The original That Place on Bellflower menu was upscale continental. A few of these dishes have remained, such as Filet Mignon in Bearnaise Sauce and Beef Wellington. Now, there's a much more international flair, including flavors of Cuba and the Pacific Rim. If that doesn't fit your palate or your budget, never fear. Order a Bellflower Burger and Fries. With its location near Cleveland's cultural district and medical mecca, there's something for everyone.

VEAL AND LEEK STRUDEL

1 pound ground veal
1 cup leeks, chopped coarse
1 egg
1 teaspoon salt
½ teaspoon white pepper
½ teaspoon nutmeg
1 sheet puff pastry
1 egg yolk
Béchamel Sauce (see below)

Preheat oven to 400 degrees. Brown veal over low heat. In a large bowl, mix veal with leeks, egg, salt, pepper, and nutmeg. Place puff pastry on a baking sheet. Form veal mixture into a loaf shape on top of pastry. Wrap pastry around veal mixture to completely enclose it. Seal edges with a little water. Bake for 45 minutes. Brush top of strudel with a little egg yolk. Place back in oven for 15 minutes until top is browned. Slice and serve with Béchamel Sauce. Serves 4.

BÉCHAMEL SAUCE

¼ cup butter
¼ cup flour
1 cup milk
1 cup heavy cream
1 teaspoon chicken bouillon granules
½ teaspoon nutmeg
salt and pepper to taste

Melt butter over low heat, then add flour, whisking constantly until mixture is completely smooth. Using a wire whisk, slowly add milk, cream, and bouillon. Add nutmeg and heat until thickened. Add salt and pepper. Yields about 1½ cups.

VEGETARIAN COUNTRY-STYLE SPAGHETTI

1 pound spaghetti
1 tablespoon oil
1 cup plum tomatoes, chopped
1 cup green olives, sliced
½ cup red onion, chopped
¼ cup Poblano peppers, chopped
4 cloves garlic, crushed
½ pound feta cheese, crumbled
1 cup dry vermouth
½ teaspoon saffron
3 tablespoons cracked black pepper
3 eggs, beaten

Cook spaghetti al dente. Rinse, drain, and set aside. Heat oil in a large sauté pan. Add tomatoes, olives, onions, peppers, and garlic. Sauté approximately 1 minute. Add feta, vermouth, and saffron and sauté another 2 to 3 minutes. Add spaghetti and black pepper. Cook uncovered for 5 minutes. Add eggs and toss quickly to combine. Remove from heat and place in serving bowls. Garnish with additional black pepper if desired. Serves 4 to 6.

CLUB ISABELLA

2025 UNIVERSITY HOSPITAL DRIVE
CLEVELAND, OH 44106
216-229-1177

At the turn of the twentieth century, this section of Euclid Avenue—indeed, this area of Cleveland—was abundant with lovely Victorian homes of wealthy and successful families. Today, Club Isabella stands as a lonely reminder of those times. When it was constructed, the building was the carriage house for the Douby family estate. Records indicate that Mr. Nathan Douby was the first businessman to run the May Company retail stores here in Cleveland. After the mansion was torn down, the carriage house was donated to an order of nuns, who used it as their nunnery. Around the time of Prohibition, the structure did a real about-face, becoming a speakeasy. It's rumored that Bob Hope once performed here during its heyday.

Today, the small structure is surrounded by concrete giants. Club Isabella sits just outside the main entrance of University Hospitals. Its proximity to Case Western also encourages students and faculty to frequent the restaurant. As one local reviewer put it, from "local docs to post-docs," they're all here. In addition, the establishment is close to the Cleveland Museum of Art, the Cleveland Historical Society, the Cleveland Museum of Natural History, and Severance Hall, home of the Cleveland Orchestra, so it also has a following in the community's cultural sector.

The restaurant's ambiance is casual. Club Isabella is a perfect place to kick back and relax. The live jazz that can be enjoyed almost any night of the week further adds to the mellow atmosphere. The original stable doors open from the main dining room on to patio seating in a garden-like setting, where tables are nestled near ivy-covered walls. This was quite popular the day we visited, with several tables of guests lingering in the warm sunshine.

Inside, interesting dividers sit in several locations. Their top halves are constructed from leaded-glass squares, while the bottom halves are typical of common stall dividers. A splash of color is provided by large paper flowers twined above the simple bar. Potted palms placed throughout soften the angular lines of the very open main dining room. The original posts and beams are still intact, as is the narrow wooden-slat ceiling. Offsetting the rustic feel of the carriage house is an eclectic mix of contemporary portrait paintings.

The menu is appropriately simple, yet offers a variety that includes something for everyone. The Russian Salmon Salad Sandwich, served on pumpernickel bread with a side dish of Potato Salad, was a popular choice with Debbie, as was the Almond-Crusted Chicken Strips. The Triangle Duck Cakes, served with

Mint Hollandaise Sauce, caught Karen's eye. And those were just the lunch choices. For dinner, the menu tends more toward an Italian influence. Choices include Calamari Fritti, Mussels Basilico, and Spaghetti ala Frutti di Mare.

As we left, we waved to the chef, visible behind a large picture window set into a brick archway in one wall of the building. It provided an interesting contrast—an individual plying his trade in a century-old structure, able to look out over the hustle and bustle related to medical technology and the modern world.

BOMBALOTTI

2 cups penne pasta
1 cup Italian sausage
½ cup button mushrooms, sliced
½ cup fresh peas
1 tablespoon olive oil
½ teaspoon fresh garlic, chopped
salt and pepper to taste
1 cup heavy cream
½ cup chicken stock
¼ to ½ cup Parmesan

Cook penne according to package directions. Drain and set aside. In a sauté pan, sauté sausage, mushrooms, and peas in olive oil and garlic. Drain excess oil. Season sausage mixture with salt and pepper. Add cream and chicken stock. Simmer 5 to 8 minutes until sauce thickens. Add pasta and toss to mix. Top with Parmesan and serve. Serves 2 generously.

SHRIMP PROVENCALE

10 large shrimp, peeled and deveined
1 tablespoon olive oil
1 tablespoon fresh garlic, chopped
½ cup white wine
½ cup tomato juice
½ teaspoon fresh basil
½ teaspoon crushed red pepper
1 cup tomatoes, chopped
salt and pepper to taste
2 slices French bread

In a sauté pan, sear shrimp in olive oil and garlic. Add wine and tomato juice. Add basil and red pepper. Allow to cook down approximately 4 to 5 minutes. Add tomatoes and season with salt and pepper. Pour over French bread. Serves 2 as an appetizer.

CHAPTER 3

Once Upon a Tavern

The Heritage Restaurant

Back in the old days, a tavern wasn't just a place to stop in for happy hour. It was typically the hub of activity for a town. Certainly, a great deal of information was exchanged over a pint or two, and more than a few deals were struck. These taverns served as the post office and stagecoach stop, as well as the best place in town to get a good meal. That last part hasn't changed. Their ambiance today ranges from laid back to upscale, and the cuisines vary from sandwiches to crepes. They've evolved but stand ready, as before, to meet the needs of society's broad spectrum.

137 COURT AVENUE SW
CANTON, OH 44702
330-453-8424

Benders Tavern advertises itself as the place "where fine food and the best of service have been nationally famous for over 95 years." The slogan is right—this is a place that is serious about food. There are four dining rooms and a taproom in which you can enjoy the very extensive selection of items. The menus change daily, and there are never fewer than nine or ten seafood specials each day. Karen selected the Char-Broiled Tasmanian Salmon with Tomato Caper Relish, Bender Fries, and Coleslaw, while Debbie opted for the Baked Mushroom-Chicken Noodle Casserole. Both choices were delicious. The Bender Fries, which are a kind of scalloped-potato hash browns, were unusual and so good that we were forced to have a second helping. Benders serves a selection of pies and cheesecakes for dessert, but its specialty is the Benders Sundae, served with homemade Peanut Chocolate Sauce.

We sat and chatted with Jerry Jacob, the current owner. He showed us one of his old postcards of the taproom from 1902. Very little has changed since then. The brown and white hexagonal tiles are all still there, as is the ornate tin-tile ceiling. The large bar is still in use,

only now it is surmounted by an enormous blue marlin. The unbelievably intricate mural surrounding the taproom is impressive. Painted in 1907 by an itinerant Dutchman in exchange for room and board, and based on illustrated chapter headings from a German book, it used to contain German quotations and satirical quips that have unfortunately long since been painted out.

Sadly, a fire in 1988 destroyed the upstairs banquet rooms—and also the murals on those walls. However, guests can still enjoy the priceless marble, the tiger-oak paneling, and the tin-tile ceilings—each more ornate than the last—in the four dining rooms that remain. Jerry chatted about his childhood. He recalled visiting Benders when ladies and gentlemen entered through separate doorways into different dining rooms. We were in the main dining room, which had once been for gentlemen only. Ladies were occasionally allowed, but only if escorted, and rarely even then. If a gentleman visited Benders with his wife or family, he was expected to eat in the ladies' dining room. Back then, a couple of the favorite menu items were Sardine Sandwiches and Peanut Butter and Bacon Sandwiches.

Many famous people have visited Benders over the years. Newspaper articles tell of guests such as Billy Graham, Tom Poston, and Joel Rose. Football celebrities have included Jim Thorpe, Lou Groza, and Brian Piccolo. Karen would have been thrilled to meet Olympic swimmer Johnny Weissmuller, best known for playing Tarzan. Debbie wondered if more recent visitor Dan Quayle enjoyed the Bender Potatoes (with an *e*).

It was a delightful meal. Clearly, the clientele shared our appreciation of "Canton's oldest and finest restaurant and tavern." As we stepped back outside to Court Avenue and placed our feet on the well-worn front step, we reflected on the thousands of people who had walked this path before us.

YELLOW PICKEREL CAMP KAGEL-STYLE

salt and pepper to taste
½ teaspoon paprika
2 yellow pickerel, heads and tails removed, deboned
2 tablespoons flour
¼ lemon, cut in half
2 tablespoons fresh parsley, chopped fine

Sprinkle salt and pepper and paprika over fish. Roll fish in flour and place flesh side down in a buttered ovenproof skillet. Brown fish over medium heat for about 2 minutes, then turn fish over and place skillet in a 400-degree oven for 15 minutes. Remove fish from skillet. Squeeze lemon pieces into skillet, add ½ of parsley to the drippings, and sauté for 1 minute. Arrange pickerel on 2 plates and pour drippings over top. Sprinkle with remaining parsley and serve at once. Serves 2.

BENDERS TURTLE SOUP

½ cup oil
1 cup carrots, diced
1 cup celery, diced
2 medium onions, diced
3 medium cloves garlic, chopped fine
⅓ cup flour
7 cups fish stock
1 tablespoon pickling spices
1 cup tomato paste
½ teaspoon thyme
½ teaspoon basil
¼ teaspoon black pepper
¾ teaspoon salt
1 tablespoon parsley flakes
¼ teaspoon dill weed
¼ teaspoon MSG, if desired
⅓ teaspoon rosemary
½ teaspoon sugar
2½ pounds turtle meat, diced
½ cup sherry wine
2 tablespoons lemon juice

Heat oil in a large stockpot and sauté carrots, celery, and onions. Add garlic and continue to cook. Gradually stir in flour. Whisk in stock a little at a time until well blended. Add rest of ingredients except turtle meat, sherry, and lemon juice. Simmer for 2 hours, stirring occasionally. Ten minutes before serving, add final 3 ingredients. Continue to cook, stirring frequently to break up turtle meat. Serves 8 to 10.

COURT STREET GRILL
112 COURT STREET
POMEROY, OH 45767
740-992-6840
WWW.COURTSTREETGRILL.COM

Former Jefferson Airplane band member Jorma Kaukonen occasionally stops by to play a riff. Other nationally known musicians such as Eddy "the Chief" Clearwater have also performed at the Court Street Grill. Artists on their way from a performance in Pittsburgh to their next show in Cincinnati or Indianapolis frequently play for an evening. The restaurant, in conjunction with the Pomeroy Blues & Jazz Society (known as PB&J), sponsors free summer concerts.

PB&J is a part of owner Jackie Welker's life in more ways than just the music society. This traditional children's favorite is a popular item of the Court Street Grill's menu. It all started years ago when Jackie and his mother saw a recipe in *Better Homes and Gardens* magazine for a grilled peanut butter and jelly sandwich. The two tried the creation and thought that heating the peanut butter really made the sandwich much better than the cold lunchbox variety. When Welker bought the restaurant, he served the sandwiches just as he and his

mother used to make them. However, he took quite a bit of ribbing for having PB&J on the menu, so he decided to upscale it by slathering the filling on a flour tortilla, rolling it, and then deep-frying the whole thing. Neither Karen nor Karin Johnson of the Meigs County Tourism Board, who was dining with us, is a peanut butter fan, but we all loved Jackie's creation.

Karen also tried the soup of the day, Chicken Tortilla, topped with shredded cheddar cheese and a dollop of sour cream. It had just enough zing and was delicious. We shared the Court Street Griller, a large grilled ham sandwich topped with melted Swiss, cheddar, and provolone cheeses. It was served with light, crunchy potato chips on the side and a large stack of napkins. The food here is meant to be enjoyed right down to the last drop on your chin. We also sampled the Yamma Damma Doo's, french-fried sweet potatoes glazed with a brown-sugar mixture. Debbie may have finally found a way to get her family to eat sweet potatoes for Thanksgiving!

After all that food, we certainly didn't have room to try the famous Bungtown Burger, a past winner at the Amsterdam Burger Festival. The name *Bungtown* comes from the community of Burlingham, just down the road from Pomeroy. It seems that during Prohibition, many of Burlingham's influential women went around removing the bungs, or corks, from their husbands' stashes of liquor. Word spread, and from that day on, locals have called the area Bungtown. As we sat and enjoyed the casual atmosphere of the restaurant, Jackie said he didn't even know Bungtown wasn't the formal name until someone mentioned Burlingham to him when he was in high school.

The restaurant was fashioned from a building constructed in 1864. The space once housed a pharmacy but has been a restaurant of some sort since 1935. Jackie says he and his regulars enjoy the distressed look of the original brick walls, the plank floor, and the once-painted tin ceiling. It's an unpretentious tavern with faithful customers greeted by first name as they walk in.

 SUPER SECRET SLAW

½ head cabbage
4 red peppers
4 green peppers
½ pound carrots
½ bunch celery
3 medium onions
1½ cups coarse salt
6¼ cups sugar
1 cup white vinegar

Shred vegetables and mix thoroughly in a large bowl. Add salt and stir. Let stand for at least 4 hours. To strain remaining salt out, place vegetables in a colander and rinse; press and squeeze firmly to remove salt. Return vegetables to bowl. Add sugar and vinegar, mixing thoroughly. Serves 12 generously as a side dish.

Note: The grill serves this on its Bungtown Burger, Court Street Reuben, and Super Secret Slaw Dog.

 PACO STIX

$1/3$ cup peanut butter (smooth or chunky)
$1/3$ cup jelly
2 8-inch flour tortillas
vegetable oil
powdered sugar

Spread peanut butter and jelly equally on each tortilla. Roll once, tuck in sides, and continue to roll. Secure with toothpicks. Heat oil to about 350 degrees in a medium pot. Place rolled tortillas in oil and deep-fry for about 3 minutes. Sprinkle with powdered sugar and serve. Serves 2.

 YAMMA DAMMA DOO'S

vegetable oil
2 large sweet potatoes, peeled and julienned
2 tablespoons brown sugar
1 tablespoon butter, melted

Heat oil to approximately 350 degrees in a medium pot. Deep-fry sweet potatoes for 3 to 5 minutes. Remove from oil and drain. Sprinkle with brown sugar and drizzle with butter. Serves 2.

Heritage
Restaurant

7664 WOOSTER PIKE
CINCINNATI, OH 45227
513-561-9300
WWW.THEHERITAGE.COM

Howard Melvin is full of stories. Not the pull-your-leg type, but interesting tidbits that relate to The Heritage Restaurant, which he and his wife, Janet, have owned since 1959. The restaurant was once the home of Edgar and Martha Scott, who purchased this tract of land—situated along what was to become the Wooster Turnpike—in 1827. The Little Miami Railroad eventually came past. With all the riverboat, railroad, stagecoach, and wagon traffic, the herds of animals going to market, and even racehorses out for their daily exercise, this was a busy place!

At the turn of the twentieth century, the home became a well-known restaurant. In actuality, Kelly's Gardens was a roadhouse, but it was one of the area's first and finest, and so enjoyed a popular following. After paying for a meal or a drink, customers were given change in coins and told, "We're out of paper money." This practice increased the likelihood that the clientele would use the slot machines on the premises. Anna Victoria and Frank Kelly were

more commonly known as "Ma" and "Pretty" Kelly, the latter nickname referring to Frank's wardrobe of two hundred suits and a wagonload of hats, a clear indication of the couple's success.

Circus owner John Robinson wintered his show at nearby Terrace Park. Since the Kellys owned many of the circus concessions, they were good friends with the circus people, among whom was a contingent of pickpockets so savvy they even had special equipment for removing diamonds from the jewelry of victims. The reward from the Kellys for a diamond was two dollars or a shot of whiskey. Two-quart measures full of gems were evidence of their success. Pretty Kelly also trained prizefighters, including Kid McCoy, and dabbled in politics. Upon his mysterious death in 1919, his son Cornelius, known always as "Corny," stepped in.

The roadhouse continued to operate successfully during much of Prohibition. A small frame dwelling still in use today had a cellar filled with Canadian beer, and the barn held whiskey beneath its straw-covered floor. Some of the steps leading to the second-floor dining room were hinged, creating additional space to stash potables. Local law enforcement closed the operation down once, but Ma Kelly got a permit to reopen with a promise that no liquor would be served. Corny, however, served a drink one night to a "nice guy" who just happened to be a federal liquor-control agent, after which Kelly's was closed for good.

Today, the Melvins have certainly shed

that roadhouse image. They brought Cajun cuisine to Cincinnati and were the first to offer Free-Range Chicken. The Heritage is a lovely white wooden structure with black trim that offers fine dining within its doors. The dining rooms are small and fairly intimate. Each is named for some significant part of the building's history. Upstairs is the Scott Room, where an original brick wall was discovered after a 1968 fire, and where the original doorway has been converted into a display case for local artifacts. A first-floor dining room showcases the work of wildlife artist John Ruthven, a family friend.

The menu offers such items as Duck Breast wrapped in Apple-Smoked Bacon and served with Szechuan Peppercorn Honey Sauce, as well as Chinese Pork Tenderloin with Hot-Hot Mustard. Once a year, the restaurant cooks up its Wild Game Festival, which features appetizers such as Smoked Pheasant and Bison Salad. Entrées of Venison Noisettes, Elk Chops, and Wild Boar Tacos certainly pique the curiosity. Whether it's the wonderful history or the delectable menu that intrigues you, we hope you're curious enough to go and experience all that The Heritage has to offer.

SMOTHERED GROUSE

1½ cups flour
1 teaspoon dried thyme (powdered or ground)
1 teaspoon salt
½ teaspoon pepper
4 grouse, split
4 tablespoons butter
1 pound mushrooms, cleaned and sliced
2 cups whipping cream

Combine flour, thyme, salt, and pepper in a paper or plastic bag. Mix well. Shake each half grouse in flour mixture until well coated. Set aside. Melt butter in a large skillet. Sauté mushrooms and remove from skillet. Add grouse to skillet. Brown each half lightly. Place birds and mushrooms in a baking dish. Heat cream to boiling and pour over grouse. Cover and bake at 350 degrees for 1 hour until tender. Serves 8.

CINNAMON-BAKED CARROTS

2 pounds carrots
1 cup butter
1 cup sugar
1 teaspoon salt
2 teaspoons cinnamon
1 cup water

Wash and peel carrots. Cut into 4-inch sticks. Place carrots in a deep baking dish. Melt butter and sugar together in a medium saucepan. Add salt and cinnamon. Stir. Add water. Heat mixture until it starts to bubble. Pour over carrots. Bake 1½ hours uncovered at 350 degrees. You may either serve with a slotted spoon or serve baking juices with carrots. Serves 8 to 10.

210 EAST EIGHTH STREET
CINCINNATI, OH 45202
513-421-6234

Arnold's has an unimposing facade with gray paint peeling off the red bricks underneath. The only exterior change since 1848 was the removal of the wrought-iron balustrade surrounding the first floor. Reputed to be Cincinnati's oldest tavern in continuous operation, Arnold's Bar & Grill continues to serve fine, made-from-scratch meals in an atmosphere redolent of the past.

There are several dining areas on the ground floor, each with a character of its own. We entered the bar area through what used to be the door for gentlemen only. This part of the building housed a barbershop until Simon Arnold opened his saloon in 1861. A simple wooden backbar runs almost the whole length of the room. The tables are gaily covered with red-and-white gingham tablecloths. Visitors are watched over by a voluptuous temptress depicted in stained glass over the entrance.

We sat at one of the booths in the second dining area (which used to be a feed store) and looked at the myriad photographs of Victorian ladies. The walls and floors here are attractively shabby. The old linoleum has been worn away in many places to reveal the original wooden floor below. Throughout the establishment, an eclectic collection of curios, antiques, and old photographs catches the eye. Ronda Roell, one of the owners, told us that the most popular place to eat is the covered courtyard, bounded on two sides by brick walls. Guests sit at the small wooden tables and listen to some of the best folk and bluegrass music to be found.

When the Arnold family moved to Cincinnati, the five brothers and their wives and children all lived above the bar on the second and third floors of the building. For ninety-eight years, they prospered by operating Arnold's. During Prohibition, most of the family moved out of the building to allow dining rooms on the second floor. Elmer Arnold, a descendant of the original brothers, remained on the third floor. It is rumored that he used the bathtub on the second floor to brew illegal gin. The bathtub is still there—but unfortunately, the gin is not!

Before deciding what to eat, we consulted our helpful waitress, Debi, who makes all the desserts in her spare time. She encouraged us to choose the Greek Spaghetti Deluxe, a house specialty. It certainly lived up to its reputation. The spaghetti is lightly tossed in butter, olive oil, and Garlic Sauce and topped with olives, bacon, and tomatoes, a totally delicious combination. The menu offers a large selection of sandwiches, salads, and burgers, as well as many pasta choices. The Muffaleta Sandwich—with capacola, salami, provolone, mozzarella, tomato, and lettuce, dressed in Three-Olive Relish—caught our eye. We also noticed that a number of the salads may be ordered over fettuccine, an unusual twist to an old favorite. We completed our meal with a slice of Chocolate Opera. This dessert's filling is created from Opera Creams, made right here in Cincinnati. It was a slice of heaven on earth.

ARNOLD'S FAMOUS CORNBREAD

2 cups flour
2 cups buttermilk
4 eggs
2 cups cornmeal
½ cup honey
2 tablespoons baking powder
¾ cup oil

Preheat oven to 375 degrees. In a large bowl, combine all ingredients except oil. Add oil and mix again to combine. Pour into a deep 11-by-13-inch baking dish. Bake for at least 30 minutes, until inserted toothpick comes out clean. Serve warm. Serves 12.

ARTICHOKE-STUFFED MUSHROOMS

8-ounce can artichokes, drained and chopped medium
¼ cup mayonnaise
½ teaspoon garlic, minced
1/8 cup Romano cheese, grated
4 large portabello mushrooms, stemmed and scraped

Heat oven to 350 degrees. In a medium bowl, combine artichokes, mayonnaise, garlic, and Romano. Mound ¼ of mixture in center of each mushroom. Bake for 10 to 15 minutes until golden brown. Serves 4 as an appetizer.

CRÈME BRÛLÉE

4 egg yolks
4 tablespoons sugar
pinch of salt
2 cups heavy cream
4 tablespoons brown sugar

Preheat oven to 350 degrees. Beat egg yolks in a medium bowl until slightly thickened. Add sugar and salt and beat to combine. In a medium saucepan, heat cream to a simmer. Pour hot cream into egg-yolk mixture and beat well to combine. Pour mixture into custard cups. Place cups in a deep baking pan and fill with water halfway up cups. Bake for 60 minutes until a knife inserted in cups comes out clean. Set aside to cool, then place in refrigerator to chill.

Just before serving, sprinkle with brown sugar and caramelize with a kitchen torch. Serve immediately. Serves 4.

A Cincinnati tradition since 1865

302 EAST UNIVERSITY AVENUE
CINCINNATI, OH 45219
513-221-5353

Mecklenburg Gardens has been a Cincinnati tradition since 1865. It was originally named Mount Auburn Garden Restaurant and Billiard Saloon under owner John Neeb, who created a prominent gathering place for German immigrants and singing societies. The grape arbor outside the front door became a *biergarten* where famous sopranos and baritones gathered to entertain their countrymen. In 1881, headwaiter Louis Mecklenburg purchased the restaurant. He was determined to teach his fellow immigrants about American traditions, and thus the fictional town of Kloppenburg was created. Mecklenburg's restaurant was the "town hall," and mock elections were held to teach the locals about the American political process. It is said that Kloppenburg was named after the noise that patrons made when banging their empty beer steins on the tables to indicate their need for a refill.

Over the next fifty years, Louis Mecklenburg and eventually his son Carl continued to host the rich and famous, as well as their faithful regulars. Local rumor states that during Prohibition, the Mecklenburg family informed faithful customers about the availability of strong libations by the northward or southward direction of the ship placed over the bar. If you sit at the bar today and check out the unbelievable collection of German beers, you will spot a replica of that ship on the back wall.

The restaurant has passed through many hands, both German and non-German. However, in the 1960s, as the public's desire for fine dining declined, there was no longer a call for German favorites such as Hasenpfeffer (a country-style rabbit dish) or Mrs. Mecklenburg's famous Kartoffeln (potato pancakes) or, indeed, steins of German lager. Despite this, the historic building survived through a variety of cuisines until the current owners, the Harten family, initiated the rebirth of this symbol of German heritage.

We sat in the charming main dining room, which was once the old grill room. Guests can still see parts of the old chimney, and the antique oven still stands in the center of the far wall. The room is surrounded by hand-hewn paneled walls. A hand-painted grapevine winds its way around the room, which overlooks the fully restored *biergarten* and the street beyond. In one corner, glass-fronted shelving abounds with steins.

The extensive menu offers a full range of German favorites and American creations. Debbie chose the Mecklenburg Sampler and thoroughly enjoyed its many appetizers, including Potato Pancakes, Crab Cakes, and Sauerkraut Balls. Karen chose the Chicken Strudel, which consisted of chicken, spinach, and feta cheese in a light Cream Sauce, wrapped in puff pastry. It was an unusual and extremely good dish. The servings were large, so we decided to have a slice of the Apple Cinnamon Strudel to go. We lasted about an hour before we broke down and devoured the strudel and the carton of Caramel Sauce that came with it. It was definitely the best strudel either of us had ever tasted.

CHICKEN SCHNITZEL

6 4- to 6-ounce chicken breasts
½ cup flour
2 eggs, beaten
1 cup breadcrumbs
¼ cup oil
Dunkelwisen Sauce (see next column)

Pound chicken breasts until ¼ inch thick. Dredge chicken in flour, then dip in egg, then dredge in breadcrumbs. Heat oil in a skillet and pan-sear chicken for 5 minutes on each side.

Place chicken on plates and pour Dunkelwisen Sauce over top. Serve immediately. Serves 6.

DUNKELWISEN SAUCE

¾ cup white wine
½ cup beer
2 cubes chicken bouillon
¼ cup lemon juice
⅔ cup capers
3 14-ounce cans artichoke hearts, quartered
4 sticks butter

In a medium saucepan, combine all ingredients except butter. Stir together over medium-low heat. Remove pan from flame. Cut butter into small chunks and add to pan. Stir until creamy. If sauce is thin, add more butter. Keep sauce at room temperature when serving over chicken.

★★★

3 EAST SHARON AVENUE
GLENDALE, OH 45246
513-771-5925

When Larry Youse was working in business management and his wife, Cindy, was an advertising art director, friends urged them to open a restaurant. Finally, in the spring of 1975, the two were convinced and went out looking for a location. On their first outing—actually within the first hour of searching—they found the site that was to open on August 6, 1975, as the Grand Finale.

The building they've revitalized had been purchased around the turn of the twentieth century for $750 by J. J. Kelley. He established a saloon, which quickly became a popular stop along the main thoroughfare between Cincinnati and Dayton, now Route 747. Photos show a horse-drawn Wiedermann beer wagon making deliveries in front of the tavern. Prohibition closed the bar, but Kelley's daughters remained in business by running a grocery store on this street corner in Glendale. Many residents remember stopping in for penny candy after school. Kelley's Corner Grocery remained until 1970.

When the Youses made their discovery in April 1975, canned goods still lined the shelves.

Larry and Cindy chose to restore much of what remained, including the tin-tile ceiling, today painted a fresh cream. Carpeting in a Victorian-inspired pattern and antique tables and chairs round out the décor of the main dining room. Upstairs is a veritable treasure trove of antiques. This is the bar area of the restaurant, no doubt called "the Attic" because it is full of an eclectic mix of memorabilia such as photographs, prams, skates, bowling pins, and much, much more.

We were seated in an enclosed back-porch area, where French doors opened to a popular warm-weather courtyard. Hanging plants gave the room a garden feel, and a collection of birdcages added a whimsical touch. Artwork was displayed throughout. The rotating exhibit by Cincinnati artists changes every four to six weeks.

When the restaurant first opened, crepes and desserts were the mainstays of the menu. Examples of the crepes include Shrimp Lawrence Crepes, consisting of shrimp and diced asparagus in a mild Paprika Sauce, and Crepes Coq au Vin, filled with chicken breast in White Wine Sauce with toasted almonds. The crepes were—and continue to be—well received, but customers wanted a wider variety of tasty offerings. The menu has expanded to include such dishes as Artichoke Fritters, Chicken Ginger, and Veal Morel. Other items that we found particularly tempting were the Chicken Sausage Orzo and the Salmon Pancake.

The name *Grand Finale* was chosen for the

restaurant with the intention of showcasing Larry's luscious desserts. Chocolate Cordial Pie, Caramel Custard, Red Raspberry and White Chocolate Fudge Pie, and Coconut and Macadamia Nut Fudge Pie are all available for your sweet tooth. We opted for the Limelight Pie, a fresh lime pie in a Hazelnut Crust. What will your grand finale be?

STEAK SALAD ANNIE

6-ounce filet mignon, trimmed
¾ cup vinaigrette dressing
3 cloves garlic, diced fine
3 shakes hot sauce
3 cups mixed salad greens
½ cup mushrooms, sliced thin
½ cup Swiss cheese, cubed
12 medium Gulf shrimp, cooked and chilled
4 strips bacon, cooked until crisp, crumbled
1 scallion, chopped fine
1½ teaspoons parsley, chopped

Char-grill filet mignon medium rare. Slice very thin into bite-sized pieces. Combine vinaigrette, garlic, and hot sauce. Marinate meat in this mixture for 30 minutes, stirring occasionally.

Arrange greens in a chilled serving bowl. Top with mushrooms and cheese. Arrange shrimp in a circle, then place filet mignon in center. Sprinkle with bacon, scallions, and parsley. Use reserved marinade to dress salad. Serves 2 as an entrée or 4 as a side salad.

GRAND TRIFLE

4 cups pound cake or yellow cake chunks
1 cup fresh or frozen strawberries in syrup, thawed
½ cup port wine
½ cup cream sherry
8 large scoops vanilla ice cream
1 cup fresh or frozen raspberries in syrup, thawed
1½ to 2 cups heavy cream, whipped
¼ cup slivered almonds, toasted
8 maraschino or chocolate-covered cherries for garnish

In 8 large brandy snifters or a 2-quart clear-glass bowl, layer first 8 ingredients in the order given. Garnish with cherries. Chill at least 1 hour to blend flavors. Serves 8.

THE ZOAR TAVERN & INN

162 MAIN STREET
ZOAR, OH 44697
330-874-2170
WWW.ZOAR-TAVERN-INN.COM

Religious persecution was a significant cause for many Europeans to emigrate to America. The group of German separatists that exited Wurtemberg in April 1817 was no different. Four months later, they arrived in Philadelphia. Aided by the Quakers there, the group was able to purchase fifty-five hundred acres of land in the Tuscarawas Valley. A small group of men set out for that territory, leaving the rest to winter in a more comfortable environment. By spring, the men had constructed enough dwellings to house their families. The name *Zoar* comes from the biblical story of Lot, who went to Zoar seeking refuge from Sodom.

Since life in the new land was incredibly harsh, the settlers created the Society of Separatists of Zoar. Men and women possessed equal political rights within this society, which managed the goods and services within the community for the mutual benefit of all.

In 1827, the society was contracted to dig seven miles of the Ohio & Erie Canal, which cut across its land. The canal opened the village to commerce. At one point, the Zoarites operated four canal boats. By the mid-1800s, the society had accumulated more than $1 million in assets. But after the death of its spiritual leader, Joseph Bimeler, the society began to decline. By the late 1800s, the group was no longer commercially viable, thanks largely to increased industrialization. It ultimately disbanded in 1898. In the split, each member equally received land, housing, and goods.

Today, the village is still home to about seventy-five families, who can be seen almost daily at the community post office, since there is no home delivery. The United Church of Christ occupies the meeting house built in 1853. The Ohio Historical Society maintains many of the buildings, including the bakery, the wagon shop, and the blacksmith shop. Others are privately owned and serve as quaint shops. House #23, built as the home of the village doctor, Clemens Breil, was later converted to a tavern where Zoarites could relax. Today, villagers and tourists alike enjoy it as The Zoar Tavern.

We stopped by on a late afternoon and tucked ourselves away at a corner table across the room from the high-backed dark wooden booths. Red-and-cream pads on the benches matched the curtains hanging at the narrow windows. Simple lamps in coordinated colors hung above. The menu here is quite varied, ranging from traditional appetizers such as Potato Skins and Buffalo Wings to soups such as Spatzle and Sausage and Lentil. We found the Mahogany Chicken Breast, served in Plum Sauce, and the Portabello and Red Pepper Sandwich quite appealing. Whether you opt for the modern or the traditional, a trip to Zoar will definitely be enlightening.

SPATZLE SOUP

3 quarts water
3 pounds chicken, cut into large pieces
2 medium onions, chopped
2 cups celery, diced
2 cups carrots, diced
1 teaspoon salt
¼ teaspoon white pepper
1 batch Spatzle (see below)
5 sprigs fresh parsley, chopped

Bring water to a boil in a large stockpot. Add chicken, vegetables, salt, and white pepper. Bring back to a boil, then turn down heat to medium-low and simmer for approximately 1 hour. Remove chicken. Debone and chop meat. Add uncooked Spatzle to simmering stock. Add chopped chicken and parsley and serve. Serves 12 to 16.

SPATZLE

3 cups flour
1 cup milk
3 eggs

Thoroughly combine ingredients in a medium bowl. Push dough through a spatzle maker or a colander into chicken stock. Simmer Spatzle for approximately 2 minutes until they float.

CHICKEN SCHNITZEL

¼ cup flour
1 teaspoon salt
¼ teaspoon white pepper
1 egg, beaten
3 tablespoons milk
1 cup breadcrumbs
salt and pepper to taste
4 boneless chicken breasts, pounded to ¼-inch thickness
4 tablespoons butter

Combine flour, salt, and white pepper in a small bowl. In another small bowl, beat together egg and milk. In a third bowl, season breadcrumbs with salt and pepper. Lightly coat each chicken breast with seasoned flour. Shake off excess, then dip chicken breasts in egg mixture, then roll them in breadcrumbs. Sauté in butter over medium heat for 5 to 7 minutes per side. Serves 4. The Zoar Tavern & Inn serves this dish with sautéed Spatzle and cabbage.

GREAT LAKES
BREWING CO.
CLEVELAND, OHIO

2516 MARKET AVENUE
CLEVELAND, OH 44113
216-771-4404
WWW.GREATLAKESBREWING.COM

McClean's Feed & Seed Co. and the Market Tavern were established circa 1865. The tavern became a popular spot for tradesmen and Cleveland's legal and civil-service professionals. One of its most famous patrons was Eliot Ness, who first gained fame as the leader of Chicago's Untouchables, the renowned Prohibition agents. Ness is credited with reining in Al Capone's gang. After those successes, he came to Cleveland, which was teeming with organized crime and government corruption during that time. After a favorable tenure as Cleveland's director of public safety, he ran unsuccessfully for mayor. Today, a picture of Ness hangs on the wall of Great Lakes Brewing Co., and one of the beers served here bears his name.

The barroom retains much of its nineteenth-century charm, with its simple booth seating and its lovely tiger mahogany bar, which is riddled with bullet holes attributed to an exchange between Eliot Ness and an unknown assailant. The rooms on the second story above the bar figured in the life of another famous individual. Today, this space is used as banquet rooms. At one time, however, it served as the law offices where a young clerk named John D. Rockefeller got his start before moving onward and upward to found Standard Oil.

Great Lakes Brewing Co. opened for business on September 6, 1988, becoming the first microbrewery in the state of Ohio, and the first brewery to open since Prohibition. Although the buildings at 2516 Market Street had never been a brewery, tradition was nearby. German immigrant Leonard Schlather established Schlather Brewing Company in 1878 on the corner of Carroll Avenue where Dave's Supermarket now stands. The brick structure across the street from Great Lakes Brewing Co. was once the horse stables for the Schlather operation. In March 1998, Great Lakes Brewing Co. expanded its operations, incorporating the horse stables into its new state-of-the-art brewing plant.

The restaurant was quite busy the day we visited. The sidewalk dining area, the main dining room (located in the old feed store), and the bar area were all full. A wait for a table would have been more than twenty minutes, which our tight schedule didn't allow. Instead, we hoisted ourselves onto barstools and enjoyed the ambiance à la Mr. Ness. In addition to the amber lager called Eliot Ness, the brews for the day were Dortmunder Gold, Burning River Pale Ale, Edmund Fitzgerald Porter, and

Westside Wheat Ale. An extensive list of Pub Exclusive Brews and several seasonal beers were also available.

We chose to share the Barbecued Brewery Shrimp, skewered and served on a bed of tasty Onion Straws, and the Walleye Bites, delicious bits of Lake Erie walleye battered, fried, and served with Cocktail Sauce and spicy Creole Sauce. On another visit, we might choose the Cajun Chicken Barley Salad, the Tap Room Tortellini Salad, or the Apple Pork Tenderloin Salad, all of which sounded wonderfully unique. There are plenty of selections to suit every appetite, but don't miss the Walleye Bites. They're habit forming!

PRETZEL AND CONFETTI CHICKEN

1 cup Parmesan
2 cups pretzel crumbs
5 boneless chicken breasts
2 tablespoons oil
Mustard Ale Sauce (see next column)
Confetti Vegetable Relish (see next column)

Preheat oven to 350 degrees. Combine Parmesan and pretzel crumbs. Dredge chicken breasts in pretzel mixture. Heat oil in a large sauté pan and brown chicken on both sides. Remove from pan, place in a baking dish, and put in oven for approximately 20 minutes.

To serve, place a chicken breast on each of 5 plates. Drizzle Mustard Ale Sauce on top of or under chicken, then sprinkle chilled Confetti Vegetable Relish over top. Serves 5.

MUSTARD ALE SAUCE

¾ cup ale
²/₃ cup water
½ teaspoon chicken base
½ teaspoon thyme
½ teaspoon cumin
¼ teaspoon white pepper
2 cups heavy cream
2 tablespoons Dijon mustard
2 tablespoons whole-grain mustard

Combine ale, water, chicken base, thyme, cumin, and white pepper in a large saucepan. Reduce by ½. Add cream. Reduce again until thickened to sauce consistency. Add mustards. Yields approximately 2 cups.

CONFETTI VEGETABLE RELISH

½ red pepper, seeded
½ yellow pepper, seeded
½ cucumber, seeded
1 tablespoon red onion
½ cup olive oil
juice of 1½ limes
³/₈ teaspoon cumin
¼ teaspoon white pepper

Finely dice vegetables and combine with remaining ingredients. Chill until served.

CHAPTER 4

Just Millin' Around

Jay's Restaurant

In *Titus Andronicus*, Shakespeare penned, "More water glideth by the mill than wots the miller of." Early communities frequently developed along water sources for just that reason. After the general store, the mill was one of the businesses most essential to settlers. Gristmills ground farmers' crops into various food products. And the presence of a gristmill encouraged further settlement. Lumbermills soon followed, supplying lumber for construction. Some of the mills featured here are still in operation, and all satisfy the needs of modern citizens by serving up good meals.

HISTORIC CLIFTON MILL

ESTABLISHED 1802

75 WATER STREET
CLIFTON, OH 45316
937-767-5501
WWW.CLIFTONMILL.COM

There used to be almost a hundred thousand mills operating in this country. Now, fewer than fifty are still in their original condition. Antonio Satariano Sr. and Jr. take great pride in being the owners of one of the oldest of those remaining few. They share a passion for preserving history, which led them to return their mill from a state of disrepair in 1988 to its original purpose. Under their supervision, the original grinding stones were reinstalled and a replica of the original waterwheel was constructed. They repaired floors and walls and even added a covered porch from which to view the waterfall that drops to the Little Miami River.

We sat in the Millrace Restaurant, one of the two dining rooms in The Clifton Mill. The view from atop the gorge is spectacular, even more so in winter, when every inch of the mill and the gorge below is covered with 2.5 million lights. The restaurant is located in the old storage and storefront part of the building. It is full of interesting photographs of the village

of Clifton, mill memorabilia (including a fabulous collection of old flour bags), and wooden tables and chairs. It is easy to be transported back in time.

Built in 1802 and originally named after its owner, Owen Davis, this is one of the largest water-powered gristmills still in operation. The old Davis Mill was owned and operated by many different families over the years as it quietly provided a backdrop to history itself. The whole village is historic. The Old Stagecoach Inn—a stop on the Accommodation Line—is opposite the mill. The stagecoach ran from Springfield to Cincinnati. At that time, the village of Clifton was well known for its clay soil and freshwater springs. During the rainy season, boggy roads were common, making stagecoach operation difficult at best. It did not surprise us to learn that in 1836, Clifton was the site of Ohio's first recorded stagecoach accident, which took place on the northern side of the village.

The cooking is home-style. Whole-grain breads, pies, and cookies are baked daily. We visited at breakfast time to sample the famous Pancakes, made from grain ground on the premises. Opting for the Millrace Breakfast Combo—which includes Buttermilk, Cornmeal, and Buckwheat Pancakes, served with a side of Sausage—we chatted with Antonio Jr. as we ate. He told us that the mill endeavors to support the local community in its purchases for the restaurant. To that end, it buys ostrich from a local ostrich farm. Hogs raised at another local farm are used in the mill's Whole-

Hog Sausages—and jolly delicious they are, too!

There is much history to see here, both at the mill and in the village. We knew we would have to return another day for a more leisurely walk down to the narrows, where famous Indian scout Cornelius Darnell is supposed to have leapt over the gorge to escape pursuing braves. In the meantime, supporting local farmers with every mouthful, we settled down to clean our plates!

APPLE FARM BREAD

2 packages dry yeast
½ cup lukewarm water
1½ teaspoons salt
1 tablespoon pasteurized honey
1 tablespoon maple syrup
1/3 cup vegetable shortening, softened
½ teaspoon cinnamon
12/3 cups hot water
1¼ cups applesauce (not chunky)
2/3 cup powdered milk
5 cups all-purpose flour
2 cups whole-wheat flour

In a small bowl, dissolve yeast in luke-warm water. Set aside to activate. In a large mixing bowl, combine salt, honey, syrup, shortening, cinnamon, and hot water. Mix thoroughly. Gradually stir in applesauce, then powdered milk. Add dissolved yeast and mix well. Stir in flours a cup at a time until dough is stiff but not tacky.

Lightly flour a breadboard and knead dough for at least 10 minutes. Place dough in a lightly greased bowl and cover with a moist cloth. Put bowl in a warm place and let dough rise for approximately 1 hour until it doubles in size.

Uncover and punch dough down. Cut dough in half and place each half in a lightly greased 9-by-5-inch loaf pan. Let pans stand for 30 minutes to allow dough to rise again. Bake for 45 minutes in a preheated 400-degree oven. Yields 2 loaves.

ARTISTS' SUGAR MAPLE THREE-LAYER CORNBREAD

1 cup cornmeal
½ cup whole hard wheat bread flour
½ cup white flour
2 teaspoons baking powder
½ teaspoon sea salt
1 brown egg, well beaten
¼ to ½ cup molasses or honey
¼ cup vegetable oil
3 cups milk or buttermilk

Preheat oven to 350 degrees. In a large mixing bowl, combine all dry ingredients. In a medium bowl, combine all wet ingredients. Pour wet ingredients into large bowl and combine thoroughly; mixture will be very liquid. Grease a 9-by-9-inch pan and pour in batter. Bake for approximately 50 minutes until top springs back when touched. Serves 10 to 12.

1995 BROADWAY AVENUE
STOCKPORT, OH 43787
740-559-2822
WWW.STOCKPORT.COM

The only remaining hand-operated lock system in the United States is here on the Muskingum River in Stockport. Its influence has been felt both in the community and in the Stockport Mill Country Inn. The day we visited, we shared the dining room with the Hook family, descendants of Captain Isaac Newton Hook, a Muskingum riverboat pilot. He died in 1906, the year the current mill was built. But he was around to see the first mill here, built in 1842 and then rebuilt in 1849 after a fire destroyed the original. After operating for fifty-four years, the rebuilt structure also burned down.

When the Dover brothers put up the current building in 1906, a young lad by the name of Fred James declared it to be "plenty sturdy." He and Ray Devitt eventually bought the mill and subsequently sold it to the Farm Bureau. In 1979, the operation was taken over by Robert and Jack Grove. During their tenure, the mill was involved in many 4-H projects. This venture lasted for almost twenty years, until the doors closed in 1997. They didn't stay that way for long.

In August 1998, Laura and Randy Smith were on a motorcycle ride, pursuing Randy's hobby of collecting antique autos. What they ended up with was an antique mill instead. During the renovation, Laura used as much of the mill and its machinery as possible. The original flooring and beams are evident. Old gears have been used as table bases. Rather than being painted or stained, one wall is covered with slate tiles once used as roofing.

There were a lot more knickknacks and pieces of old equipment to take in as we glanced over the menu. Karen chose the Morgan County Chili, topped with red onions and cheese. Debbie opted for the House Salad and the Crock of River Mud—blue crabmeat mixed with seasonings and cheeses, baked in a crock, and served with pita wedges. All were tasty. The dinner menu features such favorites as Veal Oscar and Chicken Piccata. Laura is proud that the restaurant is known for its Certified Black Angus Beef, served in a variety of ways, including topped with Whiskey Butter. As we sat at a table with a picturesque view of the river and the locks, we were very glad the Smiths had taken that fateful motorcycle ride. Wanting to linger awhile longer, we decided to share dessert, choosing the Muskingum Mudslide, an Oreo Cookie Crust filled with Praline Ice Cream and topped with Caramel Sauce. It was rich, and half a slice was perfect!

We chatted with Laura and quickly came to appreciate the intensity of her devotion to the mill and to this community. Each of the lovely guest rooms upstairs is named for a significant part of the area's past, highlighting the connections between the mill's history and Stockport's legacy. She proudly showed us the papers certifying government approval for the mill to generate its own power, which will ultimately be available to the townspeople as well. She envisions myriad tourism opportunities to augment the boating and fishing already in place.

LAURA'S MASHED POTATOES

8 to 10 medium potatoes
4 8-ounce packages cream cheese, room
  temperature
4 sticks butter at room temperature, divided
16-ounce carton sour cream
paprika

Peel potatoes and cut them into small chunks. Place in a saucepan and cover with water. Bring water to a boil and cook potatoes until done. Drain and mash thoroughly. Mix in cream cheese, 3½ sticks of the butter, and sour cream. Combine well. Place mixture into a large casserole dish. Scoop out a well in center of potato mixture and add remaining ½ stick of butter. Sprinkle top with paprika. Bake for 30 minutes until a crust forms on top. Serve hot. Serves 10 to 12.

MOM'S TOMATO SOUP

16 medium vine-ripened tomatoes
½ bunch celery, chopped
3 medium carrots, chopped
1 large onion, chopped
1 teaspoon granulated garlic
1 tablespoon sugar
1 teaspoon paprika
salt and pepper to taste
1 tablespoon cornstarch
1 tablespoon water

Nick skin of each tomato and immerse in boiling water for 3 minutes. Drain water and leave tomatoes to cool for 30 minutes. Peel skin off tomatoes and discard. Dice tomatoes and place in a large stockpot. Add celery, carrots, onions, and garlic and cook down over medium heat for 30 minutes. Add sugar, paprika, and salt and pepper and bring back to a boil. Thicken soup if required, using a slurry made from cornstarch and water. Serves 8.

HONEY CINNAMON BUTTER

5 sticks butter, room temperature
½ cup honey
¼ cup cinnamon

Place butter in a large bowl and whip until smooth and creamy. Add honey and cinnamon and whip for another minute. Place mixture in a sealed container and refrigerate until needed. Yields 3 cups.

JAY'S RESTAURANT
225 EAST SIXTH STREET
DAYTON, OH 45402
937-222-2892
WWW.JAYS.COM

When we arrived at Jay's at seven-thirty on a Thursday evening, it was packed. Those waiting assured us that it was definitely worth the delay. How very true that was. Jay's Restaurant was unveiled in 1976 and quickly became renowned for its wine list and its seafood. The wine list reads like poetry, and Karen enjoyed perusing it thoroughly. It is so comprehensive that it even has several pages at the front explaining the different types of wine, for those unsure of exactly what they should select. There are also maps with descriptions of various wine regions, all there for customers' education. On Fridays and Saturdays, bottles of wine are available for sale from the restaurant. Five different bottles are opened each of those days for customers to sample and purchase. This overall approach reflects owner Jay Haverstick's passion for excellent wine.

This excellence is reflected in the seafood as well. Seven or eight selections are available baked, char-grilled, or blackened. Monkfish, Tuna, Swordfish, Salmon, Halibut, Scrod, and Lake Erie Walleye were among the choices the night we dined. For landlubbers, there are chicken and steak options, but Jay's and seafood really are synonymous. We opted for the Crab Cakes, which were fabulous. They had tiny bits of red cabbage and red pepper mixed in, which added an interesting texture and just a bit of flavor. The cakes were served with Remoulade Sauce and Asian Vinaigrette. Debbie preferred the rich ginger flavor of the Asian sauce, although both were excellent. For dessert, Karen was tempted by the Chocolate Coffee Torte, but we ended up sharing a piece of Jay's famous Lemon Sour Cream Pie. Both of us delighted in the light, not-too-sweet finish to our meal.

Jay's Restaurant is located in the Joseph Kratochwill Dayton Corn and Gristmill, built in the 1850s on the banks of the Miami-Erie Canal. At one time, this mill provided Dayton and much of the Midwest with the Snow Flakes and New Process brands of flour, which were well known for their outstanding purity and fineness. The latter half of the 1900s was a prosperous time for Dayton's Oregon District. Commercial and residential development here left an architectural legacy unparalleled throughout the city. Visitors to the district—which is Dayton's oldest neighborhood—can still see the mansions of the wealthy standing among the simpler homes of laborers and craftsmen.

The interior of the restaurant is appealing in its simplicity. The brick walls of the old mill stand fairly unadorned. The beautiful light fixtures are of the time period of the mill's construction, and the railings were saved from the Old Xenia Hotel. In one corner of the room is an enormous fifty-four-hundred-pound Honduran mahogany backbar. It was commissioned for the opening of the Pony House Restaurant, an establishment where John Dillinger was a regular and where Buffalo Bill Cody is said to have ridden his horse right up to the bar! The bar serves a slightly more refined clientele today, but Jay's is popular with just about everyone, so you never know whom you might see!

DUNGENESS CRAB CAKES

2 tablespoons fresh ginger, chopped
½ to ¾ cup mayonnaise
2 tablespoons unsalted butter
½ red bell pepper, diced fine
½ yellow bell pepper, diced fine
1 pound Dungeness crabmeat
3 tablespoons fresh cilantro, chopped
1 cup radicchio, chopped
1 cup water chestnuts, diced
1 cup carrots, diced fine
1½ cups panko (Japanese breadcrumbs), divided
salt and freshly ground black pepper to taste
olive oil
Asian Vinaigrette (see next column)

In a small bowl, thoroughly combine ginger and mayonnaise. Set aside. Melt butter in a small sauté pan and sauté red and yellow peppers until soft but not brown. In a large bowl, combine crabmeat, sautéed peppers, cilantro, radicchio, water chestnuts, and carrots.

Add 1 cup of the breadcrumbs and enough mayonnaise mixture for ingredients to stick together. Add salt and pepper.

Form mixture into 8 patties and lightly coat with remaining breadcrumbs. In a large sauté pan, heat olive oil over medium heat. Once oil is hot, sauté Crab Cakes for 3 to 4 minutes on each side until golden brown.

To serve, whisk Asian Vinaigrette and drizzle ¼ cup onto each plate. Place a Crab Cake in the center of each plate and serve immediately. Serves 8.

ASIAN VINAIGRETTE

½ cup fresh lime juice
½ cup shallots, chopped fine
2 tablespoons soy sauce
1½ tablespoons fresh ginger, chopped fine
¼ cup jalapeño peppers, chopped fine
½ tablespoon fresh garlic, chopped fine
2 tablespoons honey
1½ tablespoons curry paste
2 tablespoons sesame oil
1 cup olive oil

Whisk together all ingredients in a small bowl. Set aside until needed. Yields 2 cups.

PEERLESS MILL INN
319 SOUTH SECOND STREET
MIAMISBURG, OH 45342
937-866-5968

Once a water-powered lumbermill on the bank of the Miami-Erie Canal, this charming inn is an ideal choice whether dining with a large group of friends or seeking a romantic dinner for two. The rustic hand-hewn timbers and enormous beams of dark wood give the six dining rooms and tavern a cozy, intimate feel. The large wood-burning fireplaces in most of the rooms and the flagstone floors enhance the historic ambiance, as do the wrought-iron chandeliers and the pewter chargers. Floral tablecloths and the assorted pieces of artwork adorning the walls lend a touch of warmth.

A favorite gathering place for the townsfolk, it was fairly full on the day we visited. The menu selections all looked good, from the Seafood Casserole Gratinée to the Lemon Pepper Marinated Roast Pork Loin. We opted for the Peerless Mill Inn's signature Seven-Layer Mill Salad and a homemade loaf of bread. Debbie enjoyed her Veal Piccata with Lemon Cilantro Butter, while Karen savored the Roast Duckling with Cranberry Orange Glaze and Blended Wild Rice. Both selections were served

with delicious Pecan-Glazed Carrots. The homemade desserts all sounded as wonderful as the entrées. Hot Peach Crisp à la Mode topped Karen's list, with Black Bottom Pecan Pie running a close second. It was a leisurely meal orchestrated by an attentive staff. We had plenty of time to investigate the small wooden curio boxes around the room, each filled with antique glassware and china.

Built in 1828, the lumbermill sat side by side with a gristmill. The Miami-Erie Canal had just been built, and these mills—locally known as the Great Peerless Mills—made a substantial contribution to the local economy. Named for the Miami tribe of Indians, who had once roamed the local hills, Miamisburg was a growing village and a small but important center for cultivating tobacco. Wheel and carriage factories, binderies, and paper makers were among the local industries.

The sawmill was powered by a large overshot waterwheel turned by the waters of the canal. Giant logs were dragged in from nearby woodlands and turned into beams and planks. Over the next seventy years, a city built from the products of the sawmill grew. The gristmill also prospered, wagons continuously passing through to pick up meal or flour. In 1938, the gristmill closed its doors for the last time, and the building was destroyed. Visitors now park their cars on what was once the site of that picturesque building. The lumbermill was converted into a restaurant called the Peerless Pantry. That prosperous business was eventually renamed the Peerless Mill Inn. Today, the inn is proud to be called a living part of the history of Miamisburg.

TOURNEDOS DUMAS

1 cup onions, chopped
2¼ cups cream
1 tablespoon butter
1 tablespoon flour
salt and pepper to taste
4 4-ounce beef fillets
4 toast rounds
4 slices ham
2 ounces Gruyère cheese, grated

In a medium pan, simmer onions in cream. In a second pan, melt butter and stir in flour. Cook over medium heat for 1 minute. Add onion mixture and cook until thickened. Add salt and pepper.

Broil or pan-fry fillets to degree of doneness desired. Place on toast rounds and top with onion sauce, ham, and cheese. Place under broiler for about 30 seconds until cheese is melted. Serves 2.

APPLE DUMPLING CAKE

1½ cups oil
2 cups sugar
3 eggs
2 teaspoons vanilla
3 cups flour
1 teaspoon salt
1 teaspoon baking soda
1 teaspoon cinnamon
3 cups apples, diced but not peeled
1 cup nuts
1 cup brown sugar
1 stick butter, softened
¼ cup milk

Preheat oven to 350 degrees. In a large bowl, combine oil, sugar, eggs, and vanilla. Add flour, salt, baking soda, and cinnamon and stir to combine. Add apples and nuts. Stir mixture well and pour into a Bundt pan or an 8-by-12-inch cake pan. Bake for 1 hour.

In a small bowl, combine brown sugar, butter, and milk. Pour mixture over top of cake as soon as it is removed from oven. Let set for at least 1½ hours before removing cake from pan. Serves 12.

GOSHEN'S MILL STREET TAVERN
120 EAST MILL STREET
AKRON, OH 44308
330-762-9333

Born in Germany in 1822, Ferdinand Schumacher immigrated to Ohio in the mid-1800s. He started a notions shop in Akron, which soon evolved into a grocery store. Back in Germany, he had ground oats and sold the meal, so he decided to try that here. In 1856, after just two years, his product was so popular that he bought an old factory and installed machinery that allowed him to grind about twenty barrels of oats per day. At the onset of the Civil War, Schumacher's business expanded even further, as he sold his oatmeal to the army.

Schumacher next built the Empire Barley Mill. Then, in 1872, the New German Mill joined his conglomerate. The year 1883 saw the construction of the Jumbo Mill, a full eight stories high. At that point, Schumacher's operations stretched from Mill Street down Broadway to what is now Quarry Street, covering an entire city block. He was so successful that by 1885, Akron's downtown was comprised mainly of his businesses. After a disastrous fire in 1886, Schumacher merged with the Akron Milling Company. A few years later, they joined with other mills to form the American Cereal Company, the precursor of the Quaker Oats Company. Most Americans are familiar with Quaker Oats. At that time, it was an innovative company in its approach to packaged foods and merchandising.

Today, what was formerly a cluster of thirty-six turn-of-the-twentieth-century grain silos is a collection of luxurious guest rooms and suites of the Akron Hilton at Quaker Square. Other restaurants and shops built from the old factories incorporate some of the original brick walls and timber. The Mill Street Tavern is located in what was once the cellar of the F. Schumacher Milling Company. The sandstone walls are two to three feet thick and date back to the 1860s. The blocks came from a quarry that Mr. Schumacher also owned, which allowed him to precisely specify how the millstones used in his factories were produced. The restaurant is full of vintage items, from the original oak support beams to the milling equipment. The railing on the staircase and much of the woodwork in the tavern came from Schumacher's mansion, which at one time stood just three blocks from today's Quaker Square. The breathtaking collection of stained glass throughout the dining room was garnered from turn-of-the-century churches and mansions in the Akron area.

The restaurant is known for its Prime Rib, which you can order off the menu or have in conjunction with the fabulous buffet. We opted instead for Ferdinand's Penne, tossed with chicken, sugar snap peas, roasted red peppers, tomatoes, and basil and coated in delicious Tarragon Cream Sauce. Many famous individuals have visited the restaurant, and it's easy to understand why. Luciano Pavarotti, Shari Lewis, Bill Cosby, Yanni, Florence Henderson, Vincent Price, Jacques Cousteau, and Simon and Garfunkel are but a few who have dined here. You won't find our pictures on the wall just yet, but the wait staff treated us like celebrities nonetheless.

BREAD PUDDING

4 cups milk
1 cup half-and-half
2 cups heavy cream
8 eggs
1¼ cups brown sugar
7 teaspoons cinnamon
¼ cup vanilla
¾ teaspoon salt
1 loaf French bread
1½ cups blueberries

In a medium bowl, combine all ingredients except bread and blueberries. Cut up bread into 1½-inch cubes. Place bread in a large baking dish and sprinkle with blueberries. Pour milk mixture over top and mix until bread is saturated. Cover dish and bake for 20 minutes. Uncover and bake an additional 20 minutes until top is golden brown. Serves 8 to 12.

HONEY LIME VINAIGRETTE

½ cup plus 1½ tablespoons red wine vinegar
2¼ teaspoons olive oil
2 ounces Dijon mustard
2 cups vegetable oil
juice of 1 large lime
¾ teaspoon garlic, puréed
¾ cup plus 1½ tablespoons honey
¾ teaspoon oregano
¼ teaspoon salt
$^1/_8$ teaspoon pepper

Place all ingredients into a medium bowl and whisk together. Pour into an airtight container and refrigerate until needed. Shake well before using. Yields about 3 cups.

OLD MILL WINERY

403 SOUTH BROADWAY
GENEVA, OH 44041
440-466-5560

As you drive on Route 534, you can't miss the freshly painted barn-red buildings high-lighted in crisp white trim that comprise the Old Mill Winery. We arrived after a long day on the road, so the casual, laid-back atmo-sphere was quite welcome. Tables for four pro-vided ample seating throughout the spacious interior of this old feed mill. The original wooden floor echoed with a warm resonance as guests moseyed up to the bar to get a drink or order a bite to eat.

We opted for one of the Wednesday-night specials, steamed Peel-and-Eat Shrimp, served in a basket with Red Potatoes, Corn on the Cob, and Garlic Bread. As our food was being prepared, we wandered through the interior, looking at the antique cash registers, stoves, trunks, and wooden buckets. We even discov-ered the Christmas bell that helped dress the holiday windows at Macy's Department Store in downtown Cleveland during the early 1900s.

The J. E. Goodrich family started a milling

business in this building sometime in the early 1860s. The plastered and wallpapered rooms on three floors at the back of the building prob-ably functioned as the Goodrich residence. During the early 1900s, the mill was owned by George Brown, and then by Farmer's Sup-ply Corporation. In 1937, General Mills took over the operation, using the mill to turn out ingredients for its wide array of products. All in all, the mill supplied the needs of the area for almost one hundred years.

At the time the mill was constructed, Ohio led the nation in the production of wines. Mr. and Mrs. Richard Kinkopf converted the mill into a winery in 1980, recapturing a piece of Ohio's history. Paul Cantwell and Alan and Joanne Schnider became subsequent owners. The Schniders bought the business to provide money for a unique spiritual concept they call their "Faith Foundation." The Old Mill Winery has sixteen wines on its list, including Geneva Blanc, a fruity, semisweet wine excellent for Sangria Coolers, and Grindstone White, a sweet dessert wine made from popular native Niagara grapes and similar in flavor to French Sauternes. In addition, the mill produces and bottles altar wines for church consumption in the Cleveland and Akron Catholic Diocese. A real highlight for the establishment came when Mrs. Schnider had the opportunity to offer a bottle of Old Mill wine to the pope!

Many people ask how the Old Mill Win-ery can offer home-style meals at such bargain prices. Whether you go on Tuesday night for Soup Night, visit on Thursday evening for Pasta

Night, or order off the menu, the price is definitely right. The Schniders' philosophy is to "tempt them with food and keep them with wine and great entertainment." Everything from Irish folk music to classic rock can be heard. Sunday is the night when local performers (sometimes after a glass or two of wine) are encouraged to take center stage. But any night of the week, fun is on the menu!

CHAMBOURGIN DRESSING

½ cup sugar
1½ cups oil
½ cup Chambourgin wine or other dry red wine
1 cup balsamic vinegar
1 teaspoon granulated garlic
1 teaspoon black pepper, ground
½ teaspoon basil
1 tablespoon salt

Combine all ingredients with a whisk in a large bowl. Store in an airtight container in the refrigerator. Yields approximately 3 cups.

ALFREDO SAUCE

2 cups heavy cream
½ cup Chablis
1 teaspoon fresh basil, chopped
1 teaspoon garlic, chopped
1 teaspoon fresh parsley, chopped
1 cup Romano cheese, grated
salt to taste
3 egg yolks

In a medium saucepan, heat heavy cream slowly. *Do not boil.* Gradually add next 6 ingredients, whisking well. When cheese is just about completely melted, slowly whisk in egg yolks. Yields approximately 4 cups.

MEAT LOAF

2 pounds freshly ground sirloin
2 pounds freshly ground pork
2 cups fresh breadcrumbs
1 large green pepper, diced fine
1 large red pepper, diced fine
2 cups marinara sauce
2 teaspoons black pepper, ground
2 teaspoons granulated garlic
1 tablespoon fresh parsley, chopped
½ cup sweet red wine
4 large eggs
1 large onion, diced fine

Combine all ingredients in a large mixing bowl, kneading until thoroughly mixed. Form into 4 small loaves and place in a shallow baking pan. Bake in a 350-degree oven for 45 minutes to 1 hour until centers are 155 degrees. Serves 10 to 12.

255 RIVERSIDE DRIVE
TIFFIN, OH 44883
419-448-0100
WWW.THEPIONEERMILL.COM

The Sandusky River, source of power for the Pioneer Mill, is one of only five rivers in the world to flow northward. Two large metal drive wheels located in the basement of this old mill were put in place shortly before the mill closed in 1951. The electricity generated by one of these wheels is enough to supply power for heat for the entire winter to the house across the street from the mill. During a power outage, the restaurant can obtain enough juice from the other wheel to continue operating. These metal wheels replaced the wooden handcrafted drive wheels that supplied the power for most of the mill's history. Today, the wooden wheels are displayed throughout the restaurant. Many are now in service as unique chandeliers.

The mill was built by Josiah Hedges, founder of the town of Tiffin. Begun in 1822, construction of the frame building and the raceway took two years to complete. When fire destroyed much of this flour mill and gristmill in 1875, it was rebuilt using brick. But that was not to be the only disaster facing the mill. In 1913, the town of Tiffin was devastated by a flood. As the waters receded, a two-acre island comprised of debris—primarily bricks and stones—was formed beside the mill. Today, bits and pieces of brick can still be seen on the island. In 1937, a disastrous fire swept through the building. Charring is visible on many of the heavy wooden posts and beams that still support the structure.

We were seated in the main dining room, called the Millstone Room, at a table overlooking the water. The large, deep-set windows provided an ample view of the property and the river. Intrigued by the items adorning the walls, we wandered, as we are prone to do. Our most interesting discovery was the "swing sifter," a type of elevator in which small buckets were attached to a four-inch-wide cotton belt. The belt stretched from the basement to the third floor. The small containers on the belt would pick up grain and carry it upward, where it would be ground into flour, bran, or middling. We also enjoyed the printed quotations and bits of information about the mill's history displayed throughout the building.

Debbie's Broiled Walleye Sandwich was made with fish straight from the Great Lakes. Karen chose to experience the other end of the country for her lunch, ordering the Texiana Salad. It consisted of a chicken breast basted in Barbecue Sauce and seasoned with Cajun spices, served over a bed of greens, all of which was topped with shredded cheese, crisp bacon, and onion slices. The luncheon buffet was a popular choice with many diners. On the day we visited, it featured Tomato Bisque and Broccoli Cheddar Soup, several salads, Liver and Onions, Sliced Beef, and several dessert choices. Prime Rib is the house specialty for dinner, and we can't think of a more fitting environment in which to enjoy it.

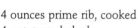

PRIME RIB AND FETA SPUDS

4 ounces prime rib, cooked
4 potatoes, baked
¼ cup mushrooms, sliced
¼ cup onions, diced
¹/₃ cup feta cheese

Cut prime rib into small cubes. Cut potatoes in half and scoop out insides, reserving skins. Place insides in a medium bowl and add prime rib and rest of ingredients. Stir to combine. Divide mixture into 8 portions and mound inside the 8 potato skins. Place under broiler for about 30 seconds until golden brown. Serve immediately. Serves 4 as an appetizer.

PIONEER SIGNATURE CUT

4 8-ounce Delmonico steaks
¼ stick butter
1 cup onions, chopped
8 ounces mushrooms, sliced
1 teaspoon Magic Spice
1 teaspoon garlic salt
1 cup Worcestershire sauce
1 cup soy sauce
1 tablespoon red wine vinegar
8 slices provolone cheese

Char-grill steaks to desired doneness. While meat is cooking, melt butter in a large skillet. Add onions, mushrooms, and all spices and liquids to pan. Cook until vegetables are soft and liquid is reduced by ¹/₃. Put steaks on plates. Pour ¼ of mushroom mixture over each steak and top with 2 slices of cheese. Place under broiler for 30 seconds to melt cheese. Serve immediately. Serves 4.

CHAPTER 5
All Around the Town

Engine House No. 5

As settlements grew, farming was still the main source of income in Ohio, but labor did diversify. In each town, it was necessary to have churches, schools, banks, and other businesses to meet the needs of the growing population. This chapter features restaurants with cuisines and ambiance that are as varied as the businesses that once occupied their locations. From gentlemen's clubs to the jail, there's something for everyone.

1092 BETHEL ROAD
COLUMBUS, OH 43220
614-451-9774
WWW.THEREFECTORYRESTAURANT.COM

As we prepared to take our first bite of dessert, the background music eased its way into the strains of "My Favorite Things" from *The Sound of Music*. Karen's Apple Tart with Rosemary was phenomenal, and Debbie's Chocolate Pistachio Torte was equally satisfying. We both started with soup, tasting the Butternut Squash Velvet Soup and the Creamy Asparagus. That was followed by an entrée of Salmon, served with Truffled Potatoes Napoleon, and Swordfish Tournedos. Everything was absolutely delicious.

The Refectory is housed in what was once Bethel United Methodist Church. The congregation began in 1842 in a defunct distillery. A barn at the corner of Francisco and Kenny Roads, housed the worshipers until 1858. Eventually, noise from the nearby train tracks forced the church to be moved so sermons could be heard. It was relocated next to the Perry Township schoolhouse, which eventually was used as a Sunday school. Only for the last thirty

years have the two structures been connected. In 1966, the church family felt it had outgrown this structure and made a decision to relocate once again. December 1971 saw the completion of a new church and the sale of the old building to a group of individuals interested in starting a restaurant. When they signed the deed that created The Olde Church-House, the deed stated that the building could never again be used as a church. But thanks to the stained-glass windows, the high beam ceilings, and the candlelight, the serenity of the building continued to be felt. The name was changed from The Olde Church-House to The Refectory in 1980.

During our visit, sacred music played softly and candlelight flickered almost in tune to the music. We were seated in the main dining room, which was once the sanctuary. We would have been equally happy to sit in the Bistro du Nord, located in the old schoolhouse, where diners enjoy a special three-course prix fixe menu.

The gastronomic delights are creations of chef Richard Blondin, a native of Lyon, France, and a protege of chef Paul Bocuse. Among the clientele for Blondin's memorable meals are old parishioners. Choir members and Sunday-school graduates happily stroll through the hallways and reminisce. One former pastor has celebrated several wedding anniversaries in the very place where he once presided over his congregation.

BUTTERNUT SQUASH SOUP

1 medium-sized leek
1½-pound butternut squash
2 tablespoons unsalted butter
¼ cup onion, chopped
2 tablespoons celery, minced
3 cups whole milk
salt and freshly ground black pepper to taste

Trim leek at both ends, leaving 2 to 3 inches of light green stalk. Slice lengthwise, pull the layers apart, and rinse thoroughly. Chop into ½-inch-thick slices, rinse again, and drain. Peel squash, then cut in half and remove seeds by scraping with a soup spoon. Cut squash into ½-inch cubes.

Heat butter in a large saucepan. Sauté leeks, onions, and celery over medium heat for about 8 minutes. Add squash and sauté another 4 minutes. Add milk and bring to a simmer. Cook uncovered for 30 minutes. Let mixture cool slightly, then purée in 2 or 3 batches in a blender until very smooth. Add salt and pepper. Return mixture to saucepan and keep warm.

Ladle into bowls and garnish each bowl with fresh chives. Serves 6 to 8.

 WARM APPLE TARTS
WITH ROSEMARY

1¼ sheets puff pastry, frozen
5 Golden Delicious apples
¹/₃ cup plus 4 tablespoons sugar, divided

½ cup unsalted butter, divided
½ teaspoon fresh rosemary leaves, chopped fine
3 tablespoons powdered sugar, sifted
4 unblemished mint sprigs

Thaw pastry and roll it out to ½-inch thickness on a floured surface. Cut out 4 5-inch rounds. Transfer to a baking sheet lined with parchment paper and refrigerate for at least 35 minutes.

Peel, core, and finely dice 1 apple. Place in a small saucepan with ¹/₃ cup of the sugar and half the butter. Cook over low heat until apple is very soft and sugar is dissolved to make a spreadable compote. Set aside to cool.

Preheat oven to 350 degrees. Cut four 6-inch squares of parchment paper. Arrange squares on a baking sheet and sprinkle 2 tablespoons of sugar evenly over sheets. Place chilled pastry rounds on top of sugar and prick dough with a fork. Spread a tablespoon of cooled apple compote over each pastry round. Sprinkle rosemary evenly over compote. Peel, core, and thinly slice remaining apples. Fan out slices in a circular pattern on top of tarts.

Melt remaining butter and using a pastry brush, coat tops of tarts carefully. Sprinkle remaining 2 tablespoons of sugar over tarts. Bake for 18 minutes until apples turn a light golden brown. Serve hot dusted with powdered sugar and garnished with mint sprigs. Serves 4.

121 THURMAN AVENUE
COLUMBUS, OH 43206
614-443-4877
WWW.MUER.COM/ENGHOUSE5

Located in the center of German Village is the Gothic structure known as Engine House No. 5. Built in 1892 at a cost of fifteen thousand dollars, it housed a crew of men, a steam-engine pumper, a hose wagon, and, of course, the four horses that pulled them. It even included a hayloft used to store fodder for the horses and to provide the occasional fireman with a place to take a nap. From the front of the structure, the most prominent feature is a tall brick tower designed for the surprising purpose of hanging out hoses to dry.

Many such fire stations were built in German Village, mostly due to the limited distances that horses were able to pull firefighting equipment. Engine House No. 5 saw a long life of service. However, the advent of motorized transport decreased the need for such a large number of fire stations, and Engine House No. 5 was closed in 1968. The empty building was slated for destruction when Chuck Muer purchased it at auction and transformed it into a unique restaurant that opened its doors in 1974. Engine House No. 5 has since

maintained a reputation for excellent gourmet seafood.

I visited in early January. Concerned about being caught away from home in a snowstorm, Debbie and I had agreed to dine separately. I sat in the main dining room, which originally housed the pumper engine and the hose wagon. Large bay windows containing circular tables are located where the two arched doorways used to be. The polished brass pole—still the pride of the place—is used for the delivery of birthday cakes, much to the surprise of guests. The walls of this delightfully large room are tastefully adorned with fire-station memorabilia, much of it from the Central Ohio Fire Museum. The room is painted in peach and muted green. The high tin-tile ceiling with its egg-shaped period lighting fixtures adds to the feeling of spaciousness and elegance.

The extensive menu here contains a significant number of seafood items, as one would expect. I opted for the daily special, Martha's Raspberry Chicken, served with seasonal vegetables and Rice Pilaf. Everything was superb, from the swift and unobtrusive service to the warm, freshly baked bread to the delightfully tangy taste of the chicken.

Guests will also enjoy the atmosphere in the other dining rooms, of which there are several. Upstairs in the old hayloft are a dozen tables where diners can overlook the piano bar. A large, hand-carved oak table adjacent to the loft is dedicated to Chief Walter Strickfadden, who was once stationed here and who gave sixty years to the fire service in and around Columbus. On the lower level, guests may visit "The Spot," where more casual—but every bit as delicious—meals are served. The original slate floors and the stone foundation give diners a unique glimpse at yet another aspect of this wonderful old property.

STUFFED FLOUNDER

16 small flounder fillets (about 4 pounds)
salt to taste
1 batch Crabmeat Stuffing (see next column)
½ pound crabmeat, preferably Maryland backfin
  lump crabmeat
½ stick butter, melted
½ teaspoon paprika
rice pilaf

Season fillets lightly with salt. Place ¼ cup Crabmeat Stuffing between 2 fillets. Roll double fillet up and place on a baking sheet lined with parchment paper, with ends of fillets underneath. Make a cut lengthwise through top fillet and stuff with ⅛ of the crabmeat. Repeat with remaining fillets. Brush fillets with melted butter, lightly dust with paprika, and season with salt. Cover and refrigerate until ready to bake.

Preheat oven to 350 degrees. Bake fish for 12 to 15 minutes until it flakes with a fork. Divide stuffed fillets among 4 plates. Serve with rice pilaf. Serves 4.

CRABMEAT STUFFING

¼ cup plus 1½ tablespoons clarified butter, divided
1½ tablespoons flour
1½ cups milk
½ cup onions, chopped fine
1 pound backfin lump crabmeat, shells removed
¾ cup dried breadcrumbs

In a small pan, cook 1½ tablespoons of the butter and flour together over low heat to form a roux; do not brown. Set aside. Heat milk and slowly add roux. Cook over low heat for 3 to 5 minutes until thickened. Cool cream sauce to room temperature.

Heat remaining butter in a small saucepan and sauté onions until translucent. Place onions and butter in a mixing bowl and set aside. In a medium bowl, toss crabmeat gently with breadcrumbs. After onions and butter have cooled, fold them into cream sauce, then fold cream mixture into crabmeat and breadcrumbs, mixing gently with a rubber spatula. Be careful not to break up crabmeat. Refrigerate until ready to serve. Stuffing will keep for up to 5 days. Yields 2 cups.

215 NORTH WALNUT STREET
WOOSTER, OH 44691
330-262-3333

The first jail to be constructed in Wayne County was made of timber and had walls twenty-six feet in length. It was completed in August 1817. Twenty-two years later, a second, solid, dungeon-like building was erected. It came to be known as "the Stone Jail." It burned during the Civil War, on December 18, 1863. Its replacement was built in the early 1870s on the northwest corner of North Walnut and North Streets. Wayne County historian Benjamin Douglas described it as "one of the finest edifices of its kind in the state." He went on to say that "it was constructed of brick, stone, and iron at a great cost." The actual sum is not known, but an 1899 addition cost taxpayers fifteen thousand dollars.

Guests access the restaurant through an upstairs entrance, where attractive banquet rooms have been fashioned from what was once the sheriff's living quarters. Just off the hallway, down a steep flight of steps, and between thick brick walls is the Olde Jaol Brewing Company. The restaurant prides itself on presenting a limited menu focused on consistent excellence. However, I'm sure the choices are more varied than they were for "guests" more than 130 years ago. My meal was certainly more upscale than the bread and water some prisoners must have received, although I did dine in one of the cells.

The unique structure and its excellent food create a first-rate dining experience. From the moment I entered, I tried to count the brick archways in an attempt to ascertain how many prisoners may have been housed here. Looking around the particular cell in which I was seated, I could easily imagine one man existing in the space, but I wondered how crowded it actually got, particularly since the entire jail was much roomier than I'd expected. Subtle lighting and occasional barred doorways completed the ambiance. Old photos of faculty members from nearby Wooster University and a vintage photograph of the jail provided further perspective.

Although I arrived before five o'clock, guests were already seated at several tables, taking advantage of the "Early Parole Dinners," the Olde Jaol's rendition of early-bird specials. The choices that particular evening were Chicken Piccata, Prime Rib, Salmon, Orange Roughy, and Beef Bourguignonne. I opted to order from the regular menu, choosing the Sirloin, an extremely tender cut of Certified Black Angus Beef garnished with deliciously thin, crispy Onion Rings and served with Garlic Red-Skinned Mashed Potatoes. At the suggestion of the staff, I also enjoyed a serving of Upside Down Apple Cinnamon Walnut Pie, accompanied by Vanilla Ice Cream. I was sorry that Karen wasn't there to dig into that with me.

Guests wanting a more casual atmosphere can stop by the Olde Jaol Tavern, once the carriage house for the jail. There, the menu includes Bail Burgers, Steak Escape Sandwiches, and other choices such as the Sticky Fingers Basket of chicken fingers and the Call out the Dogs Basket, consisting of a chili dog topped with onions and cheddar cheese. If I were sentenced to the Olde Jaol Brewing Company, I'd never seek parole!

JAOL HOUSE CHICKEN

2 4-ounce chicken breasts
½ cup mushrooms, sliced
½ cup demi-glace
2 2-ounce slices Canadian bacon
2 slices Monterey Jack cheese

Place chicken breasts in a broiler pan and broil for 10 minutes, turning halfway through. While chicken is broiling, sauté mushrooms in demi-glace. Reduce to warm and set aside. Top chicken with Canadian bacon and cheese. Return to broiler until cheese is melted.

To serve, make an oval of mushroom sauce on each plate and top with a chicken breast. Serves 2.

CHEDDAR AND ALE SOUP

2 tablespoons vegetable oil
4 slices bacon, diced
½ onion, diced
2 stalks celery, diced
2 carrots, peeled and diced
6 cups milk
2 15-ounce cans cheese sauce
1 heaping tablespoon chicken bouillon granules
2 teaspoons basil
2 to 3 capfuls Worcestershire sauce
2 to 3 shakes Tabasco sauce
1 heaping tablespoon Lawry's salt
2 teaspoons pepper
1 cup beer
¼ cup cornstarch
¼ cup water

Heat oil in a large pot and sauté bacon and vegetables until cooked. Add milk and cheese sauce, stirring until well combined. Add bouillon, basil, Worcestershire, Tabasco, Lawry's, and pepper. Bring to a simmer. Add beer. Combine cornstarch and water in a small bowl to make a slurry. Thicken soup by adding 1 to 2 tablespoons slurry at a time until it reaches desired consistency. Serves 8.

THE PRECINCT

SINCE 1981

Good Food · Good · Fun · Good Friends

311 DELTA AVENUE
CINCINNATI, OH 45226
513-321-5454
WWW.THEPRECINCTINC.COM

Police Patrol House No. 6 was designed and constructed by Samuel P. Hannaford and Sons in 1901. Designed in the Romanesque style, the distinctive brick building has remained unchanged. Among its distinctive features are a corner turret, arched windows, a winged gable dormer, and a corbeled chimney. The architecture is truly outstanding, as would be expected from the firm that designed the Cincinnati Music Hall, Cincinnati City Hall, and Cincinnati General Hospital.

Back in the early 1900s, horses pulled patrol wagons. Police equipment was carried in the wagons, as were medical supplies sometimes. When this patrol service was instituted, it made Cincinnati only the second city in the nation to have its streets patrolled by policemen. Visitors can still see the old station sign. They can also see where the huge double doors used to open to let the horses into the stable. Remodeled by entrepreneur Jeff Ruby in 1981, the stable has now become the main dining room.

We entered the building via the lobby, which was once the office area for the two-man shifts. At the far end of this room was a small bar with a leaded-glass surround. We sat in the corner turret and sipped our drinks while admiring the many artifacts, which included a large number of black-and-white photographs of police officers. Regulars consider this to be a mecca for top-quality American cuisine. This is witnessed by the numerous photos of exceptionally famous guests. Visitors might bump into anyone from Tom Selleck to Liza Minnelli, or even Sparky Anderson or Johnny Bench.

Entering the dining room, we walked past the life-sized poster of a policeman on the original brick wall. This room is elegantly furnished with white table linens and ornate Victorian bowl-style chandeliers and lamps. The lighting is muted and the service impeccable. Ably assisted by our server, Zach, we decided to sample the appetizers. Freshly baked bread arrived first, accompanied by Hazelnut, Pear, Parmesan, and Gorgonzola Butter. We sampled the Crab Cakes with Creole Mustard Sauce, the Mixed Mushroom Garlic Toast, the Crisp Fried Frogs Legs, the Alaskan King Crab Legs, and the Tiger Shrimp, served with The Precinct's Fresh Horseradish Cocktail Sauce. All of the appetizers were superb.

Our entrée, Steak Diane, was prepared table-side while we savored the Asparagus and Green Bean Salad, served with Maytag blue cheese and a dressing of bacon, and hazelnuts. Both the steaks and salads were excellent, and we agreed that dessert was now out of the question. We should have known better. Our table was barely cleared when dessert arrived. We shared an enormous helping of Jeff's Grandmother's Cheesecake, served in a pool of Raspberry Coulis, and Karen's favorite, Bananas Foster. The bananas had been flambéed in a banana liqueur together with walnuts and cinnamon. It was a truly delectable concoction. What a tremendous combination—an exceptional meal in luxurious surroundings. You can't ask for better than that!

PRECINCT CRAB CAKES

2 pounds lump crabmeat, drained and picked
¼ cup sweet onion, chopped
¼ cup red onion, chopped
2 eggs
pinch of dry mustard
pinch of nutmeg
1 cup breadcrumbs, divided
2 tablespoons mayonnaise
salt to taste
white pepper to taste
cayenne to taste
1 tablespoon olive oil
1 tablespoon butter
Crab Cake Sauce (see next column)

Gently combine crabmeat, sweet onions, red onions, eggs, mustard, nutmeg, and 2 tablespoons of the breadcrumbs. Reserve remaining breadcrumbs for dredging. Add mayonnaise, salt, white pepper, and cayenne to crabmeat mixture, being careful not to overseason. Form into 4-ounce balls and refrigerate for 1 hour.

To cook, lightly dredge crab balls in remaining breadcrumbs, pressing lightly to flatten slightly. Place cakes in a preheated, nonstick skillet with olive oil and butter. Cook for 2 minutes on each side at medium-high heat. Place in a 450-degree oven for 2 to 3 minutes. Pour Crab Cake Sauce over cakes and serve immediately. Serves 4.

CRAB CAKE SAUCE

½ cup heavy cream
2 tablespoons sherry wine (not cooking sherry)
4 tablespoons Creole mustard (coarse mustard or Dijon may be substituted)
2 tablespoons butter
salt and pepper to taste

Stir cream, wine, and mustard into a hot skillet. Bring mixture to a boil. Reduce heat and cook until reduced by ½. Add butter and season with salt and pepper. Yields ½ cup.

Teller's
OF HYDE PARK

2710 ERIE AVENUE
CINCINNATI, OH 45208
513-321-4717

The original settlers of this area were war-weary Revolutionary War veterans entitled to buy land at $1.50 per acre. A deed signed by President George Washington included what is now Hyde Park in the Miami Purchase land grant of more than three hundred thousand acres, acquired by John C. Symmes. Mr. Symmes deeded a large tract to Isaac Ferris. The transaction was dated 1798, but Ferris's residence in the area is documented prior to that date, when he helped found Columbia Baptist Church in 1790. It was purportedly the first Protestant church in the Northwest Territory.

The area remained fairly rural until 1892, when a syndicate of citizens purchased almost all of the property in the triangle bounded by Edwards Road, Observatory Road, and Madison Pike. The vision of James Mooney, Colonel A. S. Berry, T. B. Youtsey, John Zumstein, Wallace Birch, and Charles H. and John Kilgour was to create an elite suburb, one of many around the nation made possible by the expansion of electric streetcar lines.

As successful professionals and their families moved to the area, the Madison Road Improvement Association was formed. The Hyde Park Business Club grew out of that organization. Its five hundred-plus members sought fire protection, a branch library, and improved streets with incandescent lighting, among other things. The first village meeting, with Louis E. Ziegle presiding, was held after the election of officials in 1896 in the space eventually occupied by the Hyde Park Savings Bank. It was also in that building that the first city council was organized.

Not only did Mr. Ziegle serve as the first president of the Hyde Park Business Club, he was also the president of the Hyde Park Savings Bank. The bank continued in operation until 1971. At the time of its closing, it was part of the Fifth Third Bank. After that, the bank space was converted into the Left Bank, an arcade of upscale boutiques. During the transition, a fifteen-by-forty-five-foot skylight that had been covered during Fifth Third's tenure was unveiled. Today, that skylight floods the interior of Teller's of Hyde Park with sunlight. Healthy-looking philodendrons hang nearby. The restaurant uses what is left of the Hyde Park Savings Bank in interesting ways. An old safe serves as the reception desk; bar-style seating on the main floor utilizes the iron-barred teller windows; and the vault is used as a cozy seating area.

We dined on the upper balcony, likely the office space from yesteryear. Karen chose one of the day's specials, the Caramelized Onion and Potato Frittata with Gorgonzola cheese. Debbie, in an Eastern mood, paused over the

Cantonese Chicken Salad before finally deciding to sample the Thai Chicken Pizza. The menu and atmosphere obviously appeal to a wide range, as we dined near tables of senior citizens as well as families with young children. The restaurant is an interesting mix of old and new, and we're certainly glad that we had the opportunity to cash in.

HYDE PARK CHOP WITH MAYTAG BLUE CHEESE SAUCE

1 cup port wine
½ cup heavy cream
1 slice bacon, diced fine
1 shallot, diced
1 tablespoon flour
½ cup Maytag blue cheese
½ cup veal demi-glace or reduction
2 10-ounce bone-in porkchops, butterflied
salt and pepper to taste

Pour port into a medium saucepan. Place on stove over medium-high heat. Simmer until reduced by ½. Add cream and reduce again by ½. Sauté bacon in a skillet until fat is rendered. Add shallots and cook until caramelized. Add flour to skillet to create a roux. Whisk roux into the reduction and stir until well blended. Add blue cheese and demi-glace. Cook porkchops on a grill for 4 to 5 minutes per side. Season with salt and pepper. To serve, spoon sauce over porkchops. Serves 2.

GOAT CHEESE-STUFFED SHRIMP

10 shrimp, 16-20 count, tails on
2 tablespoons olive oil
½ cup goat cheese
1 tablespoon plus 1 teaspoon cilantro, minced
2 teaspoons garlic, minced
Tomato Coulis (see below)

Butterfly the shrimp. Place shrimp on a baking sheet and brush with olive oil. Combine goat cheese, cilantro, and garlic and place evenly on shrimp. Bake at 400 degrees for approximately 8 minutes. While baking, prepare Tomato Coulis. To serve, pool coulis in center of 2 plates. Arrange shrimp, tails outward, around coulis. Serves 2.

TOMATO COULIS

2 cups Roma tomatoes, diced
2 tablespoons olive oil
2 teaspoons cilantro
juice of 2 limes
2 teaspoons sugar
2 teaspoons crushed red pepper

Sauté tomatoes in olive oil over medium heat until they break down. Add remaining ingredients and cook to heat through. Place in a blender or a food processor and purée. Yields approximately 1 cup.

The Phoenix

812 RACE STREET
CINCINNATI, OH 45202
513-721-8901
WWW.THEPHX.COM

Cincinnati's finest example of Italian Renaissance architecture was built in 1893 as The Phoenix Club, the first Jewish businessmen's organization in this area of the country. The architect was Samuel Hannaford, well known for Cincinnati landmarks such as city hall, St. George Church, and what is today The Cincinnatian Hotel. Nothing was spared in The Phoenix Club's interior details. Cherubs, filigree, and scrollwork adorn much of the woodwork. All of the marble, imported from Germany, is original. The grand staircase, made of white marble, is one of the finest examples of its kind in North America. Lovely arched stained-glass panels are situated above the curving staircase, adding further elegance to the entrance.

The Phoenix Club was purchased as a sports annex in 1911 by the members of the Cincinnati Club, located just around the corner. A full-length lap pool and a bowling alley were located in the basement. The Archway Ballroom, on the second floor, became the Billiards Room, holding approximately twenty-five pool tables. Located on the third floor, the Grand Ballroom with its thirty-three-foot ceiling became a basketball court with a balcony for spectators on three sides.

After ninety years as a private club, the building was closed in 1983 when interest in such clubs declined. It was sold, boarded up, and left untouched for three years. In 1986, it was sold again, this time to owners interested in helping The Phoenix rise again to its original beauty. The restoration took two years to complete. One of the difficulties was the stained-glass windows in the Archway Ballroom. Sometime between 1984 and 1986, they were stolen—dismantled and carried away without anyone's noticing. The person suspected of the theft was ultimately charged and tried for his misdeed. During the trial, some unknown individual placed the missing windows in the hallway of the courthouse. The case was then dropped, and the windows were returned to their rightful place. Only a few pieces were not recovered. Their replacements are recognizable by their darker shade of brown. It seems that modern technology couldn't reproduce the original color.

Dinner is served in the former Reading Room, now called the President's Room. The huge, hand-carved breakfront was built entirely on site and spans the width of the room. The Phoenix's starters, listed on the menu as "First Plates," include a pleasant combination of traditional favorites such as Jumbo Shrimp, served creatively with Tomato Cocktail Sorbet, and a Crab Cake accompanied by Bacon, Leek, and

Potato Salad. The Smoked Salmon and Grilled Asparagus in a homemade Lasagna Noodle was too good to pass up. Our "Second Plate" choices were Shrimp Tempura and Roast Amish Chicken with Asparagus and Crimini Risotto. The service was excellent, the atmosphere opulent, and the food sumptuous. It was like Cinderella going to the ball without having to worry about pumpkins or glass slippers.

ROAST ARTICHOKES

3 artichokes
juice of 1 lemon
½ cup olive oil, divided
3 cloves garlic, minced
1 cup white wine
1 cup water

Peel the hard green outer leaves off the artichokes, leaving the tender greens intact. Trim stems with a paring knife, reaching the tender yellow area. Using a spoon, scoop the choke out of the center, leaving the soft, smooth surface. Rub gently with lemon juice to slow down the oxidation process. Heat ¼ cup of the olive oil in a medium saucepan. Place garlic in the pan with the artichokes. Lightly sauté, bulb sides down. Cover with wine, water, and rest of olive oil. Cook covered until tender. Serve or chill and reserve until needed. Serves 1 as an appetizer.

TOMATO COCKTAIL SORBET

3 Roma tomatoes, peeled, seeded, and diced fine
1 shallot bulb, minced
1 clove garlic, minced
½ cup horseradish, grated
juice of ½ lemon
pinch of cayenne pepper
salt and pepper to taste

Combine all ingredients and mix well. Freeze in ice cube trays. Remove from freezer a few minutes before serving. Serves 5.

NEW ENGLAND CRAB CAKES

8 ounces jumbo lump crabmeat
8 ounces crab claw meat
2 teaspoons Dijon mustard
½ cup mayonnaise
¼ cup chives, chopped
¼ cup parsley, chopped
pinch of cayenne pepper
salt and pepper to taste
1 cup dried breadcrumbs

Combine all ingredients but breadcrumbs and mix well. Chill for 4 to 6 hours. Form into 4 cakes. Roll in breadcrumbs until fully coated. Sear in a pan, then place in oven for 10 to 15 minutes until cooked through. Serves 4 as an appetizer or 2 as an entrée.

6892 CLOUGH PIKE
CINCINNATI, OH 45244
513-624-7800

Flora Hess opened her first restaurant on Beechmont Hill in 1925. At that time, she and her staff raised, slaughtered, and prepared all the meats served there. In 1943, she bought the old Clough Pike School from Mount Washington American Legion Post 484 and moved her tavern to this location. "Miss Flo," as she was called, was a devout Catholic who enjoyed people. Each year, she entertained the graduating class from nearby St. Gregory's. In 1983, when Flora Hess was forced to retire due to failing health, she was the oldest active businesswoman in Hamilton and Clermont Counties, as well as the oldest woman in Ohio holding a state liquor license. The tavern passed to her great-nephew Charles Sutter. A long succession of pubs and taverns has since occupied the site.

Gary Sammons decided to take the old school building in a new direction when he opened Clough Crossings in 1997. The two-story brick structure is attractively painted in cream and white, while the interior of the restaurant is suited for casual or fine dining. The walls are simply decorated with framed black-and-white photos of earlier events and scenes from around Anderson Township, named for the area's surveyor, John Clough Anderson. Two old school desks intertwined with flowers decorate the center of the room.

At one end of the room is a remarkable bookcase that served as the backbar in this location when Miss Flo was operating her tavern. The piece, hand-carved in Germany, was one of a matched pair owned by Charles Wolff. Before libraries were provided by the township, most wealthy residents endeavored to create their own. Mr. Wolff owned one of the most extensive collections of books in the area. At the time his palatial residence was built in 1858, he also owned the old Stephen Davis-Stephen Corbly Home. On the land surrounding that home, he constructed a special build-ing to house his rare books, which inclu_ _ an impressive variety of rare Bibles. The bookcase at Clough Crossings and its mate were used to display a portion of Mr. Wolff's fine collection.

We were seated at the opposite end of the room from this lovely piece of furniture, and so could easily admire its craftsmanship. There was also much to look at on the menu, including many tidbits of history, among them an 1898 program from "Cluff" Principal School. We were so engrossed in the history that it took awhile for us to order. The Almond-Crusted Salmon, served in Ginger Saffron Sauce, is one of the most popular entrées, as is the Cajun Seafood Fettuccine. Debbie was in the mood for a light meal, so she selected the Creamy Turkey Vegetable Soup and a side salad. The soup was deliciously full of bite-sized pieces of turkey and assorted vegetables. Karen chose the Tarragon Porkchop topped with Horseradish Sour Cream, attractively served with Wild Rice and Sautéed Vegetables. It was certainly not the type of meal either of us was ever served in the school cafeteria!

ALMOND-CRUSTED SALMON

¾ cup sliced almonds
2 6- to 7-ounce salmon fillets
½ cup flour
1 egg, slightly beaten
2 tablespoons oil
Saffron-Ginger Sauce (see next column)
rice
fresh vegetables

Preheat oven to 350 degrees. Place almonds in a single layer on a baking sheet and lightly toast for 2 minutes. *Do not overbrown.* Allow to cool. Lightly crush almonds by placing in a sandwich bag, sealing, then squeezing between hands. Pour into a shallow container.

Dredge salmon in flour, dip in egg wash, then roll in crushed almonds. Heat oil in an ovenproof skillet over medium heat. Sauté salmon in pan until almonds start to brown. Bake in skillet in oven for 3 to 4 minutes on each side. Remove salmon from pan, set aside, and keep warm.

Using the same pan, make Saffron-Ginger Sauce. When sauce is done, pour ½ cup of sauce into center of each of 2 plates. Place salmon in center over sauce and serve. The chef suggests serving with rice and fresh vegetables. Serves 2.

SAFFRON-GINGER SAUCE

¼ red bell pepper, diced fine
1 teaspoon garlic, minced
1 teaspoon shallots, diced fine
1 teaspoon fresh ginger, minced
½ cup white wine
pinch of fresh saffron
1 cup heavy cream

Sauté peppers, garlic, shallots, and ginger until tender. Add wine to deglaze pan. Reduce by ½. Stir in saffron. Add cream and bring to a simmer. *Do not boil.* Continue cooking until sauce is reduced and thick enough to coat the back of a spoon. Yields 1 cup.

THE SCHOOLHOUSE RESTAURANT
Camp Dennison, Ohio

8031 GLENDALE-MILFORD ROAD
CAMP DENNISON, OH 45111
513-831-5753

How many children do you know who would voluntarily go to school on a Sunday evening? There were quite a few at Camp Dennison School the night we visited. In 1962, when Don and Phyllis Miller converted the school building into a family restaurant, her vision was to provide an establishment where children were welcome. If our experience is any indication, she has certainly met her goal. Octogenarians dined with their children, grandchildren, and great-grandchildren at many of the round tables throughout the old classroom.

The cursive alphabet still runs atop the chalkboard, but instead of seeing lessons printed on it, guests can find the menu for the evening. The entrées here include Schoolhouse Chicken (which Karen ordered), Country Fried Steak, Ham, Fried Shrimp, Baked Salmon, Prime Rib, Top Round Roast, Meat Loaf (which Debbie enjoyed), and Chicken Livers, among others. The side dishes are served family-style

atop lazy Susans in the center of the gingham-covered tables. Before our dinners arrived, we enjoyed Coleslaw, a salad in the delicious Sweet French House Dressing, and Corn Fritters, served piping hot. Bowls of Green Beans, Mashed Potatoes, and Stewed Tomatoes arrived along with our Fried Chicken and Meat Loaf. The Stewed Tomatoes, not typically a favorite of either of us, were so flavorful that both of us had a second helping. Sadly, neither of us had room to enjoy the homemade pies or cobblers for dessert.

The dining room is remarkably like the classrooms in which both of us were educated. Large windows softened by blue-and-white gingham curtains fill the exterior wall. Pictures of Abraham Lincoln, who once visited the school, abound, as do likenesses of George Washington and other presidential personages. A potbelly stove sits against the opposite wall. The high shelf that runs around the room holds tinware, cast-iron cooking utensils, and other paraphernalia.

The school was built in 1863 and is thought to have been the first two-story school in the Midwest. It was named for the Union camp nearby, which was used for the recruitment and training of more than thirty thousand Northern soldiers during the Civil War. It also served as a hospital for the wounded when needed. One of the few military actions—and the only known death north of the Ohio River occurred in Camp Dennison. John Hunt Morgan and his Confederate raiders burned government wagons, resulting in the death of

Daniel McCook, who was riding with Union troops as a volunteer.

An old picture of the building shows that the structure has changed very little. Guests can even sit at old desks while they wait for a table to become available, since reservations are not accepted. Many families choose to feed the goats and the geese housed at the back of the property. Still others while away the time gamboling around the school grounds, just as children more than 130 years ago must have done. Some things never change!

BAKED CRUMB COD

6 saltine crackers
3 tablespoons Parmesan, grated
4 6-ounce Icelandic cod fillets
2 tablespoons butter, melted

Preheat oven to 450 degrees. Place crackers into a sandwich bag and crush. Put cracker crumbs in a medium bowl. Add Parmesan and stir to combine. Place each fillet in a buttered individual serving dish. Sprinkle crumb mixture on top of fillets, then top with butter. Bake for 15 to 20 minutes until firm and flaky. Serves 4.

MEAT LOAF

6 slices bread, broken into 2-inch pieces
¼ cup milk
2 pounds lean ground beef
1 medium onion, chopped
1 medium green pepper, chopped
2 eggs
1 teaspoon salt
1 teaspoon pepper

Preheat oven to 350 degrees. Place bread in a medium bowl, pour milk over top, and set aside for bread to absorb all the liquid. Combine remaining ingredients in a large bowl. Add softened bread and stir to combine. Place mixture in a large loaf pan and bake for 1½ hours. Serves 8.

GREEN BEANS

3 pounds canned green beans with liquid
1 medium onion, chopped
½ cup ham, chopped fine

In a large saucepan, combine all ingredients and bring to a boil. Reduce heat to low and simmer for 30 minutes. Serves 12 to 16.

SMEDLAP'S SMITHY

RESTAURANT
Waterville, Ohio

205 FARNSWORTH ROAD
WATERVILLE, OH 43566
419-878-0261

The history of Smedlap's Smithy that is printed on the menu reads like a tale of Paul Bunyan or Pecos Bill. Smedlap Effingtass came to Ohio from Georgia in 1793, leaving the South to escape a lynch mob. Good old Smedlap set up a still, selling the output to the Indians. From that moonshine, he, according to the menu, made enough to build the Commercial Building in Maumee in 1836. (Isn't it actually Levi Beebe who is credited with that venture?) At some point, Smedlap stowed away on a canal barge headed for Waterville, where he met the daughter of the town blacksmith. As the story goes, he settled down, took over for his father-in-law, and became somewhat respectable.

What we actually do know of the structure is that it was built in 1840 and that, through the years, it served as a blacksmith shop, a livery stable, and a horse-drawn hearse business. A picture taken on August 13, 1841, shows the exterior of the building looking very much like it does today. Inside, what was the hayloft during the building's livery days is now a dining room with seating for about fifty. Guests can access this dining room using the stairs near the bar, but many choose to come down via the large playground slide that spirals from the loft to the main floor. The restaurant is full of tools and other items of the period. A yoke, a saw, an ice pick, old wagon wheels, and an anvil are among them. A collection of smoking pipes is displayed at the far end of the restaurant. A playful map is along the same wall. Drawn in the style of nineteenth-century maps, it combines local sites, period advertising, and modern-day features such as Interstate 75.

As I perused the menu, the Thai Cobb Salad caught my eye. It certainly sounded like a new twist on a perennial salad choice. The Warm Chicken Salad, served with mandarin oranges, cashews, and Honey-Ginger Sauce, also sounded appealing. The menu has a lengthy list of sandwiches, such as the Bistro Burger and the Steak Caesar Sandwich. There are pasta dishes, too, including Cajun Chicken Alfredo and Thai Chicken Pasta. The list of entrées boasts several cuts of Prime Rib, along with selections like Raspberry-Roasted Pork Loin, Fried Shrimp, and Barbecued Spareribs, which happened to be an all-you-can-eat special the night I visited. However tempting all these dishes were, I was told that Smedlap's is especially known for its plank cooking. So, of course, that's what I tried. My New York Strip Steak was cooked and served on a one-inch-thick, well-seasoned oak plank. Steamed Carrots, Green Beans, and Duchess Potatoes accompanied the steak. The meat was wonderfully tender and perfectly accented by Bourbon Whiskey Sauce. Other plank choices included Chicken, Orange Roughy, and Salmon. Since Karen couldn't accompany me that day, the chef generously gave me the recipe so she could "walk the plank" at home!

PLANK FISH

2 7-ounce pieces orange roughy
2 plank boards
2 tablespoons butter
salt and pepper to taste
4 Duchess Potatoes (see next column)
½ cup White Wine Mustard Sauce (see next column)
2 tablespoons Parmesan

Place orange roughy on the planks. Rub each piece with 1 tablespoon of the butter and season with salt and pepper. Place Duchess Potatoes on board on opposite sides of fish. Bake at 350 degrees for 15 minutes until fish is flaky. While fish is cooking, heat White Wine Mustard Sauce. When fish is done, pour sauce over fish and return to oven for 5 minutes. Sprinkle with Parmesan. Serves 2.

Note: To cure planks, soak them in vegetable oil for 1 hour, season heavily with salt, and place in a 350-degree oven for ½ hour. Oak, maple, or cherry wood may be used.

DUCHESS POTATOES

4 large potatoes
2 teaspoons garlic, minced
4 tablespoons butter
salt and pepper to taste
parsley for garnish
paprika for garnish

Peel and quarter potatoes and place in a medium saucepan filled with water. Cook approximately 12 minutes until tender. Drain. Place in a large mixing bowl and mash. Combine with garlic, butter, and salt and pepper. Spoon into a pastry bag with a star tip. Pipe out two mounds of potatoes for each serving. Garnish with parsley and paprika.

WHITE WINE MUSTARD SAUCE

1 small yellow onion, chopped
1½ teaspoons cooking oil
¼ teaspoon garlic, chopped
3 cups white wine
1 cup heavy whipping cream
2 heaping tablespoons Dijon mustard
2 tablespoons fish stock
1 tablespoon cornstarch

In a large pan, sauté onions in oil until translucent. Add garlic. Add wine and cream. Continue cooking until reduced by ½. Stir in Dijon. Make a slurry by whisking the fish stock and cornstarch together. Add to sauce to thicken. Yields approximately 2 cups.

CHAPTER 6

We've Got the Goods

The Levee House Café

These restaurants certainly do! All were stores during some part of their existence. Today, however, instead of racks of clothing or cases of merchandise, they offer up a wide selection of menu items. Even though penny candy and the pickle barrel are gone, we met a few people who'd worked in those old emporiums. And we even saw one or two checkerboards ready for a game.

OLD WAREHOUSE RESTAURANT AT

Historic
Roscoe Village

400 NORTH WHITEWOMAN STREET
COSHOCTON, OH 43812
740-622-9310
WWW.ROSCOEVILLAGE.COM

In 1816, James Calder laid out a town named after him, called Caldersburgh. Fourteen years later, in 1830, Leander Ransom and Noah Swayne petitioned the state legislature to rename the village Roscoe, in honor of William Roscoe, an English author and abolitionist of the period. The opening of the Ohio & Erie Canal at that time had a strong impact on the community, transforming it from a humble settlement into one of the largest wheat-shipping ports along the 308-mile waterway. Canals continued to operate until the great flood of 1913. But the flood, along with the success of the railroads, marked the passing of the Ohio & Erie Canal's heyday.

The idea for a historical restoration in Roscoe Village was born at the dedication of a mural painted for Coshocton County's sesquicentennial celebration. The artist, Dean Cornwell, had chosen an 1850s canal scene as his subject. Seeing this rendition, local industrialist Edward Montgomery and his wife, Frances, were inspired to return the town to its proud past.

Today, Route 16 runs where the canal once did. Alongside it is a four-story building that once housed grain, wool, hides, and produce on the lower floors and dry goods on the floors above. It is now an eatery known, appropriately, as the Old Warehouse Restaurant. Arnold Medbery purchased this property in 1838 from Ransom and Swayne and built an establishment he called The Mill Store alongside the canal. The lowest floor was open at the back, so barges could pull up and transfer their cargo easily.

We arrived not by canal barge but by car, driving through the village before parking in front of the restaurant. Mindy Feikert, who coordinates special events at Roscoe Village, met us at the front door of the restaurant and escorted us on a tour of the building before joining us for lunch. Just inside the front door is a charming waiting area, complete with a potbelly stove. Downstairs, the massive sandstone blocks of the original foundation are still in place. Antique implements hang on the walls. Many of them have to do with the making of apple butter, which is a big event in this area during the fall.

The main dining room is to the right of the entryway. Its plank flooring and rough-hewn beams are original, as are some of the bills of sale and deeds that hang on the walls. You'll also see wagon wheels, feed sacks, and other items of the mid- to late 1800s. Debbie's meal choice was in keeping with the time period and the chilly weather outside. A delicious bowl of Ham and Bean Soup followed—at the recommendation of our server, Bill—by an Apple Dumpling made her feel as if the calendar might just have been turned back. Karen's lunch of Stuffed Pork Loin, served with Mashed Potatoes and Sautéed Vegetables, was every bit as good. We left completely sated, wishing we had more time to spend enveloped in the delightful past of Roscoe Village.

MARINATED SMOTHERED CHICKEN

1 cup olive oil
1 teaspoon fresh garlic, minced
¼ teaspoon Italian seasoning
¼ teaspoon onion powder
salt and pepper to taste
4 chicken breasts, boned
1 large onion, chopped coarse
1 large green pepper, chopped coarse
4 ounces mushrooms, sliced
2 tablespoons butter
8 slices provolone cheese

In a large bowl, combine oil, garlic, Italian seasoning, onion powder, and salt and pepper. Marinate chicken in this mixture in refrigerator for at least 6 hours or overnight. Remove chicken and grill to 165 degrees. Discard marinade. Sauté onions, peppers, and mushrooms in butter for about 5 minutes. Top each chicken breast with sautéed vegetables and 2 slices of provolone. Place under broiler until cheese bubbles. Serves 4.

BREAD PUDDING

1 loaf white bread
½ cup raisins
6 eggs
3 cups milk
⅓ teaspoon cinnamon
pinch of ground cloves
½ cup sugar
¼ cup cinnamon sugar
vanilla ice cream

Preheat oven to 350 degrees. Tear bread into pieces. In a large, shallow bowl, whip together remaining ingredients until thoroughly combined. Add bread and let sit for at least 2 hours. Grease a 16-by-9-by-2-inch baking dish and add mixture. Bake for 20 to 25 minutes. Sprinkle with cinnamon sugar and serve hot with vanilla ice cream. Serves 8 to 10.

THE LEVEE HOUSE CAFÉ

127 OHIO STREET
MARIETTA, OHIO 45750
740-374-2233

Marietta, established in 1788, was the location of the land-grant office for the Northwest Territory. Consequently, the town was a hub of activity as settlers passed through, full of hope and the promise of a better future, picking up their deeds at a wooden structure that still stands today.

During that time, the Ohio and Muskingum Rivers were a major source of transportation and trade. The riverbanks were lined with shops, hotels, taverns, and restaurants. Today, the only original river-front structure that remains is the building that houses The Levee House Café. It was completed around 1826 for Dudley Woodbridge, the first merchant in the Northwest Territory, and was used originally as a dry-goods store. Because of the Flemish-bond brick pattern used in the construction, the building has been credited to Colonel Joseph Barker, whose most famous work is the Blennerhassett Mansion.

The oldest part of The Levee House Café contains the Blue Room, a cozy dining room with wooden flooring and interesting seating made right in Marietta. The eye-catching blue chairs are a special design once made for Chester A. Parsons' Virginia Street Tavern, a place notorious for its bar brawls. Mr. Parsons went through so many chairs that the manufacturer created this special design with no glued joints, so the parts of the chair could easily be put back together after a fight. Other décor in the room has a history as well. The ceiling came from an old clothing store and the light fixtures from a hardware establishment. The marble window sills once served as teller counters in a local bank.

We dined in the Green Room, a sunny addition from 1911 that houses an Underground Railroad display for about nine months of the year. Partner Harley Noland shared his impressive knowledge of local history as we perused the lunch menu. He chose his favorite, Pasta Verde, and offered us a sample before we all dug into our individual meals. It was a delightful combination of spinach, chicken, ricotta cheese, and fettuccine. Pasta was the order of the day, as Debbie had the Barbecued Shrimp Pasta, sweet and tangy, while Karen enjoyed one of her favorite flavor combinations in the Chicken and Cucumber Pasta.

Faithful employee Margaret makes desserts on the premises. She'd been off for a couple of days when we visited, so Noland apologized for the selection—eight choices instead of the normal twenty! The kitchen sent out a sampler, and the three of us nibbled on Chocolate

Pear Tart, Rum Coconut Custard Pie, Fresh Apple Cheesecake, Pumpkin Pie, Oreo Cheesecake, Chocolate Chip Walnut Tart, Truffles, and Black Magic Cake, which has been declared "the Best in Ohio" by *Ohio Magazine*. With such dessert choices, entrées made to order, and a lovely river view, The Levee House Café is a treasure for today that allows guests to also treasure its yesterdays.

CHILLED CHERRY SOUP

½ cup raisins
6 thin slices orange
6 thin slices lemon
¼ cup lemon juice
1 stick cinnamon
2 cups water
2 cups peaches, sliced
1½ cups sweet or sour cherries, pitted
½ cup sugar
dash of salt
1½ tablespoons cornstarch
whipped cream for garnish

Place raisins, oranges, lemons, lemon juice, cinnamon stick, and water in a large stockpot and bring to a boil. Turn down heat and allow to simmer for 20 minutes. Remove cinnamon stick. Add peaches, cherries, sugar, and salt and bring to a boil. Blend cornstarch with a little water and add it to the fruit. Cook for about 1 minute until clear. Adjust sweetening if necessary. Set aside to cool, then refrigerate. Garnish with whipped cream just before serving. Serves 6.

COCONUT MOUSSE

3 cups plus 6 tablespoons milk, divided
2 cups sugar
pinch of salt
6 egg yolks, beaten
2 tablespoons cornstarch
2½ tablespoons gelatin
1½ cups coconut, grated
3 cups heavy cream, whipped
1 tablespoon vanilla
toasted coconut for garnish

Place 3 cups of the milk, sugar, and salt in a saucepan and bring to a boil. Reduce heat to simmer. In a small bowl, blend egg yolks, cornstarch, and 3 tablespoons of the milk. When blended, stream mixture slowly into simmering milk and stir continuously until thick. Remove from heat. Dissolve gelatin in remaining 3 tablespoons of milk. Slowly add hot milk mixture and stir well. Place in refrigerator to set. When firm, beat with an electric mixer until smooth. Add coconut, whipped cream, and vanilla and blend well. Spoon into serving glasses and garnish with toasted coconut. Serves 8 to 10.

161 NORTH HIGH STREET
COLUMBUS, OH 43215
614-228-0500

Reading a description of the Elevator Brewery as we drove toward Columbus, we anticipated enjoying its architecture. The Elevator Brewery & Draught Haus is housed in the old Columbia Building, a structure built in 1895 for commercial purposes. The Bott Brothers Manufacturing Company moved into the space in 1905 after commissioning the architectural firm of Stribling and Lum to design and build the storefront. Stained-glass arches in the Tiffany style span the front windows, with leaded-glass bands that spell out the names *Bott Brothers Billiards* and *Bott Brothers Cigars*.

The Bott brothers made and sold billiard tables, bar fixtures, refrigerators, and other equipment for cafés and billiard halls. By 1909, they were conducting the largest and most prosperous business in the city. Although the brothers outfitted many bars throughout Columbus, the only remaining examples of their work are in the Elevator Brewery.

From 1905 until Prohibition in 1919, what was considered one of the finest cafés in the United States operated on these premises. During Prohibition, the establishment served milk shakes, and patrons entertained themselves by playing chess or checkers. After Prohibition's repeal, the café reopened as The Clock Restaurant, in honor of the large timepiece just outside the front door. Even today, many Columbus residents refer to the location by that name.

The Elevator Brewery & Draught Haus, owned by Richard Stevens and his son, Ryan, takes its name from their brewery business, which they began several years prior to delving into the restaurant world. At the far end of the restaurant are antique pool tables from the eatery's earlier days. Today, guests may enjoy a game of billiards or step up to the dartboards while waiting for their meal. Hanging on the wall nearby is a picture commissioned by Richard Stevens that depicts what the second story must have looked like in its heyday, when men fought over and bet on what happened at the forty billiard tables lining the room.

Rather than knock around the eight ball, we relaxed in our booth and enjoyed the collection of art on the walls. The senior Mr. Stevens, who has quite an eye, enjoys displaying his acquisitions for the clientele. He chatted with us until lunch was served, promising to return after we'd finished. We both thoroughly enjoyed the Potato and Bacon Soup and the Spinach, Pear, and Almond Salad. The Smoked Chicken Egg Roll, served with Apricot Dipping Sauce, was absolutely the most delicious of its kind that either of us had ever tasted.

On our way out, we looked at old photographs and marveled at how like the original the room still is. The ceiling overhead is lovely in its opalescence. Behind the tiger cherry bar built by the Bott brothers, friendly bartenders still serve guests. Even the display cases still house wares. Since the Elevator Brewery's famous Chocolate Stout Cake wasn't available during our visit, we'll drive down High Street on another day and stop at the clock to give it a try.

🍃 PILSNER BEER BLANC 🍃

2 cups white wine
2 cups heavy cream
1 cup pilsner beer
4 sticks unsalted butter
salt and pepper to taste

Place wine and cream in a saucepan over medium heat and reduce by ½. Add beer and bring to a boil, then reduce heat to a simmer, whisk in butter, and season with salt and pepper. Yields 4 cups.

🍃 PANCETTA PILSNER SHRIMP 🍃

½ stick unsalted butter
8 ounces pancetta, sliced very thin
20 medium shrimp, peeled and deveined
2 cloves garlic, chopped fine
8 ounces fresh spinach leaves, stems removed
1 cup Pilsner Beer Blanc (see next column)

In a medium skillet over low heat, melt butter and begin to render pancetta. When partially cooked, add shrimp and increase heat. Continue to sauté until shrimp and pancetta are fully cooked. Remove pan from heat, put 5 shrimp on each of 4 plates, and arrange pancetta around outside of plates. Return skillet to stove and add garlic and spinach. Sauté until spinach is lightly wilted. Put spinach on plates in center of shrimp and pancetta. Drizzle with Pilsner Beer Blanc. Serves 4.

COLDWATER CAFE

35 EAST MAIN STREET
TIPP CITY, OH 45371
937-667-0007

The Coldwater Café was a treasure we discovered one day while browsing the picturesque shops along Main Street. The tiny, ten-table café is reminiscent of street-side cafés in Paris, with its French country *décor-toile* tablecloths and matching wallpaper. Visitors will note the original plank floor and the exposed bricks. One of the bricks is missing. Proprietress Betty Peachy has replaced it with an egg snuggled in its own small nest. Black-and-white plaid draperies on café rods adorn the windows, and French photographs are hung here and there on the yellow plastered walls.

One of the first things that intrigues guests about the Coldwater Café is that the chairs don't match. Written on the menu is an explanation. It seems that when Betty Peachy opened the café, she invited close friends and family to the very first dinner. The price of admission to this gala event was . . . a chair. So each chair in the dining room has its own story to tell, as do many of the other items. It is interesting to note that the name of the café

comes from Betty's late father, Joe "Coldwater" Peachy. He grew up in the small mountain community of Belleville, Pennsylvania, where he built his house right next to Coldwater Creek.

The building looks much the same on the outside as it did back in the 1800s. It was erected in 1835 and became a general store under the management of Sidney Chaufee in 1840. By 1875, Albert M. Heckner took over the store. A "Wholesale and Retail Dealer in Groceries and Provisions" was how he advertised himself, as was painted along the length of the building. Since those days, the building has housed a bakery, a confectionery and ice cream parlor, and a tailor shop. In the 1930s, the first restaurant opened here, operated by Charles Priller. It was followed by a succession of eateries until February 8, 1994, when the Coldwater Café began.

Seated at a round table in a sunny window, we prepared ourselves for a treat. A large selection of sandwiches is on the menu, all served on freshly baked breads. Or guests can choose a salad with a basket of homemade breads on the side. The Chicken Pecan Salad sounded tempting, as did the Black Bean and Rice Salad. We checked out the house specialties served in the evening. We liked the sound of the Lobster Crab Cakes with Remoulade Sauce and the Vegetable Lasagna Pinwheels, and Betty Peachy was kind enough to give us the recipes for them.

It was a difficult choice, but we eventually opted for a Chicken Pecan Salad Sandwich and a Vegetable Pita Sandwich. When they arrived, we promptly halved them so we could sample each. And we couldn't resist trying the Coldwater Café's signature dessert, the English Teacake with Warm Butter Sauce. It was fabulous. We're not going to describe it. You'll just have to visit and try it for yourself!

LOBSTER CRAB CAKES

½ pound jumbo lump crabmeat, picked and flaked
¾ pound lobster meat, cooked and chopped
¾ cup red bell pepper, chopped fine
¾ cup yellow bell pepper, chopped fine
¾ cup green onions, chopped fine
1 cup red onions, chopped fine
2¼ cups fresh breadcrumbs, divided
½ cup mayonnaise
9 tablespoons peanut oil
Remoulade Sauce (see next column)

In a medium bowl, stir together crabmeat, lobster, peppers, onions, 1½ cups of the breadcrumbs, and mayonnaise. Form into 18 cakes about 2½ inches in diameter and ½ inch thick. Place remaining breadcrumbs in a shallow bowl. Dredge 6 crab cakes 1 at a time in crumbs and transfer to a plate. In a 12-inch heavy skillet, heat 3 tablespoons of the oil over moderate heat until hot but not smoking. Cook crab cakes about 6 minutes until golden brown on both sides and heated through. Clean skillet after each batch. Cook remaining cakes in batches of 6 in 3 tablespoons oil. Serve with Remoulade Sauce. Yields 18 crab cakes.

REMOULADE SAUCE

1 small onion, chopped
1 cup mayonnaise
½ cup chili sauce
½ teaspoon mustard
dash of Tabasco sauce
1 tablespoon Worcestershire sauce
dash of paprika

Combine all ingredients in a blender and blend for 1 minute. Yields 1½ cups.

27 EAST WINTER STREET
DELAWARE, OH 43015
740-369-7111

La Canard Fortunato boasts fine French-Italian cuisine. We oohed and aahed our way through a serving of the house specialty, Spaghetti Carbonara, made especially to order. A melt-in-the-mouth mixture of eggs, bacon, onion, and Parmesan, it was the best of its kind we'd ever tasted. Chef Mark Jordan chatted with us about his love of cooking and his delight in being able to have a free hand to create delicious dishes from seasonal produce. The lunch menu is relatively short, but each item is created with care, from the Shrimp Salad-Stuffed Tomato to the Fried Egg and Ham Sandwich on Texas Toast. The large selection of entrées on the dinner menu includes the signature Potato-Encrusted Salmon, which Mark serves with Creamy White Wine Sauce.

Built in 1869 at a cost of between six thousand and nine thousand dollars, this two-story red-brick building was ornamented with galvanized-iron cornices. The three original owners each occupied a room on the first floor. Mr.

Cronkleton and his tinware shop occupied the west room. His staff and all the manufacturing equipment were located on the second floor. Records show that Mr. Hilliard and Mr. Groff occupied the other two rooms on the first floor, although no one seems to have noted exactly what their occupations were. By 1886, the three gentlemen had moved on, and the first floor housed a flourishing bar and restaurant. On the upper floors, the Central Hotel maintained a few select rooms for traveling business people. But by about 1891, and continuing to at least 1929, the hotel was known as Delaware's "entertainment center." It is easy to imagine gentlemen entering the bar on the first floor, enticed by the ladies of the evening leaning out of the upstairs windows.

Over the next several decades, the building housed a hatchery, a car dealership, and a print shop on the second floor. Through all these changes, the claw-foot tub used by the brothel remained in place. It can still be viewed today, as can a sample of the original upstairs wallpaper from the 1890s. Changes were also made to the storefront. The brickwork and the large windows were covered with shabby stucco and stonework.

Don and Pam Rankey and Bob and Tina Hoffman purchased the building in April 2000 and began renovation. The elegant original brickwork was restored on the outside of the building, which now looks much as it did during the 1800s. Inside, the walls were stripped to reveal the brickwork, and the drop ceilings were removed. Stained-glass Tiffany lamps and oak floors complete the historic look. The inside space has been divided into two areas. La Canard Fortunato, an elegant place to dine, is complemented by The Lame Duck, a tavern and more casual eatery complete with four murals depicting the owners and local councilmen. Throughout the two eateries, interesting curios hang on the walls, such as the original hatchery sign, the framed Lame Duck shirt signed by Dwight Yoakam, and tickets and pictures from his concert in Columbus. Whatever your pleasure, elegant or casual, you are sure to be charmed by the food and the atmosphere here.

POTATO-ENCRUSTED SALMON

2 medium potatoes
2 8-ounce salmon fillets
2 tablespoons olive oil

Preheat oven to 350 degrees. Pierce potatoes all over with a fork. Place on a baking sheet and bake in oven for 30 minutes. Remove from oven and set aside to cool. Peel and shred potatoes. Spread potatoes on top of salmon fillets. Heat oil in a large skillet. Place fillets potato side down in skillet and sauté approximately 4 to 5 minutes until potatoes are golden brown. Remove from skillet and place salmon side down on a baking sheet. Bake in oven for 12 minutes. Serve immediately. Serves 2.

NEW YORK-STYLE CHEESECAKE

1¾ cups graham cracker crumbs
2 cups sugar, divided
⅓ cup butter, melted
3 8-ounce packages cream cheese
4 eggs
1 tablespoon plus 1 teaspoon vanilla, divided
1½ cups sour cream

Preheat oven to 300 degrees. In a small bowl, combine graham cracker crumbs, ¼ cup of the sugar, and butter. Press mixture into the bottom of a greased 10-inch springform pan and set aside. Using a mixer, blend cream cheese and 1½ cups of the sugar for 5 minutes until smooth and creamy. Add eggs and 1 tablespoon of the vanilla and continue to mix for 10 minutes. Pour cream cheese mixture into pan. Bake for 60 minutes in center of oven. Remove from oven and allow to cool for at least 20 minutes. In a small bowl, combine sour cream and remaining sugar and vanilla. Pour on top of cooled cheesecake and return to oven for 10 minutes. Remove from oven and allow to cool completely before removing from pan. Serves 16.

13-15 WEST WILLIAM STREET
DELAWARE, OH 43015
740-369-3471
WWW.BROWNJUG.COM

Above the large bar at the back of the restaurant is a red sulky used in harness racing. That's not surprising, since the restaurant was founded the same year as, and was named for, the Little Brown Jug, a horse race run here in the town of Delaware on the third Thursday after the first Monday in September. The race, part of the Grand Circuit of harness racing, attracts top riders. It's a pacer race, which means that the front and back leg on one side of the horse must move forward at the same time. In order to compete, horses must be entered at birth, then must be kept eligible as yearlings and again as two-year-olds before finally competing in the Jug as three-year-olds.

The building in which The Brown Jug Restaurant is located started out in the late 1800s as the Cuckoo Saloon and Restaurant. When that went out of business, one side became Zack Davis' Seed Store and the other side became People's Store, a men's clothing store complete with an entire Boy Scout section. Ed Wolf, co-owner of The Brown Jug, recalls working at the store as a fourteen-year-old. At that time, the store had rolling ladders that he frequently climbed to reach the merchandise on the top shelves, just below the 17-foot tin-tile ceiling. Ed laments that the ceiling is gone now, due to building-code changes and previous "improvements." He has tried to re-create the look from tiles he garnered from the sale of an old hotel.

In 1963, the seed store left and the clothing store expanded. Seven years later, when People's Store closed its doors, The Brown Jug moved from its original location around the corner to occupy the store. At that time, the restaurant was owned by Don "Bear" Smith, who eventually sold it to Ed and his brother-in-law, Bill Stroud. Don didn't get away for long, though, coming back to manage the kitchen until 2000, when he finally retired after thirty years' affiliation with The Brown Jug.

He's credited with the Big Bear, a hearty strip-steak sandwich, and the Stromboli, which is not at all like common strombolis of today. It's a house specialty made with beef and topped with either Mushroom Sauce or Pizza Sauce. I had a delicious bowl of Potato Soup as I chatted with Ed. It was filled with chunks of potato, celery, and carrot. Unlike many potato soups, the creamy broth had a bit of a kick, which I quite enjoyed.

As I left to go pick up Karen, who was elsewhere in town, I noted a piece of railing used at the finish line of the Little Brown Jug from 1981 through 1991. It would be fun to return for the Jug—or even the Jugette, the race for fillies sponsored by The Brown Jug, run the day prior to the main event. I'm normally not a gambler, but I do like a good horse race, and I'm betting I'd have a great time!

BAYOU SHRIMP AND SCALLOP SOUP

5 slices bacon
½ cup green onions, sliced
1/3 cup carrots, diced
¼ cup green peppers, diced
2 tablespoons flour
2 cups hot water
¾ cup potatoes, diced
1½ tablespoons shrimp base
4 ounces shrimp
4 ounces bay scallops
dash of nutmeg
dash of white pepper
dash of red pepper sauce

In an 8-quart pot, sauté bacon until crisp. Do not drain fat. Add onions, carrots, and peppers and sauté for 2 to 3 minutes. Blend in flour and cook over medium heat for 2 to 3 minutes. Add water, potatoes, and shrimp base. Heat to boiling, then reduce heat to medium. Boil about 10 to 12 minutes until potatoes are tender. Add shrimp, scallops, nutmeg, white pepper, and red pepper sauce. Boil for 2 to 3 minutes, stirring occasionally. Serves 4.

PARADISE SALAD

3 cups honey smoked turkey, diced
½ cup celery, diced
½ cup pecans, chopped
¼ cup raisins
½ cup plain yogurt
1/3 cup mayonnaise
2 tablespoons fresh parsley, snipped
2 tablespoons lime juice
½ teaspoon salt
¼ teaspoon ground cinnamon
6 ripe tomatoes
leaf lettuce
red seedless grapes

Combine turkey, celery, pecans, and raisins. Set aside. For the dressing, whip together yogurt, mayonnaise, parsley, lime juice, salt, and cinnamon. Pour dressing over salad and toss lightly to coat. Cover and chill for several hours.

Core tomatoes. Cut each into 4 to 6 wedges, cutting to, but *not through*, base of tomato. Spread wedges gently apart and fill with salad mixture. Garnish with leaf lettuce and red seedless grapes. Serves 6.

80 NORTH PAINT STREET
CHILLICOTHE, OH 45601
740-779-0440

This delightful coffee house is located in the Preservation District of downtown Chillicothe. Surrounded by other historic buildings and just a short walk from Yoctangee Park, it is ideally located for dropping in for a steaming cup of coffee on a sunny spring morning. Constructed in the 1860s, the building once housed The Dreamland, a silent-movie house that was very popular with local residents at the turn of the twentieth century. Unfortunately, once talkies were in vogue, The Dreamland closed and audiences moved to larger theaters to enjoy their favorite film stars. This space was then occupied by Schlegel's Jewelers. Visitors to the building today can still see the original name in stained glass over the front door. The jewelry store was successful, continuing in business until the early 1970s. The building then remained vacant for two decades.

In the mid-1990s, Bob Etling took over the building and began a complete restoration. The second and third floors have been turned into upscale apartments, while Schlegel's Coffee House is housed on the first floor. This three-story building is typical of other stores of this era—long and thin. The first floor, painted in pale colors and complemented by a white tray ceiling, feels cool and spacious. Old-fashioned ice cream parlor seating adds charm, as do the many antiques and curios located around the room.

The current owner was careful to restore the ground floor with an eye to the past. Incorporated into the décor are the original Art Deco wall sconces and the old popcorn machine from Chillicothe's Royal Theater. An old theater seat and an automatic ticket taker also remind visitors of the building's illustrious past. Other interesting artifacts include an old coffee percolator, a coffee grinder located in the window display, and an old phone booth. The shiny copper espresso machine is located on a very attractive antique backbar restored to its original 1890s shine. Recovered from the old Miller's Café, located next to Poland Park in Chillicothe, it looks wonderful.

To the right of the backbar is a large pastry case. We stood and examined the goodies, trying to decide among Muffins, Biscotti, Cookies, and a variety of sumptuous Cakes and Tortes. Since Schlegel's advertises "the finest coffees and desserts that Chillicothe has to offer," we were looking forward to our selection. Debbie eventually chose a slice of Caramel Pecan Cheesecake, and Karen, who almost always opts for chocolate on such occasions, chose a slice of Chocolate Truffle Cheesecake.

Both selections were yummy. There was a large selection of Coffees, Lattes, Espressos, Cappuccinos, Teas, and Phosphates from which to choose. Karen picked a Mocha Latte, which was lovely. Debbie opted for the more adventurous Cherry Italian Cream Soda, which also got top marks. It is always a treat to find such a building so lovingly restored. Why don't you treat yourself to an experience you won't forget?

CAFE MOCHA

¼ cup espresso, scant
¼ cup caramel syrup, scant
1 cup chocolate milk, steamed
whipped cream as desired

Combine espresso, caramel syrup, and chocolate milk. Steam. Pour into a large mug and top with whipped cream. Serves 1.

PINA COLADA ITALIAN CREAM SODA

½ cup very small ice cubes
2 tablespoons coconut syrup
2 tablespoons pineapple syrup
¼ cup half-and-half, scant
1 cup sparkling water
whipped cream as desired

Put ice cubes into a 12-ounce glass. In a mixing cup, combine syrups and half-and-half and stir well. Mix with sparkling water. Pour over ice and top with whipped cream. Serves 1.

CHAPTER 7
It's Tea Time!

Twin Creek Tea Room

The ritual of tea is said to have been begun by Anne, seventh duchess of Bedford. According to legend, she grew tired of her afternoon malaise during the long stretch between meals. One afternoon, she asked for a tray with tea, bread, and butter. She quickly became fond of this repast, and the tradition was born. Author Henry James once said, "There are few hours in life more agreeable than the hour dedicated to the ceremony known as afternoon tea." As most serve tea during the noon meal, you need not wait until the middle of the afternoon to enjoy the establishments in this chapter.

76 SOUTH HIGH STREET
DUBLIN, OH 43017
614-764-9359

When Debbie's family lived in Dayton during the mid-1980s, her mother and friends used to make the ninety-minute trek to Biddie's Coach House for lunch once or twice a year. It seems that through the years, people have gone to considerable lengths to get to Biddie's, including the couple who came in a canoe. At the time, the nearby bridge was under construction, leaving historic downtown Dublin difficult to reach from the suburbs of Columbus. Rather than driving miles out of their way, the couple rented a canoe on the opposite bank of the Scioto River and paddled across.

The restaurant is housed in what was once Sells Hotel, built in the 1830s as a private home. The largest dining room is located to the right of the front door. Most of the tables seat two or four, but one table for six occupies "Biddie's Corner," where Louise, a friend of owner Mary Marsalka, has done a flowery mural. She's also painted the ladder-back chairs, which adds to the uniqueness of the décor. Another example of Louise's expertise decorates the walls on the

back porch. This mural depicts scenes and buildings from around Dublin. The riders in the picture's hay wagon are likenesses of all the employees who worked at Biddie's when the mural was painted.

Guests planning to dine with a party of four or more can make advance reservations to be served tea, or they can order from the regular menu, which boasts daily traditions. For example, on Monday, the delicious Cottage Pie is served. Fridays and Saturdays during the fall and winter provide an opportunity to order Biddie's hearty Potato Soup, served in a bowl of crusty bread. With Karen's English background, we opted for tea, of course. Our two-tiered tray was laden with goodies. The savory items included Ham Salad and Egg Salad Open-Faced Sandwiches, Pinwheels filled with Salmon-Dill Spread, and phyllo tart shells heaped with Chicken Salad. All were so delicious that it was difficult to choose. Everything at Biddie's Coach House is homemade, so the desserts were every bit as delectable as the sandwiches. Chocolate Petits Fours, two different types of Profiteroles, and Lemon Bread lightly laced with Cream Cheese were all quite a treat. The Lemon Bread was so good that we took two loaves with us to enjoy with our families.

Had we been selecting off the regular menu, Karen would have chosen the Burgundy Pot Mushrooms, which are sautéed in rich Burgundy Wine Sauce, then served in a crock topped with a crusty puff pastry. Fresh fruit and a choice of soup or salad accompany this unusual and delicious meal. Debbie would have been delighted with Biddie's Tea Basket, which is a sandwich assortment of Egg Salad, Chicken Salad, and Lemon Bread with Cream Cheese.

Named after Mary's mother, who ran the cash register until she was ninety-two, Biddie's Coach House is a rare find. In another time, we may have donned hats and white gloves to visit such an establishment. Today, that isn't necessary—though considering the décor and the hospitality of Mary Marsalka, who treats guests as welcome neighbors, such attire would be a perfect fit!

 CONFETTI CASSEROLE

2 pounds pork, cubed
1 pound pork sausage
16-ounce package angel hair, linguine, or other noodles
14¾-ounce can cream of chicken soup
1 green pepper, chopped
1 pimento, chopped
1 onion, chopped
16-ounce can whole-kernel corn
½ pound mild cheese, grated
1 large can mushrooms, sliced
2 tablespoons butter, melted
1 cup cracker crumbs

Brown pork in a large skillet, simmering until tender. Remove from skillet. Fry sausage, drain, and crumble. Cook noodles according to package directions. Drain. Combine all remaining ingredients except butter and cracker crumbs in a large casserole dish. In a small bowl, combine butter and crumbs. Sprinkle buttered crumbs on top of dish and bake at 350 degrees for 1 hour. Serves 8 to 10 generously.

 BIDDIE'S CHILLED STRAWBERRY SOUP

4 cups fresh strawberries, hulled and halved
16-ounce can pears in light syrup
2 tablespoons honey
3 teaspoons lemon juice
fresh mint leaves
strawberry slices

Combine strawberries, undrained pears, honey, and lemon juice in a blender or food processor. Cover and blend until mixture is smooth. Transfer mixture to a large bowl. Cover and chill for 4 to 24 hours. Garnish with mint leaves and strawberry slices. Serves 8 to 10 as an appetizer or side dish.

71 NORTH MAIN STREET
WAYNESVILLE, OH 45068
513-897-7729
WWW.ANGELOFTHEGARDEN.COM

Visitors to this address in 1879 found the Wayne Novelty Works Company. At the time, cast-iron novelties were very popular, and none more than the company's dark green frog doorstop, which doubled as a garden ornament. Unfortunately, the popularity of such items was short-lived, and the company closed its doors in 1885. The buildings were taken over by the Reed Broom Factory. Stories still abound about Waynesville's "Great Fire," which started in the Reed stables, where some children reportedly were playing with matches. The fire spread so fast that all but two of the buildings on the west side of the street were completely leveled.

In 1900, Charles Cornell, a relative of Ezra Cornell, the founder of Cornell University, purchased the lot and cleared the site. By 1902, the present Victorian two-story brick house had been erected. After Charles Cornell's death in 1918, the house had two years under the ownership of Samuel Meredith. Mr. Meredith was a buyer for the Miami Valley Leaf Tobacco Company, which was located in nearby Dayton. By 1920, Dr. D. John Witham was using the house as a home and an office. The good doctor left a number of fairly grisly objects in the house, including a complete human skeleton found in the attic. Undeterred by such evidence of the doctor's tenure, the next owners, John and Grace Gibson, refinished all of the woodwork throughout the house. This stately old home, having passed through the hands of many owners, rests today with Pamela McNeily. Pamela hopes to completely restore the inside of the building to its former Victorian splendor. The restaurant part of the structure has already been completed, and plans are in hand for the rest of the house.

When we arrived for luncheon, our server, Tim, complete with cravat and white gloves, opened the front door. It quickly became obvious that we were in for an elegant treat. Tim seated us in the octagonal front room, which is papered in pink roses. The brass angel wall sconces and the delicate lace tablecloths further enhance the genteel atmosphere. We sipped deliciously refreshing cups of Hot Ginger Tea while admiring the elaborately carved scrollwork in the doorway and the large pocket doors.

Tim gently suggested that we allow Pamela to select which of the many delicious offerings we would try. All the menu items are made from scratch, and accordingly have that wonderful freshly baked taste. We started with the Irish Soda Bread Scones, served with Lemon Curd. Karen particularly enjoyed the Tomato, Cheese, and Broccoli Quiche, while Debbie preferred the flavorful Potato and Cheese Soup. Though we both tasted a variety of sandwiches, we agreed that the highlight of our visit was the unbelievably good Chocolate Irish Cream Cake. There was a noticeable Irish flavor to our meal, and we finally realized that it was the month of March, and that Saint Patrick was being honored. We thoroughly enjoyed both the delightful meal and the Victorian elegance. It was a truly memorable occasion.

 ANGEL HUMMINGBIRD CAKE

3 cups all-purpose flour
2 cups sugar
1 teaspoon cinnamon
1 teaspoon baking soda
3 eggs, beaten
1 cup canola oil
1½ teaspoons vanilla
8-ounce can crushed pineapple with juice
2 cups chopped pecans, divided
2 ripe bananas, mashed
Frosting (see below)

Preheat oven to 350 degrees. Grease and flour three 8-inch or two 9-inch cake pans. Combine dry ingredients in a large bowl. Stir in eggs and oil until dry ingredients are moistened. *Do not overmix.* Add vanilla, pineapple, 1

cup of the pecans, and bananas. Stir well. Pour evenly into cake pans. Bake for 25 to 30 minutes. Cool and cover with Frosting. Sprinkle remaining pecans on top of cake. Serves 16.

 FROSTING

8 ounces cream cheese, softened
1 cup butter, softened
3½ cups powdered sugar
2 teaspoons vanilla

Beat cream cheese and butter until smooth. Slowly add powdered sugar and vanilla. Yields approximately 3 cups.

 ANGEL PUFF

12 eggs
2 cups cheddar cheese, shredded
2 cups Monterey Jack cheese, shredded
1 teaspoon baking powder
½ teaspoon salt
½ cup butter, melted
½ cup all-purpose flour
2 cups cottage cheese

Beat eggs until light and fluffy. Add remaining ingredients and stir gently until well blended. Pour into a 9-by-13-inch baking dish. Bake for 30 minutes at 350 degrees. Serves 6 to 8.

Twin Creek Tea Room

19 EAST DAYTON STREET
WEST ALEXANDRIA, OH 45381
937-839-5094

The lot on which the Twin Creek Tea Room sits was one of the original twenty plots laid out for West Alexandria on what is now the north side US 35. When John M. Davis planned this house, he had to see to many details, including having the bricks made. He contracted with Edgar Derby for the beautiful butternut staircase and the woodwork throughout the house. The home was completed in 1875. John Halderman and J. R. McCleaf were subsequent owners. Benjamin Kennedy and Mr. and Mrs. John Davis bought the property in 1894. After the death of Mr. and Mrs. Davis, the home passed to their daughter, Pauline, a Broadway star who performed under the name Pauline Daigneau. She sold the house in 1936 to Russell and Bess Hall, who enlarged the kitchen in order to open an eatery. The Country Cousin Restaurant operated from the late 1930s until the early 1940s, when it was forced to close due to food shortages brought on by World War II rationing. After the war, Eugene Copp and his mother, Ruth, purchased the home. She continued living here with her son and his wife, Verle, helping them raise their family. Almost three decades later, John and Elfrieda Santo bought

the residence, where they lived and operated an antique business called The Red Elephant.

In 1992, Dr. Mark and Carolyn Ulrich purchased the home and converted it to a tearoom and gift shop. Melodie Dill and Pam Morneault oversaw the food operations until 2000, when they retired. As we chatted with Carolyn during our visit, she explained that part of her vision for the venture was to provide her three daughters with summer jobs.

We certainly felt that this attractive home, painted in deep burgundy with accents of hunter and cream, would be a wonderful place to come and spend a few hours each day. Inside, the lovely butternut woodwork blended nicely with the airy rattan chairs in which luncheon guests were seated. The tables were covered in lace with an underlay of green, used during the fall, winter, and very early spring. The rest of the year, pink is used for an accent. Both coordinate beautifully with the hunter and rose floral wall coverings throughout. The ceiling is particularly remarkable, its original plasterwork looking every bit like a wedding cake.

Many delicious sandwiches filled with homemade ingredients are available for the choosing. We both chose the half-sandwich option so we'd have room to taste something else from the menu. Debbie opted for the traditional Chicken Salad and enjoyed the bowl of deliciously creamy Cheddar Chowder that came with it. Karen chose the Vegetable Sandwich and the Vegetable Soup, both of which she found delightful.

After lunch, we just had to poke around in the Ivy Corner gift shop, housed upstairs. Guests should be sure to leave time to browse. Had we not had other appointments, we certainly could have whiled away the afternoon looking at all the pretty things.

TEA ROOM
BAVARIAN BEEF SANDWICH

8-ounce package cream cheese, softened
¼ cup sour cream
2 to 3 tablespoons horseradish
12 slices rye swirl bread
leaf lettuce for 6 sandwiches
6 slices red onion
12 thin slices roast beef, warmed

Combine cream cheese, sour cream, and horseradish, mixing well until blended. Spread mixture on bread. Add lettuce, onions, and meat. Yields 6 sandwiches.

CHILLED ROYAL CARROT CAKE

2 cups sugar
1 cup oil
4 eggs
2 cups all-purpose flour
1 teaspoon baking soda
1 teaspoon salt
2 teaspoons cinnamon
3 cups raw carrots, grated
½ cup pecans, chopped
8-ounce can crushed pineapple, drained
8-ounce package cream cheese, softened
¼ cup butter, softened
4 cups powdered sugar
vanilla to taste

Preheat oven to 350 degrees. Cream together sugar and oil. Add eggs and beat until creamy. Add flour, baking soda, salt, and cinnamon. Mix well. Add carrots, nuts, and pineapple. Mix well. Bake in 2 greased 9-inch round cake pans for about 50 minutes. Remove from oven and set aside to cool.

In a medium bowl, mix cream cheese and butter thoroughly. Add powdered sugar a little at a time. Add vanilla and mix well. Spread between cooled cake layers and on top. Chill and serve cold. Yields 1 cake.

2982 ROUTE 516 NW
DOVER, OH 44622
330-343-1333
WWW.OLDEWORLDBB.COM

The George Stauffer family owned a ninety-acre farm and sold eggs and fruit from its orchard to earn a living. By all appearances, the Stauffers must have been successful, because in 1881 they built a large home constructed of a sandstone foundation, hardwood beams, and sun-baked brick. Both Stauffer children worked on the farm but were college-educated.

Gertrude Stauffer lived in her childhood home until her death in the 1960s. At that time, a local investor bought the property in its entirety. The farmland became a strip mine, and the house was rented to a tenant who treated it in such a way that it was condemned for sanitary reasons in the early 1970s.

The house sat empty until August 1992, when it was purchased by the Sigrist family. Growing up on a nearby dairy farm, Jonna Sigrist had dreamed of returning this home to its original grandeur. At the time she bought it, not one window remained in the house. Many animals had taken refuge inside, and overgrowth encroached upon the brick walls. Community members, friends, and neighbors all stopped in to lend a helping hand. Today, the five bedrooms for overnight guests, the dining room, and the parlor areas used for serving tea all proclaim that Jonna's wish has been realized.

Upon arriving, we established ourselves at a table in a sunny bay window and spent our first moments gazing across the landscape. Our attention then turned to the décor. Across the room was a fireplace surrounded by a lovely mirrored mantelpiece. Throughout the room were numerous Victorian accessories, including a floor lamp with a large, fringed shade. Our table was beautifully set, and a pot of Earl Grey and a pot of Apricot Tea promptly arrived. To Karen's delight, we were there for the British Traditions Tea, which included Quiche Lorraine, Cucumber Sandwiches, Currant Scones with peaches and Devonshire Cream, the tearoom's Queen of Hearts cookies, Gingerbread, and fresh fruit.

The luncheon menus, served to groups of six or more, have themes that reflect the décor of some of the guest rooms. For example, the Orient Express lunch is paired with the unique Oriental Room. "Lunchtime in Florence," which features Tortellini Soup, is partnered with the lovely Mediterranean Suite upstairs. Other guest rooms include the Parisian Room, where the blue walls are decorated with latticework and roses; the cozy Alpine Room, with its quilts and cuckoo clock; and the Victorian Room, which has a claw-foot tub.

A special event here is the annual Valentine's Day Progressive Dinner, in which the Olde World B & B works in conjunction with three other establishments. Guests can enjoy a different course at each of the four beautiful, romantic inns. We'd never heard of such an event outside the typical neighborhood progressive dinner, but we thought it was a wonderful idea. Jonna gave us brochures to leave in a conspicuous place at home.

EGGS BENEDICT CASSEROLE

2½ cups cooked ham, chopped
10 eggs, poached
¼ teaspoon pepper
Mornay Sauce (see below)
1 cup crushed cornflakes or fine breadcrumbs
¼ cup margarine, melted

Put ham in a 9-by-13-inch pan. Place eggs on ham and sprinkle with pepper. Pour Mornay Sauce over eggs. Toss cornflakes and margarine. Sprinkle over sauce in a rectangle around each egg. May be refrigerated no longer than 24 hours before baking. Bake in a 350-degree oven for 45 minutes. Serves 10.

MORNAY SAUCE

¼ cup butter
¼ cup flour
½ teaspoon salt
⅛ teaspoon nutmeg
2½ cups milk
1½ cups Gruyère or Swiss cheese, shredded
½ cup Parmesan

Heat butter in a saucepan over low heat until melted. Stir in flour, salt, and nutmeg. Cook until bubbly, stirring constantly. Remove from heat. Stir in milk and return to heat. Heat to boiling, stirring constantly. Boil for 1 minute. Add cheeses and stir until smooth. Yields 2 cups.

SPICED RHUBARB BREAD

1½ cups brown sugar, packed
⅔ cup vegetable oil
1 egg
1 cup buttermilk
1 teaspoon vanilla extract
1 teaspoon baking soda
2½ cups all-purpose flour
1 teaspoon salt
2 teaspoons ground cinnamon, divided
1½ cups fresh or frozen rhubarb, diced
½ cup nuts, chopped
½ cup sugar
1 tablespoon butter or margarine, melted

In a mixing bowl, beat brown sugar, oil, and egg. Add buttermilk, vanilla, and baking soda and mix well. Combine flour, salt, and 1 teaspoon of the cinnamon. Stir milk mixture into flour mixture. Fold in rhubarb and nuts. Pour into 2 greased 8½-by-4½-by-2½-inch loaf pans. Combine remaining cinnamon, sugar, and butter to make topping. Sprinkle over loaves. Bake at 350 degrees for 1 hour or until bread tests done. Freezes well. Each loaf serves 8 to 10.

Swan House

225 WEST SANDUSKY STREET
FINDLAY, OH 45840
419-429-SWAN
WWW.SWANHOUSETEAROOM.COM

I sat in the lovely dining room of Swan House and reveled in the beauty of the day, which was equaled by my surroundings. This Italianate home, known as the McConnell-Hosler House, was built in 1865. Its style was popular throughout the country during the Civil War and was the top preference among the nation's elite families. Architectural symmetry is evident on the outside of the structure in the placement of the cornice brackets and windows. Inside, the center halls, both upstairs and down, divides a floor plan identical on either side.

Peter Hosler, the Hancock County treasurer, took ownership of the home in 1880. He went on to found Farmer's National Bank, which evolved into The Ohio Bank and eventually became today's Sky Bank. A subsequent owner, Mrs. E. M. Foresman, established a tearoom in 1929, a precursor of good things to come. During the early 1930s, when the public schools were closed, Kay Potter held art classes here. For a time, the studio space was also used by students learning to tap-dance. The list of various functions for this lovely home expanded in 1933 when doctors E. E. Rakestraw and Hugh Marshall bought it for their medical offices.

By 1998, the structure had been turned into a beauty shop and seven apartments. It was purchased by three enterprising women who intended to restore its original elegance and use it as a gift shop and tearoom. Over the six months of the restoration, many amazing discoveries were made. The tops of the tall, curved windows were found. The ceiling had been lowered twice, obscuring the windows' elegant arches. The front entrance was also returned to its original splendor, as the barrel-vaulted porch and glass fan windows were uncovered. The attic housed yet another treasure. The original louvered shutters were stored there. Upon discovery, they were hand-refinished by one of the owners and her husband.

Karen was unable to travel with me that day. I was fortunate to be seated at a small, round table beside the front windows, where I had ample opportunity to take in such details. Lovely crystal chandeliers shone overhead, and beautiful sideboard pieces were placed throughout the room. Tea started with a warm Blueberry Scone tucked in a linen napkin and served on a silver platter. Everything is made on the premises. The Strawberry Jam, Lemon Curd, and Devonshire Cream that I found in the silver condiment server were all delicious accompaniments. The three-tiered tray that followed was laden with goodies. The

French Breakfast Puff, the Spinach Cheese Bread, and the Raspberry Cake Roll were my personal favorites, although all ten of the items served were luscious. The Cream Puff was particularly unique, fashioned into the shape of a swan.

After dining, I browsed through the rooms of lovely gift items. I certainly agree with the ladies of Swan House. Through their labor of love, this is an ugly duckling returned to its rightful place as a lovely swan.

DRIED TOMATO AND BASIL TEA SANDWICHES

4 ounces cream cheese, softened
1/3 cup dried tomatoes in oil, drained and minced
2 tablespoons walnuts, chopped fine
2 tablespoons Parmesan, shredded
12 slices wheat bread
½ cup butter, softened
½ cup fresh basil, chopped
¾ teaspoon sugar
½ teaspoon lemon juice
24 slices white bread

Beat first 4 ingredients in a medium mixing bowl until well blended. Spread on wheat bread. Combine next 4 ingredients and spread on 12 slices of the white bread. Place wheat bread face up on top of white bread. Put remaining 12 slices of white on top of wheat. Trim crusts and cut into quarters. Yields 48 finger sandwiches.

COUNTRY CHEESE SNACKS

1 cup mayonnaise
1 cup Parmesan, grated
8-ounce package cream cheese, softened
2 green onions with tops, minced
1 loaf party rye bread
dried dill weed for garnish

In a medium mixing bowl, combine mayonnaise, Parmesan, cream cheese, and green onions thoroughly. Spread equally on slices of rye. Place on a baking sheet about 4 inches from heat and broil for 3 minutes. Garnish with dill weed. Serves 24.

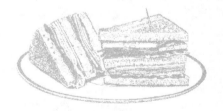

63 WEST MAIN STREET
MADISON, OH 44057
440-417-0220
WWW.TEAROOM.ORG

We received a postcard from a friend, and on the back it stated, "His Majesty's Tea Room is a place to be pampered." How right the card was. Michael Loparo, the owner of this delightful place, enthusiastically greeted us. We sat in the dining room to chat. This elegant room simply exudes Victorian charm. The tables are dressed in lace and royal blue tablecloths. The high wooden paneling and the tall sash windows give a light, spacious feel to the room. All around are gatherings of teddy bears, music boxes, and fine china knickknacks. Michael told us that she wanted to create a place that showed how much she cared about people and old-fashioned service, and she has certainly succeeded.

Originally the Madison Exchange Bank, the structure was completed in 1875 for a total cost of $4,350, including the lot, building, furnishings, and vault. A handsome one-story brick bank with an unusual rounded corner at the main entrance, it would stay in business for the next ninety-four years. The townsfolk have plenty of stories to tell about the bank, the most popular of which concerns an incident that took place on the evening of November 27, 1900, when five bank robbers broke in. Four of them kept watch while one drilled into the main safe in an attempt to get it open. A local citizen came upon the scene and was captured and locked into the coal shed behind the bank. The Methodist preacher was shot at but escaped to raise the alarm. The robbers eventually got the safe open, only to find it empty. Irate citizens forced the gang to flee into the night empty-handed. Luckily, all the money had been placed in a smaller safe that the would-be robbers totally ignored.

When the bank closed its doors for the last time, the building continued in service as an antique store and then as a clothing consignment shop before it was used as the main office for Redlin Realty. Having reached the age of one hundred, it was nominated for inclusion on the National Register of Historic Places. It has been the site of His Majesty's Tea Room since 1994. Locals and visitors alike can enjoy the Old World ambiance inside the building and the refreshing summer breezes on the patio overlooking the town square.

A large variety of delicious treats is served here. "Proper Afternoon Tea" consists of four courses, including Karen's favorite homemade Scones with Lemon Curd and Devon Cream. There are many interesting sandwiches to choose from. The Lord Vincent is a hearty roast beef sandwich with crusty bread and Horseradish Sauce. The Duchess of Cambridge is a combination of avocados, tomatoes, bell peppers, and sprouts on Health Nut Bread. Visitors always enjoy the English Ploughman's Lunch—a crusty roll with chunks of cheddar cheese and pickle—which is traditionally served to hungry farm workers at midday. But whatever you sample, be sure to try one of the large variety of special teas, many of which are flavored with dried fruits, nuts, spices, or even dried flowers!

CLASSIC SHORTBREAD

½ cup butter, softened
¹/₃ cup powdered sugar, unsifted
¼ teaspoon vanilla
1 cup flour, unsifted
vegetable oil spray

Preheat oven to 325 degrees. Using the back of a large spoon, cream butter until it is light. Mix in powdered sugar, then vanilla. Work in flour. Knead dough on an unfloured surface until smooth. Lightly spray a 9-inch circular baking pan with vegetable oil. Place ball of dough in center of pan. Working from the center, press dough into pan evenly. Prick dough with a fork and bake for 30 to 35 minutes until lightly browned. Be sure middle is thoroughly cooked.

Let shortbread cool in pan for 10 minutes before loosening edges with a knife. Flip pan over onto a cutting board. It may be necessary to tap pan hard against cutting board to extract shortbread. Cut into eighths while still warm. Serves 8.

 DEVON CREAM

1 cup heavy whipping cream
½ cup sugar
2 teaspoons vanilla extract
1¼ cups sour cream

Place first 3 ingredients in a medium bowl and whip until stiff. Fold in sour cream. Refrigerate until ready to use. Yields 2 to 3 cups.

14 EAST MAIN STREET
SPRINGFIELD, OH 45502
937-322-8961

The firm of Shepley, Rutan, and Coolidge designed the elegant Bushnell Building on East Main Street in downtown Springfield. Under contract to provide a fashionable structure for Asa S. Bushnell, who eventually became Ohio's governor, the company produced a tall building featuring arched doorways and Second Renaissance Revival detailing in the terra-cotta decorations. Even the outside is magnificent. The upper stories of multicolored brick contain intricate moldings and large overhanging eaves. Completed in 1893, the building encompasses some 165,000 square feet of office space. It housed a bank, offices for salesmen and attorneys, Wren's Department Store, and a tearoom in the basement.

A mainstay in Springfield, the department store is long gone but was remembered by everyone we spoke to. Sandra Zinger, the owner of Tapestry & Tales, recalled going shopping on Saturdays at Wren's and descending to the basement for lunch. She even got her first credit card here. The current tearoom is located in the same space as the old one. On our way, we stopped just inside the Fountain Avenue entrance to admire the white marble

walls, the marble curved stairwell with its intricately carved newel post, and the magnificent stone archways on the ground floor.

The tearoom is delightful—a charming room filled with small tables covered in lace or cross-stitched tablecloths. Napkins in assorted colors are each bound by an unusual napkin ring. A few of the tables are glass-topped and are filled with knickknacks and period pieces. We spotted letters, gloves, jewelry, photographs, combs, and much more. In the center of one wall is a display of sheet music from days gone by. At the opposite side of the room, a display of Victorian clothing and hats caught our eye. The many high shelves surrounding the room are filled with fine china, which adds to the feeling of elegance and refinement.

After perusing the menu, we opted to try the Passion Fruit Iced Tea and to share the Vegetable Herb Egg Salad and the Lemon Tarts. Both the salad and the tarts were made from scratch and were absolutely scrumptious. The buffet that day contained an assortment of salads, White Tie Lasagna, Glazed Carrots, and Mandarin Orange Cake. Although we didn't try them, we listened to the many compliments coming from the tables around us.

The Bushnell Building, listed on the National Register of Historic Buildings, contained one more surprise. We took the elevator to the second floor. One of the lawyers working there in the early 1900s was a Mr. Harry A. Toulmin, the patent attorney for Orville and Wilbur Wright. The Wrights applied for their original patent in 1903. On May 22, 1906, three years later, the United States Patent Office granted them patent number 821-393 for a flying machine. Harry Toulmin persuaded the brothers that the patent should cover their three-axis system of control, rather than just the flying machine itself. A shrewd move, it led to the handling of more than thirty patent lawsuits for the Wright brothers.

FIDGET PIE

1 pound potatoes, peeled and sliced thin
3 cups ham, cooked and diced
1 medium onion, sliced thin
2 or 3 apples, peeled and sliced thin
4 fresh sage leaves, chopped
½ teaspoon nutmeg, ground
salt and pepper to taste
1¼ cups chicken broth
9-inch piecrust

Preheat oven to 425 degrees. In a 9-inch pie plate, layer potatoes, ham, onions, and apples. Sprinkle with sage, nutmeg, and salt and pepper. Pour broth over everything and cover with piecrust. Flute edges of crust and poke a small hole in the center to allow steam to escape. Cover with foil and bake for 40 to 45 minutes. Remove foil and return to oven for another 8 to 10 minutes until crust is golden brown. Serves 6.

SALMON PATTIES

3 16-ounce cans salmon
1 stalk celery
1½ to 2 cups breadcrumbs
3 eggs
½ teaspoon salt
⅛ teaspoon pepper
2 tablespoons milk

Preheat oven to 350 degrees. Drain salmon, remove skin and bones, and flake into a large bowl. In a food processor, finely process celery. Add celery to bowl with salmon. Add remaining ingredients and combine thoroughly. Shape into twenty ¼-cup patties or ten ½-cup patties. Place on a greased baking sheet and spray lightly with cooking spray. Bake for 12 to 15 minutes until golden. Serve immediately. Yields 10 to 20 patties.

CHAPTER 8

A Cabin in the Woods

The Inn at Cedar Falls

The rough-hewn logs and crude chinking that provided rustic shelter for so many hopeful pioneers as they struggled to make a new life on the frontier have endured. Some are used today as wonderful restaurants. We found new appreciation for the hardships faced by those settlers, and we hope that you enjoy this portal into America's pioneer spirit.

THE MORGAN HOUSE.

RESTAURANT

5300 GLICK ROAD
DUBLIN, OH 43015
614-889-5703

The taupe clapboard house at the corner of Glick Road and Dublin Road is easily identifiable as The Morgan House Restaurant, even without a sign. When we visited shortly after New Year's, it was still simply decorated for Christmas, with wreaths hung at the windows from red ribbons. In addition to being a restaurant, The Morgan House sells antiques, gifts, and collectibles in such a wide array that guests might easily browse for a couple of hours before or after dining.

Meals are served in two dining rooms. We were seated in the larger of them, at a Shaker-style table situated between the stone fireplace and a Christmas tree decorated with fruit. On the wall opposite the fireplace was a mural of the Ohio countryside. Down the hall, hanging from the Shaker pegboard, were period clothing and implements. We were joined for lunch by Cathy O'Brien, a local personality well known in the food arena. She sampled the Tomato Florentine Soup, which was chock-full

of spinach, tomatoes, and other tasty ingredients. She followed that with the Chicken Casserole, as did Karen. It was accompanied by a green salad topped with Poppy Seed Dressing. A wonderful meal! Debbie chose the quiche of the day, which was filled with potatoes, tomatoes, chives, sour cream, and cheddar cheese. Not a morsel remained. We shared a piece of Layered Lemon Pie, which had a crust so flaky that any county-fair participant would have been proud. The layers—one of traditional lemon pie filling and the other of a fluffy cream cheese concoction—combined to make a perfect light dessert. Other items on the menu that tempted the palate were The Morgan House Soup, one of chef Chris Meadows's carefully guarded secrets, and Kendra's Pot Luck, a creamy chicken pot pie topped with puff pastry and baked in a terra-cotta pot.

The other dining room is actually the log cabin that once belonged to the Weaver family. Chris showed us pictures of the family sitting outside the structure, then embarked on the tale of their home. The cabin was originally situated in Morgan County. On July 22, 1863, General John Hunt Morgan and his Confederate raiders confiscated the house. Morgan slept comfortably inside, while his men camped in a nearby orchard. According to newspaper articles and Morgan County Historical Society documents, Morgan typically chose a log or stone house as his headquarters, because those materials were best for stopping bullets. Accounts say that Mrs. Weaver baked bread as Morgan slept. After he awoke and breakfasted on the porch, he kidnapped Mr. Weaver and forced him to be a scout. Eventually, Weaver escaped and John Hunt Morgan was captured, becoming one of the first residents of the Ohio State Penitentiary. Hunt's raiders subsequently helped him to flee, after which he donned civilian clothing and rode a train to Cincinnati amid throngs of Union troops. Fortunately, in the havoc that General Morgan wrought throughout Ohio, he spared this log cabin for all of us to enjoy.

STRAWBERRY CELERY SEED DRESSING

½ white onion
4 fresh strawberries
1½ cups sugar
1 tablespoon dry mustard
1 tablespoon salt
²/₃ cup vinegar
2 cups canola oil or virgin olive oil
3 tablespoons celery seed

Cut onion into 4 pieces and place in a blender or food processor. Stem strawberries and place with onions. Purée. Add sugar, mustard, and salt. Mix well. Pour in vinegar and combine. Slowly add oil to mixture. Pour into a storage container. Stir in celery seed until well combined. Dressing will keep up to 3 weeks in refrigerator. Yields approximately 3 cups.

BROCCOLI DILL QUICHE

1 cup biscuit mix
1 cup plus scant ¹/₃ cup half-and-half
3 eggs
1 cup broccoli, chopped fine
9-inch deep-dish pie shell
1 tablespoon fresh dill, chopped
2½ cups cheddar cheese, shredded

Preheat oven to 375 degrees. Place biscuit mix in a medium mixing bowl and slowly add half-and-half. Whisk briskly. Add eggs and whisk briskly until batter is smooth. Set aside. Place broccoli in pie shell and sprinkle evenly with dill. Sprinkle cheese over broccoli. Pour batter into pie shell and bake for 45 minutes. Serves 6 to 8.

21190 ROUTE 374
LOGAN, OH 43138
740-385-7489
WWW.INNATCEDARFALLS.COM

In our search for peace and serenity, we found a treasure in The Inn at Cedar Falls. The inn is comprised of two log cabins built in the early 1800s, surrounded by three of Ohio's most beautiful state parks. Hikers will enjoy the mammoth rock formations, caves, and waterfalls in the surrounding Hocking Hills.

We entered the inn through the dining room, with its primitive furnishings and its dried orange slices hanging at the windows. The chinked walls, exposed beams, and uneven floors helped transport us back to the pioneering 1840s. A cross-stitch sampler on the wall and the soft glow of candlelight gave the room a warm, homey feeling.

The central part of the double log house contains the kitchen, where guests can stop by and chat with the chef as she prepares the meals from scratch. The inn has its own organic vegetable and herb gardens, from which seasonal offerings are prepared. To the rear is a delightful sitting room, where we sat next to the fireplace and thumbed through personal journals that had originally been located in the guest rooms. Visitors of all ages had inscribed their thoughts in prose and poetry. Each page related tales of spectacular views, wonderful meals, and a common feeling of being very far from today's modern conveniences. On warm evenings, guests are encouraged to sit outside on the porch and share the breathtaking view. Bird watchers will love spotting the ruby-throated hummingbirds, yellow finches, and pileated woodpeckers.

Two and a half years in the making, The Inn at Cedar Falls was the vision of Anne Castle. Previously a successful businesswoman in the corporate world, she, together with her daughter Ellen Grinsfelder, survived a long struggle against physical, emotional, and financial blocks to create the inn. A short history of the inn is located in each room. Anne passed away in 1991, but Ellen carries on her dream of a place where guests can "come home."

We sipped our drinks and played a game of Chinese checkers until it was time to eat. As we tasted the Wisconsin Cheese Ball and Crackers and polished off a house salad tossed in tangy Maple Balsamic Vinaigrette, we chatted with Debby and Harry Brown, who were also seated at our table. It was their third visit to the inn, and they enthusiastically described their comfortable cabin to us. Debbie chose the lightly breaded Pork Tenderloin with Chardonnay Glaze and Crimson Pear Chutney, while Karen opted for the Pan-Seared Chicken Breast, served over a bed of Grits and finished with Portabello Mushroom Sauce. Both entrées were so wonderful that we barely had room to sample the Cinnamon Raisin Bread Pudding, topped with Caramel Sauce. Good food and good company made for a totally delicious evening, and we departed determined to return to this home away from home.

* * * * *

CHICKEN BREASTS STUFFED WITH ORANGE, LEEKS, AND MINT

4 leeks, white part only, cleaned and sliced thin
½ stick butter
½ cup mint, chopped medium
8 chicken breasts, skinned, boned, and pounded to ¼-inch thickness
pepper to taste
zest and juice of 2 oranges, divided
2 tablespoons oil
2 cups heavy cream

Sauté leeks in butter until soft and until liquid evaporates. Remove ⅔ of leeks from pan and mix them with mint in a small bowl. Sprinkle chicken with pepper and a little orange zest. Spread ½ to 1 tablespoon leek mixture on each breast and sprinkle with a little more orange zest. Roll up each breast and tie with string in 2 or 3 places. Brush chicken with oil and place on a baking sheet. Bake at 350 de-grees for 30 minutes uncovered. Do not over-cook. Add remaining zest and juice to remaining leeks and simmer covered over low heat for 15 minutes. Add cream, increase heat, and stir about 7 minutes until thickened. Cut each breast crosswise into 5 pieces and spoon sauce on top. Serve immediately. Goes well with rice or risotto and asparagus. Serves 8.

YAM AND APPLE CASSEROLE

2 Granny Smith apples
2 16-ounce cans yams, drained and patted dry
1 stick butter, melted
½ cup dark corn syrup
⅓ cup plus 2 tablespoons light brown sugar
2 tablespoons dry sherry
¾ teaspoon cinnamon
⅛ teaspoon salt

Preheat oven to 350 degrees. Core, peel, and slice apples and set aside. In a food processor, purée yams, 6 tablespoons of the butter, syrup, brown sugar, sherry, cinnamon, and salt. Spread ½ of mixture into a greased 10-inch pie pan or casserole dish. Arrange ½ of apples on top. Repeat with remaining yam mixture and apples. Brush top of apples with remaining butter. Bake for 45 minutes until apples are tender. Serves 6 to 8.

The Cabin

28810 LAKE SHORE BOULEVARD
WILLOWICK, OH 44095
440-943-5195

The list of early-bird entrées served Monday through Friday is lengthier than the entire menu at some restaurants. It's a sure indication that there is something here for everyone. The Honey-Roasted Chicken and the Silver Dollar Tenderloin Medallions caught our eye. All the selections are generously served with a salad, a vegetable, choice of Potato or Wild Rice, and warm Bread. The regular menu includes eight appetizer choices and a lengthy list of entrées. Shrimp Scampi, Potato-Crusted Halibut, and Breaded Sea Scallops are among the seafood options. Such favorites as Veal Oscar, New Zealand Rack of Lamb, and Baby Back Ribs are also available. Guests can't go wrong with The Cabin's signature desserts of Apple Cinnamon Napoleon and Crème Brûlée. No wonder patrons were so happy to see this local institution reopen after a devastating fire.

The restaurant burned in June 1993. Just one day before what remained of the building was to be destroyed, longtime friends Joe and Susan Durkoske and Barbara and Marty Belich rescued the structure. The enthusiasm of former patrons and previous employees got the couples through the arduous process of restoring The Cabin to its place as one of Willowick's favorite eateries. Long before the doors once again swung wide, customers were booking parties. Some people even had tailgate parties in the parking lot just to keep up the encouragement. Familiar faces were seen among the staff when the restaurant reopened. The manager and the bartender returned, as did several other employees, including a server with more than twenty years at The Cabin and a member of the kitchen staff who had been there for thirty. It seems that's the kind of allegiance the place elicits.

The Western Reserve land on which The Cabin stands was deeded in 1853. The main part of the original structure, built as a hunting lodge in 1903, was converted to a restaurant in 1933. Owner Andy Anderson was issued the second liquor license in Lake County. When he started the business, there were animal heads on the walls and beer spigots coming out of the walls, serving Wooden Shoe Beer and Genesee Ale. In 1944, Anderson took on partners Bud Handy and Betty Hylkema. Eventually, the restaurant became known for its superb steak and fish dinners. During a 1994 interview, manager Shirley Miller recalled that pike dinners were once so popular and so inexpensive that people would line up around the outside of the cabin waiting to get in. She also remembered fondly that Betty was very concerned about fairness to customers. If she found that someone had been overcharged, she'd try to identify who they were, after which she'd go to great lengths to get the money back to them. If she couldn't, the money was donated to charity.

The current owners have tried to maintain this homey atmosphere. Although oak and pine have replaced the scorched, rough-hewn logs, the old fireplace still stands. People love to come to The Cabin to recall old memories while making new ones.

THE CABIN'S TRADITIONAL SCAMPI DINNER

12 4- to 5-ounce scampi or prawns
½ cup clarified butter
¼ teaspoon salt
¼ teaspoon pepper
1 teaspoon garlic salt
½ teaspoon cayenne pepper
⅛ teaspoon onion salt
¼ teaspoon white pepper
½ teaspoon celery seed, crushed
1½ teaspoons paprika
2 tablespoons breadcrumbs

Cut shells of scampi lengthwise along middle of back all the way to tail. Pull scampi out of shells but leave tails attached. Remove black vein that runs length of back; by removing vein, you are butterflying scampi. Place cleaned scampi on a large baking sheet lined with aluminum foil. Brush with enough clari-

fied butter to coat. Combine next 7 ingredients. Season scampi lightly with mixture. Sprinkle with paprika, then with breadcrumbs. Place under broiler for 8 to 10 minutes. Serves 3.

Note: Three teaspoons Old Bay seasoning may be substituted for salt, pepper, garlic salt, cayenne, onion salt, white pepper, and celery seed.

ARTICHOKE ALOUETTE

12 whole artichoke hearts
2 8-ounce packages cream cheese, softened
2 to 4 tablespoons fresh herbs of choice (tarragon, basil, thyme, rosemary, etc.)
⅓ cup flour
3 eggs
½ cup breadcrumbs
4 cups cooking oil

Cut artichokes in half and make an indentation with thumb in the middle of each. In a small bowl, combine cream cheese with herbs. Scoop approximately 1 tablespoon cream cheese mixture into the indentation in each artichoke half. Roll stuffed artichoke in flour, dip in eggs, and roll in breadcrumbs. Dip in eggs and roll in breadcrumbs again. Heat oil to 375 degrees in a small fryer or a medium saucepan. Fry a few breaded artichokes at a time. Fry approximately 6 to 8 minutes until golden. Serves 4 as an appetizer.

COWGER HOUSE

COWGER HOUSE #9
197 FOURTH STREET
ZOAR, OH 44697
330-874-3542
WWW.ZOARVILLAGE.COM

Our meal started with a Fussel Shrub, a refreshing, fruity drink served with a scoop of ice cream and topped off with a pineapple ring and a maraschino cherry. Ed and Mary Cowger discovered the drink on a trip to Williamsburg. Within a month of their return, Ed served up the drink to guests, who promptly proclaimed, "That's our name!" It turns out they were direct descendants of Jacob Fussel, for whom the drink was named. Fussel was the first man in the colonies to commercially market ice cream.

Since neither of us elected to have an additional beverage, water arrived in a large pottery mug bearing insignias designed by the Cowgers. The central figure etched on the mug was a pineapple, the well-recognized symbol of hospitality. If, as a guest, you found a pineapple in your bed, it indicated you'd overspent your welcome.

Given the generosity of our hosts, that would have been easy to do. Our delicious dinner was served at a simple plank table in the dining room of the low-ceilinged log cabin. Garlic Bread and Cheese Bread accompanied the ample salad, tossed with Mary's homemade dressing. Entrées of Trout and Chicken Cordon Bleu followed. A tasty Baked Potato and country-style Green Beans rounded out the meal. The portions were quite generous, making it difficult to save room for the custard-filled Cream Puff that followed. Rest assured, it is something you don't want to miss.

The dining room closely resembles what it must have looked like in 1817, when the cabin was constructed by German separatists who settled in the area. It was built for the village brewmaster. Frequently, the Zoarites would gather here for refreshments before going next door for business meetings and prayer at the home of their leader, Joseph Bimeler. A fire crackled in the stone fireplace during our visit. Fox and raccoon hides decorated the walls, and an old harness hung in one corner.

Ed and Mary Cowger obtained possession of the building in 1984. For many years, they were a two-person dinner theater, staging an 1865 reenactment during the evening meal. During their tenure, the Cowgers have served more than fifty thousand guests. Mary cooks from scratch with an oven and stove just like you'd use for a typical family of four! The Cowgers have two other properties within this historic village, an 1833 post-and-beam manor and the more contemporary Amish Oak Cottage. Altogether, they provide a total of ten rooms for overnight guests. It is said that, within the Cowger House experience, guests can "rough it or plush it." We enjoyed the peaceful, rustic simplicity of our visit.

 SPINACH-STUFFED STEAKS

8 8-ounce cube steaks
2 15-ounce cans spinach, drained
2 eggs, beaten
8 slices American cheese, diced
3 slices bread
salt and pepper to taste
¼ small onion, chopped
1 clove garlic, chopped
1 tablespoon cooking oil
15-ounce can tomato sauce
1½ cups dry wine

When purchasing meat, have the meat department run it through a cuber 1 extra time. To make stuffing, combine next 7 ingredients. Place ⅛ of stuffing on each piece of meat. Roll each piece. Heat oil in a skillet. Place each roll seam side down in the skillet. Brown on both sides, carefully turning rolls over. After browning, place rolls in an ovenproof pan. Combine tomato sauce and wine and pour over meat. Bake at 350 degrees for 1 to 2 hours until done. Be sure to keep basting meat during baking. Serves 8.

RUM BUNS

½ cup sugar, divided
¼ cup shortening

1 teaspoon salt
1 cup milk, scalded
1 package dry yeast
1 egg, beaten
1½ teaspoons rum flavoring
3½ cups flour, divided
2 tablespoons butter, melted
½ cup raisins
Icing (see below)

Place ¼ cup of the sugar, shortening, and salt in a bowl. Pour milk over mixture. When mixture has cooled, add yeast, egg, rum flavoring, and 1¾ cups of the flour. Beat until smooth. Add remaining flour and beat until smooth. Cover and let rise about 2 hours until dough doubles in volume.

Divide dough in half. Roll each half into a long strip. Brush top with melted butter and sprinkle with remaining sugar and raisins. Roll up lengthwise and cut each half into 12 slices. Place slices in greased muffin tins, cover with a towel, and let rise until double. Bake at 400 degrees for 15 to 20 minutes until golden brown. Remove from oven and spread with Icing. Yields 2 dozen buns.

 ICING

1 cup powdered sugar
2 tablespoons hot water
1 teaspoon rum flavoring

Combine all ingredients until smooth. Yields ½ cup icing.

MARIO'S INTERNATIONAL SPA & HOTEL
35 EAST GARFIELD ROAD
AURORA, OH 44202
330-562-9171
WWW.PLACESTOSTAY.COM

The Grey Hotel was built in 1840. It was considered to be quite fashionable, offering excellent overnight accommodations and such amenities as a grand dining room, a bar area, and a "moving" dance floor. At some point, the building was placed on logs and pulled by a team of horses from the southwest corner of Routes 82 and 306 to its present location at the northeast corner of the intersection. The process took two days. After the move, the building became known as the Aurora House, and its use changed to that of a two-family home. It remained a family dwelling until it was purchased by Mr. and Mrs. Mario Liuzzo in 1977.

As the Liuzzos converted the Aurora House from a home to a spa, they recaptured the early heritage of the Grey Hotel. Guests today use a stone walkway reminiscent of the original flagstone path built to provide ladies clean access to the premises. The foyer area of the spa gives a view of the original staircase leading to the second floor. Those stairs allow modern-day guests to ascend the long-ago route of those on their way to a memorable evening in the dance hall.

The unique woodwork in the main hallways of the upper and lower levels came from the siding and beams of a barn once located on the property. The Cabin Restaurant, a log cabin dating to the mid-1800s, is one of the three dining options at what is now known as Mario's International Spa & Hotel. The cabin was constructed as a sugar house on a dairy and cheese farm and was later incorporated as the tavern for the Aurora Stage Coach Inn. The rustic restaurant has rough-hewn walls and wide-plank floors. The original doors of the sugar house are now displayed in the lobby. When the restaurant expanded several years ago, old barns from Geauga and Portage Counties were dismantled and used to enhance the rustic atmosphere.

The Cabin Restaurant serves a wide menu ranging from Pasta Pollo to Fletto a Portabello, a signature dish of pan-seared beef tenderloin. Gourmet pizzas have been on the menu for quite some time. Right after Mario and Joanne took a trip to Italy in the late 1980s, they had a wood-fired oven installed at the restaurant. At first, no one ordered the unusual pizzas, but the fad has finally caught on, and these selections are now some of the most requested. Because the menu items are so delicious and so beautifully presented, it's hard to believe that many of them have significantly fewer calories than you'd expect. And if you're a

Crème Brûlée fan, dessert is not to be missed. This particular item was voted the area's best by *Cleveland Magazine*.

That certainly isn't the only recognition that Mario's has received. *Conde Nast* magazine listed the establishment as one of the ten best spas nationwide. Guests such as David Letterman, Kristi Yamaguchi, Wayne Newton, and Sarah Brightman can attest to the quality of the experience. After eating our way through two states in less than three years, a little pampering from The Cabin Restaurant and Mario's was good indeed.

PASTA ALLO ZAFFERANO

16-ounce package pasta of your choice
1 onion, chopped
2 tablespoons olive oil
½ teaspoon saffron
2 tablespoons water
2 tablespoons curry powder
½ cup ricotta cheese
½ cup skim milk
1 cup fresh pineapple, diced
½ cup peas, cooked
salt and pepper to taste
fresh mint leaves for garnish

Cook pasta according to package directions. Drain. In a large skillet, sauté onions in olive oil until golden. Mix saffron with water and stir in curry. Add to onions and mix well. Sauté at low heat for 5 minutes. Stir in ricotta and milk. Heat. While stirring, gently toss in pasta. Place in a serving dish. Sprinkle pineapple and peas over top and toss gently. Season with salt and pepper. Chill. Serve cold, garnished with mint leaves. Serves 10 to 12 as a side dish.

LEMON POPPY SEED CAKE

4 cups all-purpose flour
1 cup sugar
1 teaspoon baking soda
5 teaspoons baking powder
⅓ teaspoon salt
½ cup poppy seeds
2 teaspoons lemon zest
⅔ cup oil
2 cups nonfat milk
2 eggs, lightly beaten

Combine dry ingredients in a bowl. Combine oil, milk, and eggs in a separate bowl. Lightly mix into dry ingredients. Do not overmix. Pour into a 10-inch tube pan sprayed with nonstick cooking spray. Bake at 350 degrees for 50 minutes. Serves 16.

Lake White Club

1166 ROUTE 552
WAVERLY, OH 45690
740-947-5000
WWW.BRIGHT.NET/~DICK4D

Lake White is beautiful, with broad, grassy banks and mature woodlands. This area was once Indian country. Originally a forested valley with a gently flowing creek, it attracted many settlers to its fertile ground and abundant timber. Peter Patrick discovered the valley in 1785 but was quickly attacked by an Indian hunting party. He and his companions fled, leaving only Patrick's initials carved into a beech tree next to the stream. Much later, those initials served to give the stream its name—Pee Pee Creek.

Eventually, the Shawnees moved on. By 1799, a pioneer surveyor by the name of John Beasley had recorded some seven hundred acres of this land—including the site of the future Lake White Club—on behalf of John Winston of Virginia. A log cabin was built here in the mid-1820s. It's easy to imagine looking out of the cabin's windows and watching settlers moving west, carried along the Ohio & Erie Canal, now Route 23. When John Winston died in 1837, his Richmond relatives were only too glad to sell the backwoods property for the sum of $1,829. The land subsequently passed through many owners, including the valley's first millionaire, James Emmitt.

In the early 1930s, former Ohio lieutenant governor George D. Nye acquired the property for use by Lake White, Inc. Wayne Wick bought several acres of the original tract, including the site of the log cabin. August 1935 saw the completion of the lake bed. But the occupants of the cabin knew that the lake was going to take many months to fill. Several days later, a terrific storm broke over the Waverly area, and the next morning, lo and behold, the lake was completely filled. It wasn't long before visitors from all over the state stopped by to see it. It was at that time that the kitchen at the log cabin began to serve fried chicken. In 1938, it officially became the Lake White Club. A huge screened-in porch had to be added to accommodate the large number of diners.

Today, visitors can still admire the huge original logs cut from the local woodlands and the fireplace built of large stones removed from Pee Pee Creek. We sat on the porch and enjoyed the view and the atmosphere. We also enjoyed the menu itself, which was sprinkled throughout with amusing quips and notations. Debbie selected the Fried Chicken, and Karen chose the Fisherman's Platter, a mix of deep-fried Scallops, Shrimp, and Oysters. Each came with Tomato Juice, Coleslaw, and homemade Rolls. Everything was delicious. We chatted with owner Audrey Ford about her love for the building, the staff, and her husband, Dick. It's clear that the tradition of home-cooked food and fine service is still in style at the Lake White Club.

CHERRY CREAM PIE

2 tablespoons nuts, chopped fine
9-inch piecrust
1 cup whipping cream
16-ounce can sweetened condensed milk
1/3 cup lemon juice
1/2 teaspoon vanilla
1/4 teaspoon almond flavoring
Cherry Glaze (see below)

Preheat oven to 350 degrees. Press nuts into bottom and sides of piecrust and bake for 10 to 12 minutes until golden brown. Set aside to cool. In a medium bowl, whip cream until thick and stiff. Add milk, lemon juice, vanilla, and almond flavoring and fold gently to combine. Spoon mixture into cooled shell. Top with Cherry Glaze and chill. Serves 8.

CHERRY GLAZE

2 cups canned, pitted sour cherries, drained, juice
    reserved
2/3 cup cherry juice
1/4 cup sugar
1 tablespoon cornstarch
2 to 3 drops red food coloring

Combine all ingredients in a saucepan. Cook over low heat, stirring constantly until thick. Set aside to cool. Yields enough glaze for 1 Cherry Cream Pie.

CHOCOLATE CHEESECAKE

1 1/4 cups graham cracker crumbs
2 tablespoons sugar
2 tablespoons butter, melted
6 ounces bittersweet baking chocolate
1/4 cup rum
2 8-ounce packages cream cheese
3/4 cup fine sugar
1/2 cup sour cream
1 tablespoon vanilla
4 eggs

Line outside of a 9-inch springform pan with foil, shiny side out. Butter inside of pan. In a small bowl, combine graham cracker crumbs, sugar, and butter. Press mixture evenly into bottom of pan. Refrigerate.

Preheat oven to 325 degrees. In a double boiler, melt chocolate with rum. Set aside. In a large bowl, beat cream cheese until light and fluffy. Gradually beat in sugar, sour cream, and vanilla. Add eggs and continue to mix well. Place bowl over a saucepan of hot water and stir until mixture is smooth. Place about 1/3 of mixture into another bowl. Combine remaining cream cheese mixture with chocolate mixture. Remove crust from refrigerator and pour chocolate-cream cheese mixture into it. Pour plain cream cheese mixture on top of that, then make swirls in batter with a fork. Bake for 50 minutes. Cool, then refrigerate overnight. Serves 12.

YE OLDE TRAIL TAVERN

228 XENIA AVENUE
YELLOW SPRINGS, OH 45387
937-767-7448

As we entered Ye Olde Trail Tavern, the first things we noticed were the dollar bills lining the wall opposite the bar. Most were signed by the persons to whom they once belonged, including the likes of John Lithgow. Other notables who have dined here include Coretta Scott King, Bob Hope, and Cliff Robertson. Jonathan Winters stops by on occasion, having double-dated with the mother of owner Cathy Christian. Cathy's mother also dated Rod Serling, who once tended bar at "The Trail," as locals call it, and taught a writing course in the banquet room upstairs. Cathy's grandmother put a stop to the relationship, fearing Serling would never amount to anything. Oh, for twenty-twenty hindsight!

In addition to the currency, all sorts of other items line the walls, including flasks and steins. Cathy got so many inquiries about these that they're now for sale. We enjoyed identifying the milk jugs, saddle forms, and horseshoes and guessing at the many other things we had no clue about.

Past the bar area and through a low doorway, guests enter the original log cabin. A fireplace at the far end of the room flickers, as it has for many a year. An atrium dining area has been added, and we chatted with Cathy about the restaurant there. She wanted it in part to protect the exterior wall of the cabin and also to provide a lighter alternative to the dark main room.

For lunch, we moved into the cabin and chose a small booth close to the fire. Other seating is provided at long tables and benches, carved with the names and initials of many who've visited. Pictures of presidents hang on the plaster walls, which appropriately bear the soot of fires from years past. The restaurant is known for its burgers, but after a larger-than-normal breakfast that morning, neither of us felt we could do one justice. We opted instead to share a bowl of Chili and the Most Excellent Grilled Cheese, made with three different cheeses, tomato, and lettuce. Both were very tasty and satisfying on a bone-chilling day.

Ye Olde Trail Tavern is located in the first home in Yellow Springs, known then as Forest Village. While we were visiting, we thumbed through an old book on the history of Greene County. In it was an account of a gentleman's first visit to the area. It seems that in his travels, he met a man who was planning to settle around here. He later received a letter inviting him to visit what the man portrayed as an up-and-coming village. One day, the gentleman set out on foot from his home in Dayton, arriving at what he thought was the right area by late afternoon. Not seeing the cluster of houses he expected, he asked a passerby where Yellow Springs was. The man pointed to a thicket and said, "Right there. You can't see it for the trees." There in the forest was a lone log cabin, the totality of Yellow Springs.

That log cabin eventually became a stagecoach stop for weary travelers on the Columbus-Cincinnati Trail. Cholera once swept through the town. Forty deaths were attributed to the epidemic, seven of them occurring in the tavern itself. Many others happened in the houses nearby, all of which shared a common well. With today's medical knowledge, one can assume that the single water source was likely the cause of the demise of so many.

Those deaths are thought to be one possible explanation for the female ghost that frequents the restaurant. Those who have seen her describe her either in a blue or a black dress but differ as to the style of her hair. However, all who have seen her share one thing in common—they have been men with ponytails. Perhaps the ghost is most comfortable with the men's style of her day.

The motto of the tavern is "Many pass through, few pass by." One reason is the variety of soups served, the recipes for which are carefully guarded secrets. Another reason is the well-known burgers. We encourage you to try your favorite flavor combination at Ye Olde Trail Tavern. It's more than a local watering hole.

MOST EXCELLENT GRILLED CHEESE

2 tablespoons butter
2 slices whole wheat bread
1 thick slice cheddar cheese
1 thick slice Swiss cheese
1 thick slice mozzarella cheese
1 leaf lettuce
2 slices tomato

Melt butter in a large skillet or on a griddle. Place both slices of bread in melted butter and grill until crisp. Turn bread over. Place cheddar on one slice and Swiss and mozzarella on the other. Grill until bread is browned and cheese is melted. Place lettuce and tomato on one side and top with other piece of bread. Cut in half. Serves 1.

TAVERN BURGER

$1/3$ pound ground beef
1 kaiser roll
¼ cup spaghetti sauce, heated
1 slice mozzarella cheese
1 to 2 tablespoons sautéed mushrooms

Form ground beef into a large patty and fry it to desired doneness. Drain. Place burger on bottom half of bun. Top with spaghetti sauce, cheese, and mushrooms. Broil to melt cheese if desired. Top with other half of bun and serve. Serves 1.

CHAPTER 9

Down On the Farm

Bluebird Farm Restaurant

During early United States history, farming wasn't just an occupation but a means of survival. Families had to provide for themselves, as the nearest neighbor could be a mile or two away and the nearest town farther than that. Many settlers were lured from points east by the opportunity of owning something substantial—land. The restaurants in this chapter are the vestiges of a way of life.

Klosterman's
Derr Road Inn

4343 DERR ROAD
SPRINGFIELD, OH 45503
937-399-0822

We stumbled upon Klosterman's Derr Road Inn as we were out exploring the Clark County countryside. The pristine white farmhouse with black shutters quickly found a place on the list of Debbie's favorites. It took just one glance at the menu, where Coconut Shrimp served with Mixed Berry Marmalade topped the list of appetizers. Kim Klosterman, who owns the restaurant with his wife, Karen, graciously brought us a sample as we chatted. We also tasted the Calabash Scallops, dusted in cornmeal and served with Lobster Cream Sauce. One bite was as delicious as the next as we made our way through a sampling of the Seafood Crepes, topped with Shrimp Cream.

The room in which we ate had plank walls, a barn-style door, and shutters at the windows. Attractive floral stenciling of sunflowers and lupines gave it the feel of a summer meadow. A mother bird painted atop the window was perched so that she could overlook her nest, tucked above the door frame.

The dining area to the rear of the old farmhouse has a wall of windows overlooking the deer preserve for which the restaurant has become well known. It all started several years ago, when housing developments began to drive off the deer. What had once been a nightly ritual of watching does and fawns across the hills ebbed until customers began to express disappointment at not having seen deer over the course of several visits. Kim decided to bring the deer back by fencing part of the property. Now, the deer are fed at the same time as the guests. Young diners are frequently invited to help bottle-feed the fawns.

The menu includes intriguing dishes like Hot Pecan Dip, Thai Shrimp and Scallops, Walleye with Crispy Roasted Fettuccine, and Mediterranean Trout topped with tomatoes, capers, feta cheese, and artichoke hearts. Seafood is definitely the house specialty, although many other tasty entrées are offered, including Lasagna made from Karen Klosterman's special recipe. The popular lunch buffet includes Meat Loaf, Fish Bites, Pork with Rice, Beef and Noodles, and Macaroni and Cheese, among other items. Practically any dessert your sweet tooth might crave is available.

Deeds of previous owners like the Heindl, Warner, and Smith families hang in the entry vestibule. Descendants of the Schafer family and the Langen family, who also lived here at one time, are still frequent visitors to the restaurant. Kim recalled many occasions when old Mr. Langen used to come in and tell stores about cultivating the land with a horse and plow.

Simon Kenton, known as a wilderness warrior and a cohort of Daniel Boone, once lived among Derr Road's rolling hills. During his tenure, the deer ran free. Now, thanks to Klosterman's, the rest of us can appreciate nature as Simon Kenton once did.

SEAFOOD CREPES

2 tablespoons olive oil
2 stalks celery, diced
¼ white onion, diced
¼ red onion, diced
1 bunch green onions, chopped
12 ounces fresh spinach, chopped
1 red pepper, chopped
1½ tablespoons seasonings of your choice
1½ tablespoons garlic, minced
12 ounces crabmeat
8 ounces shrimp, chopped
3 8-ounce packages cream cheese, softened
½ cup Parmesan
8 premade crepes

In a skillet, warm oil and sauté vegetables, seasonings, and garlic until soft. Remove from pan and set aside. Sauté crabmeat and shrimp until soft. Return vegetables to pan. Add cream cheese and Parmesan and stir to combine. Roll ⅛ of mixture into each crepe and serve immediately. Serves 4.

STRAWBERRY ROMAINE SALAD

¼ cup mayonnaise
1 tablespoon cider vinegar
1½ tablespoons sugar
1½ tablespoons whole milk
1 tablespoon poppy seeds
1 head romaine lettuce, cleaned
2 cups strawberries, halved
¼ large red onion, cut into thin rings

Combine mayonnaise, vinegar, sugar, milk, and poppy seeds. Place in an airtight container and refrigerate until cold. Just before serving, break lettuce into bite-sized pieces and place in a large bowl. Add strawberries and onions. Remove dressing from refrigerator and shake well. Pour over salad and toss well. Serve immediately. Serves 4.

HOT PECAN DIP

2 8-ounce packages cream cheese, softened
4 tablespoons milk
5 ounces dried beef, diced
¼ small onion, diced
½ teaspoon garlic powder
1 teaspoon white pepper
1 cup sour cream
½ cup pecans, chopped
assorted crackers

Preheat oven to 325 degrees. In a medium bowl, combine first 6 ingredients. Fold in sour cream. Place in a small ovenproof dish and top with pecans. Bake for about 15 minutes until dip begins to bubble. Serve with assorted crackers. Serves 4

BELLFAIR COUNTRY STORE

1490 NORTH FAIRFIELD ROAD
BEAVERCREEK, OH 45432
937-426-0788

In a farmhouse built just after the Civil War is the most amazing collection of stuff that either of us had ever seen. It would take several visits to get a grip on most of it, and it would be completely impossible to ever take it all in. We spent a large portion of our conversation saying, "Did you notice . . . ?" and "Did you see . . . ?" The collection belongs to Gary Deis, who fondly calls it his "stock portfolio" or his "retirement nest egg." We identified rug beaters, prams, high button boots, spades, train lanterns, old saddlebags, sieves, saws, and more. An old Hi-Arc gasoline pump stood beside the counter, while a collection of old Coca-Cola trays was displayed behind it. Toys from throughout the twentieth century were displayed in cases above the booths.

The restaurant has the feel of an old general store, with barrels and tins and cupboards in every nook and cranny. Candy is displayed as it was when it cost only a penny. Maybe if its price were still that reasonable, the young boy at the counter wouldn't have been in tears when he was told he had to decide on just one treat. The place prides itself on its "cracker-barrel hospitality" and welcomes those who come to look around, as well as those who come to eat.

Kathy Deis, Gary's wife, does most of the cooking. The recipes for her soups and her Warm Apple Dumpling Cake are well-guarded secrets. That cake was voted "Best Dessert" in the Taste of Beavercreek competition. Karen completely agreed that it deserved the honor. The cake was moist and flavorful, filled with nuts and bits of fruit, then topped with icing and pecans. Debbie opted for something from the soda fountain, deciding on a Chocolate Malt. The restaurant also serves Shakes and Phosphates of vanilla, lime, cherry, and strawberry. It still serves Sarsaparilla, too.

Ham and Bean Soup is served every day. Chicken and Rice was the special the day we visited. The Cabbage Rolls are quite popular, and very large. Many women who come in for lunch actually split an order and still take some home! The Breaded Pork Tenderloin Sandwich is just as yummy.

This whole restaurant thing started for the Deises many years ago when Gary was working in a grocery store. At the encouragement of his boss, he bought the old farmhouse and began selling antiques. Pretty soon, he added candy, jam, stone-ground flour, and the like. It's grown into what guests see today, plus the Christmas shop across the street, which is the largest in the state!

After the business began to flourish, Gary and Kathy wanted a way to say thank you to all their customers. They bounced many ideas around and came up with the Popcorn Festival, now an annual event attracting around a hundred thousand visitors. Whether you've experienced this extravaganza in person or not, we're sure you'll enjoy its recipes.

POPCORN ROAST

2 cups breadcrumbs
½ cup nuts, chopped
½ cup popcorn, popped and ground
½ cup hot water
¾ cup melted butter, divided
½ teaspoon instant minced onion
1½ teaspoons salt
¼ teaspoon pepper
1 egg, beaten

Preheat oven to 350 degrees. Butter a small mold or loaf pan. Thoroughly combine all ingredients except ¼ cup of the butter. Place in pan, cover, and bake for 1 hour, basting 3 times with remaining butter. Turn out into a hot dish and serve with your favorite sauce. May be enjoyed as an appetizer, a side dish, or a snack. Serves 4 to 6.

POPCORN CEREAL

2 cups water
2 quarts popcorn, popped
½ teaspoon salt
2 to 3 cups milk or cream, warmed

brown sugar, cinnamon, honey, raisins, or fruit for topping

Pour water into a pan and bring to a boil. Stir popcorn into boiling water. Add salt. Boil at least 5 minutes, stirring occasionally. Remove from heat, cover pan, and let stand several minutes. Serve with milk or cream. Serve with a topping of your choice. Serves 6 to 8.

POPCORN #5

2 tablespoons butter
3 to 5 drops hot pepper sauce
2 quarts popcorn, popped
²/₃ tablespoon chili powder
1 teaspoon cumin, ground
1/3 teaspoon coriander, ground
¼ teaspoon celery salt
1/8 teaspoon onion salt
1/8 teaspoon cayenne pepper
1/8 teaspoon garlic powder
1 cup cheddar cheese, grated

Preheat oven to 250 degrees. Melt butter in a small pan over low heat. Stir in hot pepper sauce and mix well. Spread popcorn in a single layer in a large baking pan. Drizzle with hot pepper butter. In a small bowl, combine remaining ingredients except cheese. Sprinkle this mixture over popcorn, then sprinkle cheese over top. Bake for 3 to 4 minutes until cheese melts. Serves 6 to 8.

190 ALAMO ROAD
CARROLLTON, OH 44615
330-627-7980
WWW.EOHIO.NET/BLUEBIRD

On the town square of Carrollton sits the McCook House. The McCook family sent two brothers and nine of those brothers' children to battle during the Civil War. One of the Christmas trees at Bluebird Farm Restaurant pays homage to this sacrifice. It is bedecked with ornaments depicting soldiers in Yankee blue and Confederate gray uniforms.

The buildings on the farm predate that conflict. They were constructed in the mid-1800s by Jacob and Louisa Kintner. One barn contains a gift shop, where items are attractively arranged even in the old cattle stalls. Another barn is the home of owner Joyce Hannon. The old farmhouse is now the restaurant. Guests enter through the original kitchen area and head up a flight of stairs to the main dining room. The plank floor is a lovely, mellow chestnut. The cream walls are trimmed with marvelous stencils of buildings, each a structure in town, done by a friend of Joyce's daughter. A corner cupboard and another built-in cupboard contain the restaurant's collection of bluebird china. I thought this might have been the inspiration for the restaurant's name, but it seems that the bluebird is the county bird of Carroll County, and

the name was chosen for that reason. The dining room on the third floor is more Victorian in its décor, which includes floral wallpaper and lace curtains over lovely arched windows. Karen wasn't able to make this sojourn, so I dined with Joyce, restaurant manager Ruth Ann, and Amy Rutledge of the Carroll County Visitor's and Convention Bureau. We ate on the enclosed second-story porch, which was a lovely setting after a fresh snowfall.

The restaurant prides itself on its hearty home-style meals. I chose the Chicken Casserole with a side dish of Cranberry Salad, which hit the spot on a wintry day. Other items ordered from our table were Spinach Lasagna Roll-Ups, which looked delicious, and Ham, Broccoli, and Cheddar Quiche, which was extremely appealing. On another visit, I might choose the BLT Chicken Salad, a favorite of many guests. When the dessert tray came, I couldn't make up my mind, so we decided to wait until after we'd toured the other buildings.

Across a short walkway, we visited the gift shop before continuing to the toy museum. Joyce's daughter, Susie, seeking a way to display her collection of antique toys, was the inspiration for the museum. The bear collection alone is unbelievable. You'll also find Madame Alexander dolls, some excellent English dolls, a wide variety of German dolls, and an impressive assortment of Steiff animals. And that's not all. Joyce has an impressive collection of hats that changes with the seasons—felts and velvets for the winter, bonnets and straw hats for the summer. Many are in the restaurant's ladies' room. Mannequins adorned in period dress, antique photos, and an antique curling iron complete the powder-room décor. I won't give away what Joyce has done with the upstairs restroom—it's whimsical, clever, and completely unexpected!

After touring, we returned to sate our sweet tooth. My Cherry Macaroon Pie with Coconut-Almond Topping was unique and delicious. Go to Bluebird Farm for lunch, a Friday- or Saturday-night date, or a traditional Sunday dinner to enjoy a down-home meal!

CREAM PUFFS

1 cup water
½ cup margarine
1 cup flour
4 eggs
Custard Filling (see next column)

Combine water and margarine in a medium saucepan. Bring to a boil. Add flour and stir well. Remove from heat. Add eggs 1 at a time, beating well after each addition. Drop by heaping tablespoonfuls onto a greased baking sheet. Bake at 375 for 40 to 45 minutes until golden brown. Allow to cool. Put Custard Filling into a pastry tube and pipe into puffs. Yields 12 puffs.

CUSTARD FILLING

4½ cups milk, divided
2 cups sugar, divided
4 tablespoons margarine
1 teaspoon vanilla
½ cup cornstarch
2 eggs

Combine 4 cups of the milk and 1½ cups of the sugar. Stir and bring to a boil. Add margarine and vanilla. In a separate bowl, combine cornstarch, remaining sugar, eggs, and remaining milk. Stir until well blended. Add to the boiling mixture, stirring constantly until thickened. Set aside to cool. Yields enough filling for 12 Cream Puffs.

CHICKEN CASSEROLE

10 chicken breasts, boned and skinned
4 cups sour cream
2 15-ounce cans cream of chicken soup
15-ounce can mushroom stems, drained
9-ounce can water chestnuts, drained
6-ounce package commercial stuffing mix

Poach chicken in salted water for approximately 10 minutes until tender. Cool and cut into bite-sized pieces. Combine sour cream, soup, mushrooms, and water chestnuts. Add chicken pieces and put in a 13-by-9-inch baking dish. Prepare stuffing mix according to package directions and spread over chicken mixture. Bake uncovered for 45 minutes at 350 degrees. May be mixed and refrigerated one day prior to using. Serves 6 to 8.

THE GRANARY AT PINE TREE BARN
4374 SHREVE ROAD
WOOSTER, OH 44691
330-264-1014
WWW.PINETREEBARN.COM

The success of Pine Tree Farm, which includes a tree farm, home furnishings and interior design, a gift shop, and a restaurant, is indirectly linked to that of immigrant August Imgard, who arrived from Germany during the 1850s. As his first Christmas in the New World approached, he observed the holiday much as he would have in Bavaria—by decorating a Christmas tree. This was very uncommon in America, but by the following Christmas, almost everyone in town followed Imgard's lead, making Wooster one of the first places in America to observe the tradition of Christmas trees.

Over the years, local farmers decided to meet the increasing demand for evergreen trees by growing them commercially. Robert Dush and his wife were one family to do so. Their son, Roger, went through college on money garnered from the tree business. He worked in Chicago before returning to Wooster to open Pine Tree Barn, an expansion of the tree busi-

ness, with his father. They set up shop in a twenty-five-thousand-square-foot Dutch bank barn. Built in 1868, it once held a significant number of livestock.

Since customers were coming to get trees, the Dushes decided to offer ornaments for sale as well. The family, realizing it was drawing business from a seventy-mile radius, also made food available for customers. At first, the restaurant was tucked into the corner of the barn where the grain bins once were. That area, with its wide-plank flooring and barn walls, is still there. Attractive sage-green bench-style seating extends around the perimeter. Additional casual side chairs slide up to the linen-covered tables, creating a cozy dining-room atmosphere. Adjacent to this, another dining room has been added overlooking the beautiful grounds and the sparkling lake.

Karen was unable to accompany me that day. As I chatted with Rita, I munched on a Lemon Crumb Muffin, a specialty of the house that was featured by Burt Wolf on a cooking segment he filmed here. I also enjoyed the Pesto Chicken and Pasta. I ended my delightful meal with a piece of Sour Cream Raspberry Pie, made according to a recipe from Roger's mother.

The Dushes and their faithful customers proclaim Pine Tree Barn to be in the middle of nowhere. Actually, this luncheon restaurant is just a few miles from Wooster, and it's well worth the trip!

MARIE'S PESTO CHICKEN AND PASTA

4 4- to 6-ounce chicken breasts, boneless
2 tablespoons olive oil
1 pound angel hair pasta
3 tablespoons lemon-infused oil
1 cup red peppers, julienned
1 cup green peppers, julienned
1 cup green onions, cut on the diagonal into
   1-inch strips
½ cup black olives, halved
1 cup homemade Pesto, divided
¼ cup Parmesan, shredded

Brush chicken breasts with olive oil. Cook pasta according to package directions. While pasta is cooking, grill chicken until juices run clear. In a large skillet, heat lemon-infused oil and sauté peppers, green onions, and olives al dente. Add ¾ cup Pesto to skillet and toss with vegetables. Remove from heat. Place pasta on 4 plates and divide vegetable mixture among them. Place chicken breasts on top. Spoon remaining Pesto over chicken and sprinkle with Parmesan. Serve immediately. Serves 4.

LEMON CRUMB MUFFINS

4 cups sugar
6 cups flour
¾ teaspoon baking soda
¾ teaspoon salt
5 fresh lemons
8 eggs
2 cups sour cream
2 cups butter, melted
2 tablespoons lemon juice

cooking spray
Streusel (see below)
Lemon Glaze (see below)

Preheat oven to 350 degrees. Sift dry ingredients together in a medium bowl. Grate rinds of lemons and set aside. In a separate bowl, whisk eggs, then add sour cream, butter, and lemon juice. Continue to whisk until smooth. Fold lemon rinds into egg mixture. Fold all dry ingredients into egg mixture. Blend well. Spray muffin tins and fill with batter. Top each muffin with 1 tablespoon Streusel and bake for 18 to 20 minutes. Remove muffins from oven and immediately poke each several times with a toothpick. Drizzle top of each muffin with a scant ½ teaspoon Lemon Glaze. Let cool slightly. Remove from muffin tins. Serve warm or allow to cool and store in an airtight container for later use. Batter can be kept up to 1 week in refrigerator. Yields 30 muffins.

Streusel

1¼ cups sugar
1¼ cups flour
⅓ cup butter, softened

Sift sugar and flour together. Add butter. Work into dry ingredients until crumbly. Yields 2½ cups.

Lemon Glaze

½ cup sugar
⅓ cup lemon juice

Combine ingredients until all sugar is dissolved. Yields ⅓ cup.

HOMESTEAD INN RESTAURANT

12203 US 250
MILAN, OH 44846
419-499-4091

Set amid the flat farmland of central Ohio, the property surrounding the Homestead Inn could have inspired the Beatles' tune "Strawberry Fields Forever." Levi Arnold was a strawberry farmer who relocated to this area from Connecticut. He built his large, two-story house in 1883, using several popular styles of the day. An intricate wrought-iron railing surrounds the widow's walk, where Mrs. Arnold is said to have kept watch on the field hands below. According to local legend, the strawberry farm was so successful that the house and its furnishings were paid for with the profits from just one year's crop. When the Lake Shore Electric Railway was completed in 1893, Arnold had a refrigerated rail car designed to ship his strawberries. The fruit was loaded on the train right at the farm, since he also had his own rail siding.

The house and farm remained in the Arnold family for three generations. Interestingly enough, current owners Mr. and Mrs. Robert Berry and Doug Berry have ties to the Arnolds. Doug's great-aunt married one of the Arnold descendants and lived in the house at the time her children were born. She was in her nineties in 1979 when the Berrys took ownership, but as she walked through the house, she told them bits and pieces about how the rooms were used and how the home was decorated. Sure enough, as they began to renovate and restore, color schemes and details she had described revealed themselves. Although the Berrys began their tenure in the late 1970s, the home had been used as a restaurant some twenty years prior to that.

Visible from the Ohio Turnpike, Homestead Inn Restaurant is popular with tourists and locals alike. We arrived from the other direction, coming north on US 250. We were immediately drawn to the gnarled trees in the yard and the contrast they provided to the lovely wrought iron of the ornate porch and the patterned slate roof.

We were seated at a cozy window table in the main dining room. Fabulous beaded gingerbread trim separated one room from the next. The intricate pattern in shades of black and tan on the inlaid marble fireplace reminded us of those done on Ukrainian Easter eggs. Even the hinges on the ten-foot doors were elaborate. Downstairs, the Rathskeller—the old cellar, built from massive stone blocks—offered a very different dining experience. There, old tools and interesting lighting that gave a candlelight effect decorated the many nooks and crannies.

We shared a cup of the Reuben Chowder,

delicious on that rainy day. It had a creamy Swiss cheese broth filled with chunks of sauerkraut, corned beef, and pickle. Karen followed it with the Smothered Crab Burger and Onion Rings, while Debbie enjoyed the Perch Luncheon, served with a Twice-Baked Potato and a dish of Coleslaw. No strawberries were on the menu, though. They just weren't in season.

DEVILED EGGS

12 hard-cooked eggs
½ teaspoon salt
¼ teaspoon pepper
3 tablespoons sugar
1 teaspoon cider vinegar
1 tablespoon prepared mustard
$^1/_3$ cup mayonnaise
2 teaspoons celery seed

Shell eggs. Cut in half lengthwise and separate whites from yolks. Place yolks in a bowl and mash with a fork or a pastry blender until they resemble fine crumbs. Add next 6 ingredients, blend until smooth, then fill whites with yolk mixture. A pastry bag works best for adding filling. Sprinkle with celery seed. Serves 24.

SWEET POTATO BREAD

1 cup fresh yams, cooked and mashed
½ cup oil or shortening
$^1/_3$ cup water
1¾ cups flour
1½ cups sugar
½ cup walnuts, chopped
1 teaspoon baking soda
1 teaspoon lemon rind, grated
¾ teaspoon cinnamon
¾ teaspoon nutmeg
½ teaspoon salt
Glaze (see below)

Combine first 3 ingredients in a large bowl and beat well. Add flour, sugar, walnuts, baking soda, lemon rind, cinnamon, nutmeg, and salt and beat well. Pour into a greased loaf pan and bake for about 1 hour at 350 degrees. Brush with Glaze while still warm. Yields 1 loaf.

GLAZE

4 tablespoons powdered sugar
1 tablespoon butter
1 tablespoon milk
1 tablespoon lemon juice

Combine all ingredients in a small bowl. Yields $^1/_3$ cup.

The Sawyer House

Restaurant & Tavern

9470 MENTOR AVENUE
MENTOR, OH 44060
440-358-0100

The stone building on the south side of US 20 was once part of a group of Sawyer family homes that sat along both sides of the avenue. Daniel Sawyer lived in this house, while his brother Joseph lived on the corner of Mentor Avenue (US 20) and Chillicothe Road. Another brother, Isaac, lived just across the way. A collage of Sawyer family pictures hangs in the vestibule near the reception desk. Three generations of Sawyers lived in this house. Longtime area residents used to talk about Daniel's son, William, trimming the front hedges. His hard work garnered him much respect, since William had a clubfoot.

The house, marked by a stone over the front entrance, was built in 1843. The construction style, in which native cut stone and cut sandstone were set in a random pattern, is quite unique. This is one of only two or three stone homes more than one hundred years old in Lake County. Some of the stones are as much as four feet by two and a half feet.

Inside, stone walls were visible in the dining room where we were seated and up the steps adjacent to the bar area. The main dining room is more modern than the building's exterior but still has vestiges of the past, including the original cellar door and a wall of weathered barn siding. A large, old-fashioned clock set above a series of booths adorns one of the end walls. Eight ceiling fans turn lazily overhead, operated by an elaborate pulley system. Off the bar area, two additional dining rooms decorated in tones of teal and mauve are located in the downstairs rooms of the Sawyers' original residence.

We were intrigued by the Graham Cracker-Crusted Calamari, served with Curry Coconut Aioli. The Veal Meat Loaf, wrapped in smoked bacon and then char-grilled, also sounded wonderful. Pork Tenderloin is a favorite of Debbie's, so she was tempted by The Sawyer House's version, which comes encrusted with rosemary and walnuts and served with Sweet and Sour Red Cabbage and Sun-Dried Cherry-Apple Relish. Ultimately, it was the Ravioli, filled with butternut squash and served in Sage Cream Sauce, that got her vote. The portion was just the right size for lunch. Karen had no difficulty in selecting the Crab Cakes, served in four petite mounds with a side of Jicama Slaw. Although we decided to curb our calorie count, the ladies' luncheon next to us gave us an opportunity to observe each of the desserts. The Cheesecake that day was a luscious-looking raspberry. The Pecan-Rolled Ice Cream Balls, served with Vanilla and Cinnamon Ice Cream and topped with Kentucky Bourbon Caramel Sauce, was enough for two people. The Double Mousse Parfait, with its layers of creamy white and dark chocolate, looked wonderful. Temptation almost won out when we saw the Chocolate Lucifer Torte, but for once, we refrained!

CRAB-ROLLED HALIBUT

1 cup mixed red, green, and yellow bell peppers, diced fine
1 tablespoon fresh basil, chopped
1 tablespoon fresh thyme, chopped
1½ teaspoons fresh rosemary, chopped
1½ pounds jumbo lump crabmeat
1 egg
¼ cup mayonnaise
2¾ cup fresh breadcrumbs, divided
2 tablespoons Old Bay seasoning
1 tablespoon granulated garlic
salt and pepper to taste
5 6-ounce halibut steaks
3 eggs, beaten
Orange-Basil Hollandaise (see next column)

Sauté peppers until half cooked. Add chopped herbs and cook until vegetables are al dente. Cool. In a medium bowl, mix by hand the crabmeat, pepper mixture, 1 egg, mayonnaise, ¾ cup of the breadcrumbs, Old Bay, garlic, and salt and pepper. Set aside. Lay out a 12-by-12-inch piece of plastic wrap. Place 1 portion of halibut on plastic, then place another piece of plastic wrap on top of fish. Using a meat mallet, pound halibut into a rectangular shape about 6 inches by 10 inches. Pull off top layer of plastic wrap. Put 6 ounces of crabmeat mixture in middle of halibut. Fold short ends of halibut to cover about ¼ of the crabmeat.

Firmly but delicately roll up halibut around crabmeat. Repeat with other halibut steaks. Dunk rolled halibut in beaten eggs, then roll in remaining breadcrumbs. In a skillet, sear all sides of halibut until golden brown. Place in a 375-degree oven and cook until fish is flaky and crabmeat is hot. Slice and place on plates. Drizzle with Orange-Basil Hollandaise. Serves 5.

ORANGE-BASIL HOLLANDAISE

¼ pound fresh basil leaves
2 cups extra-virgin olive oil
1 tablespoon granulated sugar
juice of 3 blood oranges
¼ cup white wine
6 egg yolks
1½ cups clarified butter, warmed
2 teaspoons lemon juice
1 teaspoon cayenne pepper
salt and pepper to taste

Blanch basil and let cool. In a blender, combine basil and olive oil and blend for 5 minutes on high. Strain and set aside. In a small pot or pan over medium heat, combine sugar and orange juice and reduce by ½. In a separate stainless-steel bowl, mix wine and egg yolks. Whip over simmering water until yolks form ribbons and triple in volume. Take off heat and gradually add butter, whipping constantly. Add lemon juice, cayenne, and salt and pepper. Set aside in a warm place. Yields approximately 3 cups.

750 MURPHIN RIDGE ROAD
WEST UNION, OH 45693
937-544-2263
WWW.MURPHINRIDGEINN.COM

Turning on to the country lane leading to Murphin Ridge Inn, I immediately felt conspicuous in my red rental car. Amish mothers were out strolling babies, children were playing, and buggies were transporting their inhabitants homeward from the nearby village of Unity. It was quite picturesque. And, as I was soon to find, it was only the beginning of a great evening.

Innkeeper Darryl McKenney greeted me upon my arrival, doing the duties while his wife, Sherry, was out of town. He obviously enjoyed the work, as he mingled among the guests with a refreshing blend of savoir-faire and fun. As Darryl and I explored the property, he hailed guests, built a bonfire, and showed me the original log cabin on the property. The plan is to restore it for conference space. The old smokehouse is now a gift shop. The corncrib still stands, as do a chicken coop and the old well.

Two dinner bells are located at the back of the brick farmhouse, built around 1826, that is now the restaurant at Murphin Ridge Inn.

They were once used to call farm hands to meals, but there is no need of that now, as the cuisine and the ambiance draw customers from quite a distance. Seated at the table next to me were Roy and Joyce Payne, who had driven up from Portsmouth, Ohio. Somehow, during the course of our conversation, Charleston, West Virginia, came up. It turns out that the Paynes, Darryl, and I all have roots there. In fact, Darryl's wife once taught at the high school from which my husband graduated!

Four of the five tables were occupied in the dining room where we were seated. Two of the parties were celebrating birthdays. Darryl serenaded the room with "Happy Birthday"—on the kazoo. Corporate guests were seated across the hall in what is sometimes known as the "Chicken Wing," a room that houses a variety of chicken pictures, antiques, and other bric-a-brac. All the dining rooms are quite elegant in their simplicity. White walls work together with subdued painted woodwork and smooth wooden floors. The Shaker-style dining tables have polished cherry tops that nicely offset the butter-yellow place mats and the yellow-and-rust plaid napkins.

Before being seated, I had glanced at the menu and decided to order the Three Falls Trout, which is sautéed and stuffed with Crab Dressing. Chef Renee Schuler was quite generous, suggesting I sample a variety of dishes. A meal here typically starts with soup and a salad. On that evening, the soup was a tasty Vegetable, but I was also allowed to enjoy the delicious Creamed Onion. All three of the entrées—April's Chicken, the Three Falls Trout, and e.e.'s Pork Tenderloin—were fabulous. It was fortunate that I sampled lightly, because dessert soon followed, again in triplicate—West Virginia Bluebarb Crisp (an unusual combination of blueberries and rhubarb), Chocolate Fondue (served with bananas, strawberries, bite-sized pieces of cake, and a Shortbread Spoon), and Lemon Baby Cake (filled with Sweet Cream, surrounded by Lemon Sauce, and topped with Candied Kumquats). Choosing a favorite would have been impossible.

As I left, anxious to tell Karen about what she'd missed, the Midwestern sky was a vivid pink. What could have been more perfect after my Murphin Ridge experience than rounding a corner, crossing a covered bridge, and heading off into a glorious sunset?

 FOGGY BOTTOM PANCAKES

½ cup cornmeal
½ cup whole-wheat flour
½ cup oatmeal
1½ cups white flour
½ tablespoon baking powder
½ tablespoon baking soda
½ tablespoon salt
1 tablespoon sugar
3 eggs
3 cups buttermilk
³/₈ cup canola oil
whole milk as required
maple syrup
stewed apples

Combine dry ingredients in a medium bowl. In a separate bowl, combine eggs, buttermilk, and oil. Pour wet ingredients into bowl with dry ingredients and stir to combine. Thin mixture with milk if necessary. Cook pancakes on a hot, oiled griddle. Serve with maple syrup and stewed apples. Yields 8 to 12 pancakes.

CREAMED ONION SOUP

6 large sweet onions, sliced thin
1 stick butter
8 cups chicken stock
2 cups heavy cream
2 cups Parmesan, grated
salt and white pepper to taste

In a stockpot, sauté onions in butter until transparent but not brown. Add enough stock to cover by at least 2 inches. Cook until tender. Remove ½ of mixture from pot and place in a blender. Purée until smooth. Add puréed mixture back into stockpot. Add cream and cheese. Heat through but do not boil. Season with salt and white pepper. Thin with additional stock if necessary. Serves 8.

BARN RESTAURANT AT
HISTORIC

Sauder Village

ROUTE 2
ARCHBOLD, OH 43502
419-445-2231
WWW.SAUDERVILLAGE.COM

In 1861, a large bank barn was built on the Stutzman farmstead by an Amish crew. The property was passed on to Moses J. Stutzman, then to his daughter and son-in-law, Della and Louis Riegsecker. By the time their children inherited the property, the barn was sadly run-down, an anomaly in a land of pristine farms and outbuildings. As with many of the buildings we see in our travels, it was scheduled for destruction. However, about that same time, a local industrialist and entrepreneur was saving and restoring old buildings as a hobby during his retirement. His intent was to create a living-history village bearing his name.

When Erie Sauder came to look at the old barn, he saw not the gaping holes and rotted siding but the hand-hewn timbers within. Mr. Sauder envisioned a restaurant growing from the remaining bits of woodwork. Soon, the top story of the barn was loaded onto steel beams and dollies for a two-mile trek across frozen fields to proudly take its place in Sauder Village.

The portion of the old barn that Mr. Sauder rescued was once used for hay and straw storage and as a play area for many of Mr. Stutzman's descendants. It was easy to envision the youngsters of prior generations wrestling and playing hide-and-seek here. Many transients also found their way to this barn for a bit of rest. They were called "tramps" and "hobos" by much of society, but the Riegseckers always called them "walkers" and were never surprised to find one curled up in the hay.

At the ripe young age of 115, the barn opened its doors not for livestock but for dinner guests. The granary of yesteryear is now a dining room that seats up to twenty-five. The rope-and-pulley system is still overhead, as are authentic wagon-wheel chandeliers designed by Erie Sauder.

The menu is almost as lengthy as the barn's illustrious history. Diners can choose from several appetizers and eight salad selections, including the salad bar. There are no fewer than seventeen sandwich options and thirteen dinner choices. The dinners, such as Roasted Chicken and Butterflied Pork Chops, are served with hot rolls, Apple Butter, and numerous choices for sides. The restaurant also offers a daily buffet and family-style dining, a very affordable option for families eating out.

Erie Sauder was certainly a visionary not only in his care of the barn but in his building of the village. Here, professional craftsmen use the skills of their ancestors in plying their trades. Costumed interpreters amid period furnishings tell the story of the pioneer men and women who drained the Great Black Swamp, transforming it into some of America's most fertile farmland.

PORK LOIN

6-pound pork loin, trimmed
salt to taste
garlic powder to taste
pepper to taste
Apple Chutney (see below)

Season pork with salt, garlic powder, and pepper. Place in a baking pan with sides. Bake at 350 degrees for 45 minutes to 1 hour. This will cook meat medium-well, leaving it still tender and juicy. Slice pork into $^3/_8$-inch-thick medallions. Arrange medallions on a platter, top with Apple Chutney, and serve. Serves 12.

APPLE CHUTNEY

¼ cup red wine vinegar
½ cup brown sugar
1 teaspoon cloves, ground
1 teaspoon nutmeg
½ teaspoon cinnamon
1 teaspoon garlic, minced
4 cups apples, peeled and diced
¼ cup raisins

Combine first 6 ingredients and cook on low in a large saucepan until well mixed. Add apples and raisins. Reduce heat to low and cook approximately 4 hours. This is best when made ahead. If made ahead, chutney should be refrigerated, then warmed before use. Yields approximately 2 cups.

HAM LOAF

1 cup onion, diced fine
1 cup celery, diced fine
2 tablespoons butter
1 sleeve saltines, crushed
4 eggs
1 teaspoon salt
2½ pounds ground ham
1¼ pounds ground beef
1¼ pounds ground sausage
½ cup milk
½ cup water
¼ cup honey
¼ cup mustard

Heat oven to 350 degrees. Sauté onions and celery in butter until tender and slightly cooked. In a large bowl, combine saltines, eggs, and salt. Stir in onions and celery. Add meats and mix well. Stir in milk and water. Continue mixing until smooth. Place mixture into 2 loaf pans. Bake for approximately 1½ hours. Combine honey and mustard in a small bowl. Spread on top of loaves after baking. Return to oven for 10 minutes. Slice. Serves 20.

THE BARN AT

WALDEN

700 BISSELL ROAD
AURORA, OH 44202
330-562-7136
WWW.WALDONCO.COM

Out for a Sunday drive one spring day, we found our way to the resort known as Walden. The Country Inn and Stables is a modern facility providing guests with everything they can imagine, including a state-of-the-art exercise facility, a ninety-eight-seat theater, tennis courts, an Olympic-sized pool, and a 240-by-80-foot indoor arena for horseback riding. The "Bridle Suite" here (pun intended) is a lavish, 1,500-square-foot suite that features an indoor atrium. The inn so impressed the staff of *Town & Country* that the magazine granted it the honor of Favorite Inn in April 2001.

Although there are several dining options at the Walden complex, our favorite is just down the road from the main property. The Barn at Walden was built in 1825 by Solomon Little. The land on which it sits was part of the Western Reserve Land Grant, settled by Connecticut veterans of the Revolutionary War. The farm was prosperous enough for the owners to expand the barn in 1850. Two silos, one from each construction period, still stand. The barn's primary use was in keeping the cows and storing the hay necessary to run a dairy farm. In 1971, when renovations began, Mr. Manny Barenholtz came across the original cattle troughs. Since that time, ongoing improvements to the structure have been made. The goal has been to leave as much of the original as possible, including the exposed beams dating to the 1825 construction.

Although the exterior, with its stone foundation and traditional red siding, remains much as it was, the interior is French Country, befitting the upscale flavor of the Walden complex. Windows have been added so guests can take in the lovely countryside, either from the main floor or from the loft area, which offers a panoramic view of the adjacent golf course. Reservations at The Barn can be obtained in three ways. Guests at Walden's Country Inn are welcome to dine at the restaurant, as are members of Walden's Golf and Tennis Club. If you don't play, dining-only memberships are available. In addition, special arrangements can be made for nonmembers to experience the wonderful creations before they choose to join.

Chef Thomas Dech's creations have been classified as "Cross-Cultural Cuisine." His emphasis is on top-quality ingredients, careful preparation, and beautiful presentation. What more could a dinner guest want? How about a light, low-fat approach to entrées? Selections such as Pan-Roasted Salmon, served over a colorful combination of cucumbers and tomatoes tossed in Rice-Wine Vinaigrette, and Gulf Shrimp, arranged over Tricolored Pasta tossed with garlic and basil, are typical fare. Appetizers such as Quail in Teriyaki Glacé, served with

Grilled Bok Choy, and Scottish Smoked Salmon with Citrus Vinaigrette are flavor combinations that are deliciously out of the ordinary. The menu choices are ample. As many as five soups and seven or eight desserts are available. One-third of the selections change weekly, so guests can go often to enjoy Thomas Dech's gastronomic delights.

ROAST PHEASANT

4 fresh pheasants
salt and pepper to taste
4 bay leaves, crumbled
1 tablespoon fresh thyme, chopped
2 tablespoons vegetable oil
Shiitake Mushroom Risotto (see next column)
4 sprigs fresh thyme

Season pheasants with salt and pepper, bay leaves, and thyme. Heat oil in a heavy skillet. Brown pheasant on all sides until golden brown. Place on an ovenproof rack and roast at 450 degrees for 18 to 25 minutes until juices run clear. Remove from oven and let stand 15 minutes.

Debone pheasant, heat slightly in oven if needed, and serve on Shiitake Mushroom Risotto. Garnish with thyme sprigs. Serves 4.

SHITAKE MUSHROOM RISOTTO

5 cups chicken stock
¼ cup butter
1 medium onion, chopped
1 clove garlic, minced
1 pound shiitake mushrooms, sliced, no stems
2 teaspoons fresh thyme
2 cups Arborio rice
¼ cup white wine
¼ cup heavy cream
salt and pepper to taste

Bring chicken stock to a simmer. Melt butter in a heavy saucepan. Fry onions, garlic, mushrooms, and thyme until soft. Add rice, stirring until well coated with mixture. Add a ladleful of stock and continue cooking gently. Continue stirring and adding stock until all stock is absorbed, mixture is thick, and rice is tender. Remove from heat and stir in wine and cream. Season with salt and pepper. Keep warm until served. Serves 4.

CHAPTER 10
Paths to Freedom

Emmitt House

Harriet Beecher Stowe, author of *Uncle Tom's Cabin*, was a Cincinnati resident. The book, which relates the story of an escaping slave and one of the stops she finds on the Underground Railroad, was born out of a visit that Harriet made to Kentucky. She was so moved by the conditions she witnessed in her first experience with slavery that she returned to Ohio to pen the story. The establishments in this chapter are linked by their role as stops on the Underground Railroad, where slaves on the run from authorities in the South could rest before continuing their quest for freedom.

10150 HISTORIC PLYMOUTH STREET
HANOVERTON, OH 44423
330-223-1583
WWW.SPREADEAGLETAVERN.COM

With one quick turn off US 30 on to Historic Plymouth Street, the modern world disappears. It wouldn't have surprised me if my minivan had been transformed into a horse and carriage without a single "Bibbidy, bobbidy, boo!" having been uttered. At the end of the block sits the Spread Eagle Tavern. Access to the restaurant is around back, where guests enter through an adorable log cabin. This is the restored stable of the property, rebuilt by owner Pete Johnson from authentic materials of the era. Booth seating has been crafted from old horse stalls, and a cozy nook holds the old blacksmith's fireplace. The tables were handcrafted, as was the cherry paneling on the walls. If you know where to look in a piece of wood near the door, you'll see part of a bullet found by the craftsman as he planed the wood. The slug was buried deep in a tree on his property, which he cut for this specific purpose.

As I toured, I found one dining room as interesting as the next. The one with the large kitchen fireplace is particularly homey.

Through that room and into the main part of the old inn is the Hanover Room. One of the photos on the wall is of the daughter of the first owner. According to many reports, her presence is still felt. She was quite a music student in her day and is still credited with playing the piano at odd times and with turning radios on and off inexplicably.

Across the street is Dr. Robertson's house, once a stop on the Underground Railroad. The home was built with a secret room accessible only from an exterior second-story window. Dr. Robertson didn't accept payment for his services to escaping slaves. Instead, they were required to rob graves and bring back the cadavers to further the doctor's study of his profession. Tunnels connected the doctor's house to others on the street, including the Spread Eagle Tavern.

Downstairs in the tavern is Gideon Gaver's Rathskeller, where the old tunnels and crawlspaces are lined with bricks from Mr. Gaver's mansion. Pete Johnson dismantled the home, cleaned the bricks, refired them for strength, and then put them to use in this lovely series of rooms. Upstairs once again, I ordered the Country Pâté, served with gherkins and Lingonberry Sauce. It was delicious, but quite a large serving, so I saved half to share with Karen, who was unable to accompany me. That was followed by the excellent Sierra Salad.

As I munched, I contemplated what the politicians might have chosen when they were here. Owner Pete Johnson is very active in the

Republican Party today. In fact, Republicans as far back as Abraham Lincoln have visited. George W. Bush even paid a visit while stumping the campaign trail in 2000. Regardless of guests' political affiliation, the fabulous ambiance and wonderful food of the Spread Eagle Tavern are things everyone can agree upon.

SIERRA SALAD

¾ cup olive oil
juice of 1 lime
1 tablespoon poppy seeds
½ teaspoon fresh ginger, grated
2 tablespoons vinegar
2 tablespoons soy sauce
8-ounce bag mixed greens
1 cup feta cheese, crumbled
1 cup Chinese noodles
1 cup pecans, roasted

In a large mixing bowl, whisk together oil, lime juice, poppy seeds, ginger, vinegar, and soy sauce. Just before serving, whisk once more. Add remaining ingredients and toss gently until all greens are coated. Serves 8.

 ## CHICKEN POT PIE

1 stick butter
2 cups onion, diced medium
2 cups carrots, diced medium
2 cups celery, diced medium
1 tablespoon thyme
1 bay leaf
¼ cup flour
8 cups chicken stock
2 cups potatoes, diced medium
2½ pounds chicken breasts, boned and diced
1 cup cream
1 cup frozen peas
salt and pepper to taste
8 sheets puff pastry

Melt butter in a large saucepan. Add onions, carrots, celery, thyme, and bay leaf. Sweat vegetables but do not burn. Add flour and stir. Add chicken stock, potatoes, chicken, cream, and peas. Stir. Simmer for 15 minutes. Add salt and pepper. Cut puff pastry to size required for top of individual pot-pie dishes. Place pastry on a greased cookie sheet and bake as per directions on package. Divide chicken mixture evenly among 8 individual pot-pie dishes and place a baked pastry on top of each. Serve immediately. Serves 8.

EMMITT HOUSE

1861

123 NORTH MARKET STREET
WAVERLY, OH 45690
740-947-2181

When the Ohio & Erie Canal was completed in 1832, James Emmitt quickly saw its business potential. Over the next twenty years, he made a fortune hauling grain, operating a mill, and building a distillery. Even with all this development, he felt like Waverly's economic growth would be limited as long as the county courthouse was located in Piketon. He and a group of Waverly businessmen agreed to finance the process of petitioning the Ohio General Assembly in an effort to convince it to move the county seat, a goal they later accomplished.

Emmitt was so sure of his eventual success that he commissioned a new hotel to be built along the canal, at the corner of Water and Market Streets. In the construction of the hotel, Emmitt employed a master carpenter who had come to Pike County in the early 1830s. The superb workmanship of Madison Hemings was unparalleled in the area. Not only is Hemings of interest because of his skill, but also because of his parentage. It was rumored

at the time—and never denied—that he was the son of Thomas Jefferson and a slave by the name of Sally Hemings. Research over the years has further substantiated that lineage.

Upon completion, the Emmitt House quickly developed a reputation as a fine hotel. It was a particular favorite of hardware and dry-goods salesmen, who would display their sample cases in the front room, known as the Drummer's Room.

Today, that room is still known by the same name, though it contains a dining room rather than wares. There are several other dining areas as well, including the Billiard Room, with its large mural of area sights, the casual dining room called "The Lounge," and the bar. Through the lobby in the same part of the hotel as the Drummer's Room is the Canal Room, where we were seated. It boasts lovely patterned-tin walls, in addition to the tin ceilings also visible in the other dining rooms.

Karen chose the Mexican Chicken, served with side dishes of Spanish Rice and tortilla chips topped with melted cheese. It was delicious. Debbie chose the Warm Cashew Chicken Salad, served with a wonderfully moist Carrot Muffin. When it came time for dessert, Karen's eyes were immediately alight when she noticed the Fried Ice Cream on the menu. Never one to pass up a chocolate-and-raspberry combo, Debbie was drawn to the Razz Ma Tazz, a raspberry-filled chocolate cookie served with Vanilla Ice Cream and Chocolate and Raspberry Syrups.

Prior to dinner, we'd toured the old hotel

from top to bottom. In the basement, we saw the doorway that led to a tunnel stretching under Route 23. Locals believe it was intended for escaping slaves, allowing them to move between the hotel and Emmitt's office and home down the street. We didn't meet the female ghost that many staff members and the bank employees next door have experienced.

Don't let the faces at the windows fool you. They're just a touch of whimsy left over from previous owners Charly and Bill Weil. Charly's daughter, Michele Brown, and her husband, Jason, now run the Emmitt House.

EMMITT HOUSE CHILI

3½ pounds ground beef
1 large onion, chopped
⅓ green pepper, chopped
⅓ red pepper, chopped
2 pounds canned crushed tomatoes
1 packet taco seasoning
2 cups salsa
2½ tablespoons sugar

Brown ground beef in a large pot until slightly pink. Add onions and peppers and cook over medium heat until beef is thoroughly cooked. Drain. Return mixture to pot and add remaining ingredients. Simmer slowly for at least 1 hour, stirring frequently. Serves 10 to 12.

MEAT SAUCE FOR SPAGHETTI

1 medium onion, diced
1 medium clove garlic, minced
2 tablespoons olive oil
1½ pounds ground beef
1 pound sausage
3 cups fresh tomatoes, chopped
1½ pounds canned crushed tomatoes
2 cups tomato purée
2½ tablespoons sugar
2 tablespoons fresh parsley, chopped
2 tablespoons oregano
1½ tablespoons salt
½ tablespoon pepper
1 bay leaf

In a large pot, cook onions and garlic in olive oil until tender. Add beef and sausage and cook until no pink remains. Remove from heat and drain. Return mixture to pot and add remaining ingredients. Cook over medium heat for about 1 hour. Discard bay leaf. Serves 10.

The Old Tavern

ROUTE 84 AT COUNTY LINE ROAD
UNIONVILLE, OH 44088
800-7-TAVERN

Traditions come about for a very good reason. One custom at The Old Tavern is serving every single guest a Corn Fritter topped with powdered sugar and sitting in a pool of maple syrup. Concocted from a recipe dating back to 1798, they were the most delicious fritters we have ever tasted! Sitting at our table on the porch, we could look out through the floral swagged windows to see the gazebo and the gardens. The room was light and airy, and the white linens and Tiffany lamps lent elegance to each table. We chose to partake of the buffet, located in the Blue Room, so called because of the blue paneling on the walls. We began with the tasty Ham and Great Northern Bean Soup and sampled the Roast Beef, the Roast Chicken, the Seafood Linguini, and the unusual Pasta Salad with Tuna. We helped ourselves to salads and anticipated trying the Almond Raspberry Torte or perhaps the Coffee Sponge Cake. Unfortunately, our eyes were larger than our stomachs, and although every item we tried was pleasing, we had room for only a sliver of dessert.

Back in 1798, The Old Tavern was a log cabin next to an old Indian trail on the Western Reserve land. Constructed from hand-hewn timbers, it measured twelve feet long and fifteen feet wide. The windows were covered in greased paper, and the walls were caulked with mud. It was a popular stopping point for families moving west in covered wagons. Business was so good that the owners built another cabin and a roofed walkway between the two. It is said that during the War of 1812, soldiers stayed here on their way to join the fighting. In 1818, William Whitman and Calvin Cole, who had established a stagecoach line between Ashtabula and Cleveland, bought the property. They expanded the tavern and added a ballroom that still has its original double-layered spring floor today. Patrons visited from miles around to dance quadrilles and Virginia reels. That room is now the banquet hall. Wedding guests can still tread the floor where so many have danced before.

One of the most interesting facts about this wonderful old building is that it was a station on the Underground Railroad. Runaway slaves were sheltered in secret closets and basement tunnels, some of which still exist. We were escorted down to the basement to see what remains of the tunnels. The main tunnel splits into two after just a little way. The right fork is reputed to go across the street and into the graveyard, which is across the county line in Ashtabula County, while the left fork goes toward the gazebo and the gardens. One of the real-life people upon whom Harriet Beecher

Stowe based a character in *Uncle Tom's Cabin* is said to have been involved in local politics in Unionville.

The Old Tavern has long been considered the oldest tavern in Ohio. People from all walks of life have visited, stayed, and eaten here. Even a few of the former slaves stayed on after the Civil War to become servants and field hands. The tavern is a truly memorable setting for a wonderful meal.

FAMOUS CHICKEN SALAD

5 whole boneless chicken breasts, cut into
   bite-sized pieces
1½ cups dates, pitted and chopped into thirds
1½ cups pineapple tidbits, drained
¾ cup white seedless grapes, halved
¾ cup red seedless grapes, halved
½ to 1 cup mayonnaise
¼ cup almonds, chopped

In a large bowl, combine all ingredients except mayonnaise and almonds. Add enough mayonnaise to lightly coat ingredients. Place in a serving bowl and top with almonds. Yields 10 to 12 cups.

CORN FRITTERS RECIPE OF 1798

6 eggs
¾ cup milk
¼ cup butter, melted
2 pounds whole-kernel corn
½ cup sugar
3¾ cups flour
1 tablespoon baking powder

Combine eggs, milk, butter, corn, and sugar in a mixing bowl. Sift flour and baking powder together. Add egg mixture to dry ingredients. Mixture should take on a batter form. Heat oil to 375 degrees in a deep-fryer. Drop batter by ice cream scoop into fryer and fry for approximately 8 minutes. Test by poking a fork into batter ball; fork should come out clean. Yields 24 fritters.

Rider's 1812 Inn

792 MENTOR AVENUE
PAINESVILLE, OH 44077
440-354-8200
WWW.NCWEB.COM/RIDERSINN.COM

The Prime Rib and the Potato Leek Soup are house specialties, made from recipes found in the attic of this structure. This inn, built by Joseph Rider, is situated along US 20, which was once the Oregon Trail. Stagecoach stops were located every sixty to seventy miles—the distance a horse could travel in a day. Registers from the inn show that as many as one hundred guests were there in a single day. How this was accomplished in the limited space available is quite a puzzlement until you consider that many of the stagecoach drivers stayed only about four hours, just long enough to bathe, eat, and catch a couple of hours of shuteye on narrow benches upstairs. The rooms for today's guests are much more attractive, spacious, and comfortable.

Mr. Rider came to the area as part of a surveying team for the Connecticut Land Company. He was accompanied by Mr. Moses Cleveland, Mr. Willoughby, and Mr. Paine. Their efforts made Lake County the first

planned urban community in the world. We found the history behind this absolutely fascinating. Much of Connecticut was pro-British, the government of the colony technically being a proprietorship of the king. Prior to and during the Revolutionary War, the primary currency was pounds sterling. Of course, after the war, that currency was worthless here, and an alternate way to pay the soldiers was needed. The Connecticut Land Company had investors from other states, and so had acceptable currency. The company purchased property in this area, which they used to pay the soldiers. Within five years of beginning their endeavor, these gentlemen had taken this area from log cabins to clapboard houses and an organized system of streets.

The War of 1812 impacted this area, too. A local army company was commissioned into the navy. The members of that company were attacked at Put-In Bay before they had been trained in naval tactics, so they fought as soldiers would. This caught the British quite by surprise, resulting in an American victory.

Rider's Inn also figured prominently in the Underground Railroad. Estimates indicate that three thousand slaves went through its basement. Participation in the abolitionist movement in this area was multifaceted. Some chose to help because of their abhorrence of slavery. Others, tired of being undersold by crops from slave states, participated in the Underground Railroad in an attempt to reduce competition for their Ohio crops, farmed with paid labor.

The table in the main dining room at

which we were seated was above one of the basement tunnels used for escape. The room was decorated with light blue and cream wainscoting. Karen enjoyed the creamy Lemon Cake and Debbie reveled in the White Chocolate Raspberry Cheesecake as owner Elaine Crane regaled us with one historical fact after another. Our favorite piece of information concerned Harvey Johnson. Mr. Johnson was a slave who made his way to freedom via Rider's Inn. After the Civil War, he returned to Painesville, where his son and grandson became successful businessmen. Wendell Walker, his great-great-grandson, served as the president of Painesville's city council. Now, that's a success story.

ORANGE ROUGHY STUFFED WITH SMOKED SALMON MOUSSE

4 ounces smoked salmon
1 egg
¼ cup heavy whipping cream
salt and pepper to taste
brandy to taste
2 4- to 6-ounce orange roughy fillets

Purée salmon in a food processor. Add egg and cream. Add salt and pepper and brandy. Blend well. Set aside and chill. Preheat oven to 350 degrees. Grease a baking pan. Spoon mousse equally into center of fillets. Roll and secure. Bake for 8 to 10 minutes. Serves 2.

FROSTED PUMPKIN PECAN DROP COOKIES

1 cup butter, room temperature
1 egg
1 cup canned pumpkin
1 cup sugar
1 teaspoon cinnamon
½ teaspoon salt
⅛ teaspoon allspice
2 cups all-purpose flour
1 teaspoon baking soda
1 cup pecans
Frosting (see below)

Cream together butter and egg. When light and fluffy, add pumpkin, sugar, cinnamon, salt, and allspice. Mix in remaining ingredients. Blend until smooth. Drop by teaspoonfuls onto a baking sheet. You won't need to leave a lot of space between cookies, as they won't spread. Bake at 350 degrees for 8 to 10 minutes. When cool, apply Frosting in a random pattern. Yields approximately 4 dozen cookies.

 FROSTING

6 tablespoons butter, melted
1 cup brown sugar
2 cups powdered sugar
1 teaspoon vanilla

Cook butter and brown sugar until smooth. Blend with powdered sugar and vanilla. Cool slightly before using. Yields 2½ to 3 cups.

Note: Recipes reproduced with permission of Rider's Inn.

DON'S
POMEROY
HOUSE

13664 PEARL ROAD
STRONGSVILLE, OH 44136
440-572-1111
WWW.DONSPOMEROY.COM

Ebenezer Pomeroy and his wife, Violatra, introduced "Pomeroy hospitality" when they opened a tavern in 1822. Their son, Alanson, and his wife, Keziah, continued the tradition after Ebenezer met his death upon being thrown from a wagon when his horse shied.

Alanson was active in community affairs as a Strongsville trustee and justice of the peace. In 1850, three years after building a large manor house, he established the Strongsville General Store adjacent to his home. This area was known as Town Square, because it was here that people met and socialized. Men pulled chairs up to the potbelly stove at the store, waiting for the stagecoach to bring the newspaper, which Alanson's ten-year-old daughter would read.

The citizens of Strongsville were strong supporters of the abolitionist cause. "Pomeroy hospitality" extended to escaping slaves. Harlan Pomeroy recalled seeing his mother carrying trays of food to the cellar. At the time, no explanation was given to the children. Later, Alanson explained to Harlan that slaves were

brought from Oberlin by night, hidden in a load of hay. They were then harbored in the cellar until notice was received that a "Freedom Boat" would be leaving. The runaways were loaded again amid the hay and taken to nearby Rocky Road, where they boarded a boat bound for Canada.

The Pomeroys opened their home at every turn, including Sunday afternoons. Many members of the Congregation Church traveled too far to go home between the morning and afternoon services. Those families were invited to share Sunday dinner with the Pomeroys before returning to worship.

Members of the family lived in the home until Gertrude, granddaughter of Alanson, moved to Florida in 1963. Left empty, the structure quickly began to decline. In 1966, during preparations for the town's sesquicentennial, the local Women's League developed a plan to open the house for viewing. Donations came from all corners of the community, but the effort failed to raise enough money to save the home. A second open house was held, but by the early 1970s, efforts to prevent its destruction seemed hopeless.

In June 1975, about the same time that the home went on the National Register of Historic Places, Don Strong realized the potential of this property as a restaurant. Restoration began in 1979. It included revitalizing the original interior woodwork around the doors and windows. The stair rail had to be re-created from a single spindle found floating in the flooded basement.

We were seated in deep wing chairs at a cozy table in the main dining room, known as "The Library." Across the room were booth areas, each its own separate nook complete with book-laden shelves.

Seafood is the house specialty, with choices changing daily. The Voodoo Shrimp—bacon-wrapped shrimp roasted with Jamaican Curry Marinade—made our mouths water. Never one to pass up mangoes, Karen ordered the Mango Shrimp Salad, which was beautifully presented and equally delicious. The spirit of "Pomeroy hospitality" lives on in this place full of history and excellent food.

SAMBUCA-SEARED DIVER SCALLOPS

¼ cup olive oil
20 scallops
½ cup flour
¼ cup sambuca
Roasted Red Pepper Brie Cream (see next column)
fresh greens

Heat olive oil in a sauté pan over medium heat. Dust scallops lightly in flour. Sauté scallops until brown. Pour sambuca into pan to deglaze. On each of 4 plates, place 5 scallops in a pool of Roasted Red Pepper Brie Cream. Garnish with fresh greens or other items of choice. Serves 4 as an appetizer.

ROASTED RED PEPPER BRIE CREAM

2 tablespoons vegetable oil
½ teaspoon fresh garlic, minced
1 tablespoon shallots, roasted and diced
2 cups heavy cream
½ cup lobster stock
6-ounce wheel Brie with rind
1 tablespoon tomato paste
2 red peppers, roasted
1 tablespoon fresh thyme, chopped
salt and pepper to taste

Heat oil in a medium saucepan and lightly brown garlic. Add shallots, cream, and stock. Reduce by ½ and remove from heat. Stir in Brie, tomato paste, roasted peppers, and thyme. Purée in a blender or food processor until smooth. Add salt and pepper. Yields 2 cups.

 MANGO SHRIMP SALAD

1 pound 70-110 count shrimp, cooked, shelled, and deveined
1 cup mayonnaise
1 cup mango, diced
½ cup pecans, chopped
⅓ cup raisins
½ bunch scallions, diced fine
2 teaspoons cilantro, minced
¼ cup honey
1 tablespoon red onion, diced fine
mixed greens

Blot shrimp with a towel to remove excess moisture; recipe will not work unless shrimp are extremely dry. Combine all ingredients except greens. Refrigerate. Serve atop mixed greens or as desired. Serves 4.

Dante's
PIZZA & PASTA
House

261 WEST HIGH AVENUE
NEW PHILADELPHIA, OH 44663
330-339-4444

Local residents remember the house at 261 West High Avenue as the Board of Education Building. Others have known it as the Evans or the Broadhurst Funeral Home. Today, it is Dante's Pizza & Pasta House.

At one time, Augustus Beyer owned the home. At the age of twenty-two, he entered the milling business in Michigan. In 1862, he returned home to New Philadelphia and continued his profession. He purchased River Mills and established a new milling system, the second "All Roller" mill in Ohio. The mill continued successfully for thirty-five years until fire destroyed it in 1897. Beyer rebounded by building the Tuscarawas Electric Power and Light Company on the same site. He received an exclusive contract to furnish electric lights to the communities of Canal Dover and New Philadelphia, which resulted in New Philadelphia's being labeled the "Best Lighted City in Ohio." The first home to receive electricity was that of Beyer himself.

He purchased the home in 1884 from George Dougherty, who had owned the property since 1848. The exact date of construction is unknown, although some records indicate the 1860s. Features of the house discovered during renovation for Dante's Pizza suggest that it was built slightly earlier. A tunnel leads from the basement away from the house, under what is now the parking lot. During the construction of the parking lot, a piece of machinery tipped into a room-sized space when the earth gave way. Dan Drabik, who owns Dante's with his wife, Betty, asked around to see if anyone knew about the room. A few stories circulated about escaping slaves being hidden there. Others had heard about a rock garden in that location with a large rock that pivoted to cover a hole leading to the tunnel.

The history of this home-cum-restaurant so fascinated Betty Drabik that she purchased a 1908 Tuscarawas County atlas. The book contained photos of prominent businessmen and their homes, as well as information about their personal histories. We flipped through it in the most private of the restaurant's three dining rooms. Lace curtains and valences softened the windows. Original wainscoting lined the wall, and a built-in cupboard still stood in the corner. The wooden mantelpiece piqued our curiosity, because it's said to have a secret compartment. Karen looked for that compartment, convinced of its location by a directional clue incorporated in the surrounding tile. The other dining rooms were equally attractive. The front one was graced with a beautiful black marble fireplace.

We were treated to several delicious items and can't wait to go back for more. We started with slices of Italian Sausage Braid and Roasted Vegetable Bread. Both were absolutely fabulous. We brought half of each home to our most appreciative families. We also sampled a delicious Chicken Breast marinated in the unique House Dressing. It, too, was yummy. Wonderfully gracious about our sampling, Betty sent along pieces of the tasty homemade pies being served that day—Caramel Apple and Strawberry Rhubarb. Enjoying them later in the day allowed us to experience Dante's that much longer.

BRUSCHETTA

24 slices Ciabatta or Italian bread
2 tablespoons olive oil
4 cups Roma tomatoes, diced
¼ cup onion, chopped fine
1 cup parsley, chopped
1 tablespoon garlic, minced
¼ teaspoon pepper, ground coarse
½ teaspoon salt
2 teaspoons Italian seasoning
2 tablespoons fresh basil
½ cup Romano cheese
24 slices provolone cheese

Brush bread lightly with olive oil and toast. In a large bowl, combine all remaining ingredients except cheeses. Spoon onto toasted bread. Sprinkle with Romano. Top with pro-

volone and broil just until cheese melts. Serves 2 dozen as an appetizer.

ITALIAN VEGETABLE SOUP

1 pound Italian sausage
2 cups onion, chopped
3 cloves garlic, chopped fine
6 cups beef consommé
6 cups water
1½ cups Roma tomatoes, chopped
1 cup prepared spaghetti sauce
¼ teaspoon pepper
1 teaspoon Italian seasoning
4 carrots, pared, sliced, and steamed
1½ cups zucchini, chopped
15-ounce can garbanzo beans, drained
8 ounces rotini pasta, cooked and drained

In a large pot, brown sausage, onions, and garlic. Drain fat. Add consommé, water, tomatoes, sauce, pepper, and Italian seasoning. Bring to a boil. Reduce heat and add carrots, zucchini, beans, and pasta. Serves 10 to 12.

Brandywine Inn

204 SOUTH MAIN STREET
MONROE, OH 45050
513-779-4747

The Brandywine Inn was once reputed to be the tallest building for miles around. Today, its white-painted brick exterior and stacked-stone retaining walls invite visitors to step back in time to stagecoach days. Built in 1850 by David Boggs, it was originally a stop on the Great Miami Turnpike. The ground floor was constructed into a steep hillside, forming a large, cavelike room at one end. Local legend has it that this hidden room was used to harbor slaves escaping from the South. The Red Onion Tavern was also housed on this floor. An enormous onion was displayed outside to announce the tavern's location to patrons—and to slaves who could not read the written signs. The second floor housed the dining rooms and kitchen. Guest rooms were on the third floor. On the top floor, a large hall accommodated visiting lecturers and traveling road shows. Alas, that room no longer exists. In the early 1900s, there was a fire on the top floor. The owner took the opportunity to remove the walls and reroof the building, since it was slowly sinking into the ground, thanks to its heavy, twelve-inch-thick walls.

Today, there are three dining rooms on the second floor. Debbie was unable to accompany me the day I visited. I sat in the farthest original room, which has exposed-brick and rough paneled walls. The doorways are framed with planks of wood from the original floor, complete with square-headed nails. The flickering lamps reflected off the highly polished tables, giving a cozy, intimate feel to the room.

The current owners, George and Doris Bernas, wanted to create a haven for fine dining and to make the evening meal the highlight of their guests' day. To that end, the inn serves a prix fixe dinner. The chef changes the menu every week, and the inn boasts that he has not repeated a menu in twenty years!

The meal began with a Phyllo Triangle stuffed with wild mushrooms, olives, and goat cheese. It was a tangy and flavorful start to an entirely delicious meal. My waiter, Anthony, was professional and swift, describing each course as it arrived. A tart Cranberry Ice followed, then an entrée of Roasted Pork Loin with Hazelnut-Sausage Stuffing. The serving size was restrained, allowing guests to finish each course with an expectation of being able to indulge in dessert. Chef George had concocted Sweet Pastry topped with Baked Apples, walnuts, and dried cherries and served with homemade Vanilla Ice Cream. I chatted with the charming couple at the next table, who had been eating at the inn once a week for the past eighteen years. Everyone agreed that George

and Doris have created a haven of which to
be proud.

 MAKE-AHEAD TURKEY BREAST

2 quarts turkey stock
6-pound whole turkey breast, skinned
1 teaspoon olive oil
½ teaspoon dried thyme
¼ teaspoon salt
¼ teaspoon garlic powder
¼ teaspoon black pepper
Herb Stuffing (see below)

In a large stockpot, bring stock to a boil
and add turkey breast. Return to a boil, then
reduce heat and simmer for about 1½ hours
until turkey reaches 170 degrees. Remove turkey from stock, cover, and refrigerate until
needed. Set stock aside.

Preheat oven to 250 degrees. Rub surface
of turkey with oil, then sprinkle with seasonings. Wrap turkey tightly in foil and bake for
about 2 hours until thoroughly heated. To
serve, remove turkey breast from bone and
slice. Serve with Herb Stuffing. Serves 6.

 HERB STUFFING

1 stick butter
1 cup onion, diced
1 cup celery, diced
16 cups stale bread, cubed
2 teaspoons poultry seasoning
1 teaspoon dried thyme
½ teaspoon salt
½ teaspoon garlic powder
½ teaspoon dried tarragon
½ teaspoon dried rubbed sage
¼ teaspoon black pepper
2½ cups turkey stock

Preheat oven to 250 degrees. In a large
Dutch oven, melt butter over medium-high
heat. Add onions and celery and sauté for 3
minutes. Stir in bread cubes and seasonings.
Add stock and bake for 1 hour and 55 minutes. This can be done at the same time as
Turkey Breast. Serves 6 generously.

 VANILLA SWEET POTATOES

2 pounds sweet potatoes
¾ cup 1 percent milk
¼ cup brown sugar, packed
2 tablespoons vanilla extract
2 tablespoons butter, softened

Pierce potatoes with a fork and arrange in
a circle on paper towels in a microwave oven.
Microwave on high for about 10 minutes until
tender, rearranging after 5 minutes. Wrap in a
towel and let stand 5 minutes. Peel and mash
potatoes. Combine with milk, sugar, vanilla,
and butter. Place in a 1-quart casserole, cover,
and microwave on medium for about 7 minutes until thoroughly heated. Serves 6.

CHESTER'S
Road House

9678 MONTGOMERY ROAD
CINCINNATI, OH 45242
513-793-8700
WWW.CHESTERSROADHOUSE.COM

Chester's Road House is fashioned from an old brick farmhouse situated along Montgomery Road. It has been reported that a house at the back of the property near the barn once sheltered runaway slaves. Restaurant manager Roger Courtney assured us that a substantial tunnel still exists in the basement.

Roger also talked to us about the resident ghost. One guest, a local disc jockey, was unnerved by his encounter with the spirit in the men's room. Roger had a less embarrassing experience in the attic. As he was looking through files one day, he noticed an unusual shadow cross in front of him. He turned but saw nothing. As he walked to another part of the attic, he passed through what he described as a "human-sized mass of cold air." The ghost seems to be a friendly presence that simply checks to see that all is well with this old homestead.

Around 1900, the Perin family lived in the home. More than once, Mr. Perin was heard to proclaim that he owned the land "as far as the eye can see." After the Perins, the Ratabaugh family took ownership, living in the house right up until Michael J. Comisar purchased it to create Chester's. Grandchildren of the Ratabaughs who come to dine sometimes relate memories of their childhood visits here.

The bar area of the restaurant sits along a brick wall and occupies most of the original first-floor living space. Just off this area is the parlor, used for private dining and overflow bar traffic. In it is the original fireplace, which has a mantelpiece fashioned of tiger-stripe mahogany. The front porch has been expanded and enclosed to create a bright, sunny dining room. Likewise, the garden room, just off the bar, is a cheerful place to have a meal. One fact that we found particularly interesting about the original floor plan was that today's coatroom was the first kitchen. It's hard to imagine that even a glass of water could be prepared in a space that size, much less the made-from-scratch meals that were certainly concocted in the kitchen of a farmhouse.

We were seated in the main dining room, an addition created using bricks recovered from an old hotel in Dayton. As with the other dining areas, it was bathed in light. Lots of greenery filled the room, including fig trees and spider plants in hanging baskets. The specials of the day included a choice of Black Bean or Vegetable Soup and either Grilled Chicken with Sautéed Onions, Mushrooms, and Broccoli, served in a spicy Chili Sauce, or Rainbow Trout with Sun-Dried Tomato Vinaigrette, Chive

Whipped Potatoes, and Green Beans. Debbie chose the latter and enjoyed it immensely. Karen had the Chicken Breast Salad, served not with mixed greens but with Baby Spinach, which was a pleasant change. The Sunday buffet here is extremely popular, as is the "Sea Bar," a seafood lovers' delight that includes Stone Crabs, Clams Casino, Oysters Rockefeller, Blue Crab, and more.

Even with today's traffic, it isn't nearly as difficult to get to Chester's as it was for those seeking freedom. And it's still worth the trip.

SHRIMP AND SCALLOPS WITH FETTUCCINE

1 cup extra-virgin olive oil
6 cloves garlic, minced
¼ cup shallots, minced
1 pound scallops
1 pound shrimp, 41-50 count, peeled and deveined
1 pound mushrooms, sliced
2 pounds Roma tomatoes, quartered
fresh basil to taste, minced
24 ounces fettuccine, cooked according to package
    directions
Romano cheese, freshly grated

Pour olive oil into a large skillet. When hot, add garlic and shallots and sauté until soft. Keeping skillet very hot, add scallops and shrimp. Sauté 2 minutes. Add mushrooms and tomatoes. Add basil and fettuccine. Toss. Spoon onto large plates. Garnish with Romano. Serves 6.

KEY LIME PIE

1 pound graham cracker crumbs
1 cup granulated sugar
2 sticks butter, melted
2 cups whipping cream
2 tablespoons confectioners' sugar
8-ounce can sweetened condensed milk
½ cup Key lime juice

Combine graham cracker crumbs and sugar; mix well. Slowly add butter until mixture packs together. Press firmly into a 9-inch pie pan. Set aside. Whip together cream and confectioners' sugar until hard peaks form. Add milk and mix well. Add lime juice and mix. Ladle into crust and chill for 24 hours. Serves 6 to 8.

CHAPTER 11

On the Road Again

Columbian House

When the National Road opened the way west, a good team of oxen could make only ten to twelve miles per day before having to stop and rest. No doubt, the human passengers were equally weary. Horses could do slightly better, but the need for frequent lodging along the major thoroughfares was great. Highlighted in this chapter are inns and hotels whose registers over the years have read like a veritable who's who, from drovers and past presidents to modern-day guests. Some still provide overnight accommodations, and all serve meals to sate even the hungriest of travelers.

SEVEN STARS AT

The Worthington Inn

649 HIGH STREET
WORTHINGTON, OH 43085
614-885-2600

In 1816, a Connecticut gentleman by the name of R. W. Cowles came to this part of Ohio to earn his fortune. Two years later, he married Laura Kilbourne, and together they had nine children. For the mere sum of $250, he purchased three lots in Worthington's downtown area. In 1835, he built an impressive residence on the land. Unfortunately, Cowles enjoyed it for only seven years before passing away. During his tenure as a Worthington resident, he was a prominent businessman, a county commissioner, a justice of the peace, and postmaster.

Ten years after Cowles's death, Theodore Fuller purchased and enlarged the home. Two years later, the structure was again sold, this time to William Bishop. Under Bishop's ownership, the residence operated as an inn known as The Bishop House. For just a dime, guests were served a meal of beef stew or potato soup, along with biscuits or cornbread. For an additional twenty-five cents, they could spend the night. When the property was purchased by Nicholas Van Loon, the name was changed to Central Hotel. After just three years, the hotel passed into the hands of Robert Lewis.

It became known as the Union Hotel and later as the Hotel Stand.

In 1889, the building returned to the Van Loon family when it was purchased by Nicholas's son, George, who brought back the name his father had used for the inn. It was during his time at the helm that the third story and the mansard roof were added. A fire had damaged part of the original roof, and George Van Loon thought it was a good opportunity to add a third-floor ballroom. William Van Loon, a member of the third generation of the family, took over from his father in 1926. The family retained ownership until 1936. As with many such structures, changes in ownership happened more frequently than needed maintenance. By 1983, time had taken its toll. But the inherent beauty of the building was evident when the process of restoration began.

We came in out of the snow through the side entrance and up a marble staircase that brought us into a casual eating area. The backbar took up one wall, and another wall was highlighted by a lovely stained-glass picture of the inn. The room where we were seated had a celestial décor both on the ceiling and in the carpet, as well as a copy of Van Gogh's *Starry Night* hanging on the wall. Our table looked out over the wide front porch, marked by cream-and-blue colonnades.

For breakfast, we both chose the Sticky Buns, which were served warm and gooey. We looked over the lunch menu to see what we'd miss. Choices such as the Chicken and Walnut Quesadilla, the Vegetarian Club, and the

Inn Salad—made of greens, golden raisins, sunflower seeds, cucumbers, tomatoes, and Gouda cheese—were all of interest. The dinner menu included such items as Orange and Beet Salad Compote and Parmesan-Crusted Calamari. For any meal, the Worthington Inn is worth every bite!

MUSSELS IN CHARDONNAY BROTH

1 teaspoon garlic, minced
½ cup mushrooms, diced
1 tablespoon olive oil
2 tablespoons cilantro, chopped
¼ cup scallions, chopped
½ cup yellow onion, diced
12 mussels, cleaned
3 tablespoons white wine
1½ teaspoons lime juice
1 teaspoon saffron, ground
salt and pepper to taste
1 tablespoon butter
chopped parsley for garnish

Sauté garlic and mushrooms in oil until light brown. Add next 3 ingredients and heat until onions are translucent. Remove from heat and reserve mushrooms and onions, leaving liquids in pan. Add mussels and steam until they start to open. Add 2 generous tablespoons mushroom mixture, wine, lime juice, saffron, and salt and pepper. Lightly toss to coat. Whisk in butter to smooth out sauce. Sprinkle with parsley and serve. Serves 4 as an appetizer.

DIVER SCALLOPS

2 to 3 tablespoons olive oil
24 large scallops
salt and pepper to taste
2 shots Absolut vodka
1 32 fluid-ounce bottle Bloody Mary mix
1 tablespoon water
1 tablespoon cornstarch
8 tablespoons crème fraîche for garnish
24 Parmesan chips
1 sprig rosemary

Heat olive oil in a medium sauté pan. Season both sides of scallops with salt and pepper. Sear on both sides about 3 to 5 minutes total to cook through. Pour Absolut into a medium saucepan and bring to a boil. Add Bloody Mary mix and reduce by ⅓. Combine water and cornstarch in a small bowl. Whisk into Bloody Mary mixture to thicken. Season with salt and pepper. Pour ¼ cup of sauce onto a serving plate. Drizzle plate with crème fraîche. Alternate scallops and Parmesan chips on center of plate and top with a sprig of rosemary. Serves 8.

THE BUXTON INN

Established 1812

313 EAST BROADWAY
GRANVILLE, OH 43023
740-587-0001
WWW.BUXTONINN.COM

Henry Ford's name appears on the 1938 guest register. Fifty years later, the inn was featured on the back of boxes of Uncle Ben's Rice.

The origins of this noteworthy inn extend back to 1801, when a small band of men left Granville, Massachusetts, for the more fertile land of central Ohio. One of the first settlers was Samuel Thrall, who claimed the land on which The Buxton Inn now stands. Eleven years later, the land passed to Orrin Granger, who built an inn for stagecoach travelers. Following Mr. Granger's death in 1815, the inn had a succession of owners until 1861, when James Dilley bought the building. During that time, the inn housed young women who were students at Granville Female Academy across the street. Subsequent to Mr. Dilley's tenure, Major Buxton operated the hostelry, giving it its current name. The major is one of the ghosts said to be seen around the inn. When current owners Audrey and Orville Orr first bought the inn, the staff still set a place at the dinner table for the major. He's also been seen sitting in a rocking chair by the fireplace.

Fred Sweet, son of one of the twentieth-century innkeepers, first wrote about the apparitions in a 1932 alumni bulletin from nearby Denison University. He described the ghost of Orrin Granger, encountered one night in the pantry during Sweet's quest for a piece of apple pie.

Many other ghostly experiences involve "the Lady in Blue," Ethel Bounell, who moved from New York City to the inn in 1934. Her spirit was seen walking across the balcony during the Orrs' restoration of the property. A medium from Cincinnati also described a friendly presence dressed in elegant blue that accompanied her from room to room during her visit.

Guests flock to Rooms 7, 8, and 9 in an attempt to experience these prior innkeepers. Quite by chance, we were assigned to Room 9 for the night. We anxiously anticipated what might occur. After checking in, we went downstairs for dinner, starting with the delicious Curried Chicken Soup with toasted almonds and grapes. That was followed by Karen's dinner of Wild Mushroom Stroganoff, filled with five or six different varieties of mushrooms. Debbie went traditional, dining on Ham, Green Beans, and a Baked Sweet Potato. For dessert, we shared a piece of Gingerbread topped with Lemon Sauce, very different from the English variety Karen grew up with, but equally delicious.

Before heading upstairs to settle in for the evening, we looked through the other dining rooms. The largest one, located just off the lobby, is decorated in red and has red plaid draperies hanging at the windows. Down the hall is a more casual room that has oil paintings on the wall and an interesting bar at one end. Downstairs is the tavern, festively decorated with bright quilts on each table. This is where coach drivers once cooked their own meals at the great open fireplace and slept on beds of straw. We were fortunate to have more comfortable accommodations. As has been the case to date, we slept soundly and well, meeting none of the expected ghostly personalities.

GARLIC VICHYSSOISE

2 to 3 whole heads garlic
4 cups chicken stock
4 potatoes, peeled and quartered
¾ cup celery, chopped
1 carrot, chopped
1 cup onions, chopped
1 cup half-and-half
1 cup or more heavy cream
chopped garlic chives for garnish

Put garlic and stock in a 2-quart pot and bring to a simmer. Remove garlic when soft, after about 15 minutes. Add vegetables and cook for about 10 minutes over medium heat until tender. Cool, then blend well. Taste for garlic flavor. If it's not strong enough, blend in peeled cloves of cooked garlic until flavor is how you like it. Add half-and-half and cream

until thick and creamy. Chill. Serve in chilled bowls. Garnish with garlic chives. Serves 8.

PEACH MELBA

12 scoops vanilla ice cream
6 scoops raspberry sherbet
24 fresh peach slices
1½ cups Melba Sauce (see below)
6 generous dabs sweetened whipped cream
almond slivers
6 maraschino cherries

In order, place 2 scoops ice cream, 1 scoop sherbet, 4 peach slices, ¼ cup Melba Sauce, a dab of whipped cream, almond slivers, and a cherry in each of 6 stemmed goblets. Serves 6.

MELBA SAUCE

½ cup currant jelly
1 cup raspberries, sieved, or ½ cup red raspberry jelly
1 teaspoon cornstarch
⅛ teaspoon salt
½ cup sugar
1 tablespoon brandy

Bring currant jelly and raspberry juice (or jelly) to a boil in a 3-cup saucepan. Separately mix cornstarch, salt, sugar, and brandy. Add to jelly mixture. Cook, whisking well, until mixture is clear and thick. Remove from heat, then chill well. Yields 1½ cups.

THE FORUM GRILL AT

⊔ The Vernon Manor Hotel

400 OAK STREET
CINCINNATI, OH 45219
WWW.VERNON-MANOR.COM

Since the early 1900s, The Vernon Manor Hotel has maintained a stately presence in Cincinnati's Pill Hill district, not too far from the University of Cincinnati. It was built as a retreat for wealthy Cincinnati residents.

The hotel was designed to emulate the style and character of Hatfield House, the ancestral home of the earls of Percy in Hertfordshire, England. The forward-thinking architect included the most modern conveniences, including fireproof floors and refrigerators in every room. His blueprints included large guest rooms, a variety of suites, wide corridors, and gardens with wonderful oak trees. This spaciousness attracted long-term guests and many permanent residents. Their presence helped The Vernon Manor Hotel to weather the tough times that many elite hotels of the era were unable to endure. The establishment was also fortunate to have wealthy owners during the 1950s and 1960s who liberally entertained their influential friends here. Thus, The Vernon Manor has emerged as the oldest continuously operating hotel in Cincinnati.

Through the years, notable personalities including Presidents Kennedy, Johnson, George

Bush, and Clinton, Mikhail Baryshnikov, Loretta Young, Bob Dylan, Liza Minnelli, Kevin Bacon, Keanu Reeves, Tiger Woods, and many, many others have come to enjoy the haven that The Vernon Manor Hotel offers. The Beatles stayed here when on tour during the 1960s and now have one of the fifty-eight suites named and decorated in their honor. Besides the suites, there are 119 guest rooms in this impressive facility. Sarah Jessica Parker and Matthew Broderick are regular guests when they come to town to visit relatives. In addition, the hotel was center stage for the 1988 Oscar-winning movie *Rainman*, starring Dustin Hoffman and Tom Cruise. Although he was referring to something else, the address that Hoffman's character frequently uttered, "400 Oak Street, Cincinnati, Ohio," is actually that of The Vernon Manor Hotel.

We chatted with Bob Louis, director of sales, and Jim Modzelewski, food and beverage director, as we enjoyed a bite of breakfast in The Forum Grill. The service was friendly and attentive, and we quickly felt at home. We were seated in a corner of the dining room, next to the fireplace. A coat of arms hung over the stone mantel, creating a bit of castle ambiance. Wood paneling and hunter and burgundy accents enhanced the décor. The menu here offers a wide array of selections, from sandwiches to steaks and chops. The grill offers the Friday-night Seafood Festival and one of the most renowned Sunday brunches in the city. We hope this Cincinnati tradition will continue to thrive for years to come.

CHICKEN APRICOT

4 8-ounce boneless chicken breasts, skin and fat
  removed
4-ounce package chopped spinach
¾ cup mozzarella cheese, shredded
⅓ cup cottage cheese
salt and pepper to taste
3 tablespoons olive oil, divided
1 teaspoon ginger, chopped
4-ounce jar apricot preserves

Preheat oven to 350 degrees. Lay plastic wrap over cutting board or table. Place chicken breast side down on plastic wrap. Cover with an additional layer of wrap and pound with a mallet until uniform in thickness. Repeat with remaining 3 breasts. Combine spinach, mozzarella, cottage cheese, and salt and pepper in a bowl. Mix well. Divide mixture into 4 equal portions. Place 1 portion in the center of each breast. Fold breast to cover mixture.

In a saucepan, heat 1 tablespoon of the olive oil over medium heat. Add ginger and stir about 30 seconds until it softens. Add apricot preserves and stir. Reduce heat to simmer, stirring occasionally. Reserve for later use.

Heat remaining 2 tablespoons olive oil in a heavy ovenproof skillet until it just begins to smoke. Carefully place chicken in pan. Sear chicken on 1 side, then turn over. Place skillet in oven and cook about 20 minutes until internal temperature of chicken reaches 175 degrees.

During the last 5 minutes, baste chicken with apricot glaze, reserving a little to drizzle over chicken when it's served. If chicken starts to get dark in oven, lower temperature to 325 degrees and add 2 tablespoons water. Serves 4.

ROASTED CORN AND BLACK BEAN RELISH

6 ears fresh corn or 12-ounce bag frozen corn
olive oil as needed
1 fresh jalapeño pepper (use rubber gloves when
  handling)
2 teaspoons cumin
2 teaspoons coriander
6 fresh Roma tomatoes
1 bunch fresh cilantro, stems removed
12-ounce can black beans, drained and rinsed

Preheat oven to 375 degrees. Shuck corn, remove silk, rinse, and cut from cob. In a medium bowl, drizzle a little olive oil over corn and whole jalapeño. Add cumin and coriander. Spread corn and jalapeño on a cookie sheet. Place sheet in oven and stir occasionally. Roast until corn dries and browns slightly and jalapeño blisters. Remove from oven and cool. Slice tomatoes in half and squeeze out seeds. Remove cores and dice tomatoes. Place in a bowl. Chop cilantro and add to tomatoes. Slice jalapeño in half and remove seeds and outer skin. Dice jalapeño and add to tomatoes. Add corn and mix well. Cover and refrigerate until needed. Yields 3 cups relish.

THE GOLDEN LAMB
27 SOUTH BROADWAY
LEBANON, OH 45036
513-932-5065
WWW.GOLDENLAMB.COM

When we started the research for this book, the one place everyone mentioned was The Golden Lamb. The history of what is claimed to be Ohio's oldest inn began December 23, 1803, when Jonas Seamen appeared in Warren County Court to request a tavern license for the building where he resided. Seaman's two-story log home was at the very center of the new village named Lebanon, situated at the crossroads of the main north-south and east-west trails through the area. His father had been a tavern keeper in New Jersey, so the nuances of the business were familiar to Jonas. His wife, Martha, was industrious, thrifty, and a good cook, which was certainly an immense help. Soon, the tavern gained a reputation as a good place to stop.

In 1815, a Federal-style two-story brick building replaced the original log cabin, although one of the main-floor dining rooms of today is situated where the log tavern once stood. Additions were made as the inn's popularity grew during the era of coach travel. Since many drivers and other travelers were unable to read, they were simply instructed to go to "the sign of the Golden Lamb."

Since its beginning, the inn has been host to many famous and influential people. Presidents Garfield and McKinley were guests here many times. Presidents William Henry Harrison, Benjamin Harrison, Van Buren, John Quincy Adams, Hayes, Grant, Taft, and Harding all stayed here. Mark Twain's slow drawl could be heard as he rehearsed for his performance at the Lebanon Opera House. Had you visited in 1842, you may have been as surprised as innkeeper Calvin Bradley to find that the small, rather disagreeable man sharing his negative opinions about the United States was none other than Charles Dickens. Many of these notables have bedrooms named after them, as do others such as Harriet Beecher Stowe and De Witt Clinton. Each of the eighteen overnight rooms is uniquely furnished with antiques and is open for viewing, provided no overnight guest has checked in.

We enjoyed a quiet lunch in the Dickens Dining Room. Because of the inn's reputation for traditional American fare, Debbie chose the Smothered Steak with Mashed Potatoes. It was filling and good. Karen opted for a more modern choice, the Fresh Fruit Plate. Watermelon, pineapple, strawberries, and oranges were served in a beautifully arranged portion. The Red Raspberry Sorbet that accompanied the fruit was delicious, and the Raisin Nut Bread gave the meal the perfect touch.

We finished with a piece of Sister Lizzie's Shaker Sugar Pie, although we were tempted by the Weary Willie Cobbler because of its story. Weary Willie was a name given to Union soldiers during the Civil War. Legend has it that a tired soldier once stopped at a farmhouse asking for a meal. Food was scarce, and the mistress had little even for her family. All she had managed to scrape together for them to eat that day was a cobbler of cherries and gooseberries. True? That's for you to decide.

 CELERY SEED DRESSING

½ cup sugar
1 teaspoon dry mustard
1 teaspoon salt
1 teaspoon celery seed
¼ teaspoon onion, grated
1 cup salad oil
⅓ cup vinegar

Combine dry ingredients. Add onions. Add a small amount of the oil and mix well. Add vinegar and oil alternately, ending with oil. Yields approximately 2 cups.

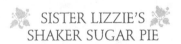 SISTER LIZZIE'S SHAKER SUGAR PIE

⅓ cup flour
1 cup brown sugar
9-inch unbaked pie shell

2 cups light cream
1 teaspoon vanilla
2 tablespoons butter
nutmeg

Thoroughly mix flour and brown sugar. Spread evenly in bottom of pie shell. Add cream and vanilla. Slice butter into pieces and distribute evenly over top of pie. Sprinkle with nutmeg. Bake at 350 degrees for 40 to 45 minutes until firm. Serves 6 to 8.

 BUTTERNUT SQUASH

3 cups butternut squash, diced
½ cup butter, divided
¼ cup plus 1 tablespoon brown sugar, divided
¼ teaspoon salt
dash of white pepper
1 unpared Jonathan apple, cored, sliced
½ cup cider or apple juice
¼ cup granulated sugar
1 cup cornflakes, crushed coarse
¼ cup pecans, chopped

Boil squash for 10 minutes. Drain. Add ¼ cup of the butter, 1 tablespoon of the brown sugar, salt, and white pepper. Heat 1½ tablespoons butter in skillet. Add apples and cider. Sprinkle with granulated sugar. Cover and simmer over low heat about 5 minutes until barely tender. Spread squash and apples in a 3-quart casserole. Mix cornflake crumbs with pecans. Melt remaining butter, combine with remaining brown sugar, and stir into cornflake mixture. Sprinkle over squash. Bake at 350 degrees for 30 minutes. Serves 8.

COLUMBIAN HOUSE
EST. 1828

3 NORTH RIVER ROAD
WATERVILLE, OH 43566
419-878-3006

When John Pray came from Rhode Island in 1817, he saw mile upon mile of unbroken forest. The nearest flour mill, in Monroe, Michigan, was almost inaccessible through the undergrowth. This prompted Mr. Pray to build the first gristmill in northern Ohio in 1821. Shortly afterward, he added a carding machine, a hemp machine, and a distillery.

In 1828, Mr. Pray built an inn on the corner of Main and Wood, today's River Road and Farnsworth Road. That one-and-a-half-story structure is currently used as the main dining room at the Columbian House. Owners Tom and Peggy Parker have oval wooden dining tables, Ohio pewter, and other period antiques. Guests enjoy Roast Chicken and Dressing, Orange Roughy with Butter Caper Sauce, and Curried Shrimp over Wild Rice Pilaf, among other entrée selections.

The property was enlarged in 1837 with a three-story addition. Mr. Pray took great pride in the inn, one of the finest examples of Federal architecture anywhere in the Midwest. He used walnut in great proliferation. The woodwork in the twenty-three guest rooms, including the doors with witch panels, is black walnut. The witch panels are wooden panels with crosses on them to repel witches. The plaster used throughout was carried on the backs of mules from Maumee.

The inn hosted a grand ball that was the premier social affair of the season. Tickets for the event, which included supper and dancing, were ten dollars per couple. Musicians were hired from Detroit for this special occasion. The third-floor ballroom, the last part of the inn to be completely restored, looks very close to the way it did at the time of those exciting events. The invitations from two balls held here at the inn hang in the private quarters of the Parker family. The second-floor rooms today exhibit period pieces as if it were yesteryear.

The first post office in Waterville was housed in the Columbian House. Mr. Pray was the postmaster. He also established a general store within the building. Eleven Pray children were reared in the structure, which welcomed many travelers and overnight guests. Mr. Pray continued as innkeeper until his death in 1872 at the age of eighty-nine. After his passing, the inn had difficulty keeping pace with the changing times. The new Miami-Erie Canal altered the dynamics of local enterprise, effectively ousting the Columbian Inn as the center of commerce and social life. The building went on to house a dressmaker's shop, a millinery, a drugstore, and the Waterville School.

Through the early 1900s, it stood vacant and was ravaged by vandals.

Fortunately, Charles Fox Capron found the inn in 1927 and purchased it to display and sell his antiques. It also attracted the attention of Henry Ford, who traveled with a party from Detroit to attend an old-fashioned ball on the third floor. By 1934, the structure was considered so important that the Historic American Buildings Survey made a complete set of plans and specifications that were placed on file with the Library of Congress. That the inn stands today, structurally sound and altered very little, speaks to the architectural genius and construction expertise of the founder of Waterville.

STUFFED ORANGE ROUGHY

5 tablespoons onion, chopped
3 tablespoons butter
1 cup fresh crabmeat
½ cup fresh breadcrumbs
¼ cup parsley, chopped
¼ cup heavy whipping cream
¼ teaspoon thyme
4 6- to 8-ounce orange roughy fillets
salt and pepper to taste
¼ cup dry white wine
¼ cup butter, melted

Preheat oven to 400 degrees. Sauté onions in butter until golden. Remove from pan and combine with crabmeat, breadcrumbs, parsley, cream, and thyme in a mixing bowl. Sprinkle fillets with salt and pepper. Form 4 equal balls of crabmeat mixture and place on fillets. Roll fillets to enclose crabmeat. Place in a baking dish. Combine wine and butter in a small bowl. Pour over fish, reserving some for basting. Bake for 30 minutes, just until fish is opaque. Baste frequently with wine sauce during baking. Remove from oven and serve at once. Serves 4.

 MERINGUES

5 egg whites
1 cup superfine sugar

Preheat oven to 250 degrees. Beat egg whites in a large mixing bowl with an electric mixer on high speed for 5 minutes until stiff but not dry. Sprinkle ¼ cup of the sugar over egg whites and beat for 3 minutes. Sprinkle in remaining sugar a tablespoon at a time. Fold in gently but thoroughly, using a rubber spatula.

Line cookie sheets with oiled brown paper. Drop mixture by heaping tablespoons about 2 inches apart onto cookie sheets. Bake for 55 minutes. Remove from oven. Immediately remove Meringues from paper onto cooling racks. Yields approximately 2½ dozen Meringues.

101 FRONT STREET
MARIETTA, OH 45750
740-373-5522
WWW.HISTORICLAFAYETTE.COM

The S. D. H. House Salad was a creation of S. Durward Hoag, whose family owned and operated the hotel from 1918 through 1974. Marietta's version of Cobb salad, it is served with warm Russian Black Bread and the house dressing, Creamy Raspberry Dijon. It was one of the items we decided to share. The other was the Chicken Salad Melt, topped with tomato slices and cheddar cheese, all baked in tender, flaky puff pastry. Both were delicious, as was the side of Potato Salad served with the Chicken Salad Melt.

The dining room at The Lafayette Hotel is known as the GunRoom Restaurant because of the private collection of flintlock long rifles that hangs on the walls. These handcrafted relics date from 1795 to 1880. Among the collection is a percussion rifle made by J. J. Henry and his sons, who accompanied Benedict Arnold in 1775.

Other memorabilia pays homage to the influence of riverboats on this establishment. As a matter of fact, the entire dining room looks like a replica of a steamboat. A captain's bell hangs by the entrance, gingerbread trim encircles the room, and black columns fashioned after steamboat smokestacks stand in the archway between the two dining areas. Even the carpet carries the motif, with paddle-wheelers and the Lafayette *L* forming a repeating design.

As more and more visitors came to town, the need for a hotel was evident. The Lafayette Hotel, named for the 1825 visit of the Marquis de Lafayette, actually began as the Bellevue Hotel, which was constructed in 1892. Unfortunately, the Bellevue burned to the ground on April 26, 1916. Two years later, Marietta businessmen rebuilt the hotel, changed its name, and hired Reno G. Hoag as manager at a salary of $150 per month, plus board for his family. It was during his tenure that one of the most interesting stories about the hotel evolved. Residents were suspicious about how a young bellhop working at the hotel could afford shiny new cars. The answer floated up the lobby steps during a flood, as several pint bottles of moonshine bobbed atop the rising water. It seems the enterprising bellhop had been acquiring and storing liquor under the stairs, then selling it to guests at quite a profit! Although Mr. Hoag fired the bellhop, the marketing skills the young man had acquired selling booze came in handy. He went on to employment with Montgomery Ward and worked his way from assistant clerk to executive vice president in just two years!

Tourism is thriving in Marietta, thanks to the town's eleven museums and its strong ties to the Underground Railroad. In fact, some claim that the Underground Railroad began here. Marietta is an official stop for the Delta Queen Steamboat Company. Several times a year, the *Mississippi Queen*, the *Delta Queen*, and the *American Queen* dock at the Ohio River levee beside The Lafayette Hotel. When the *Delta Queen* comes to town, it's particularly special, because it's the only time and place where one Historic Hotel of America visits another!

CREAMY BAKED CAULIFLOWER WITH FETA CHEESE

1 head cauliflower
4 cups heavy cream
1 cup fresh feta cheese
1 teaspoon freshly ground nutmeg
coarse salt
freshly ground pepper to taste
¼ cup fresh breadcrumbs

Preheat oven to 350 degrees. Clean cauliflower, cut or break it into large pieces, and place pieces in a small casserole dish. Pour cream over cauliflower. Crumble feta evenly over top. Season with nutmeg, salt, and pepper. Bake covered for 25 minutes. Uncover, sprinkle with breadcrumbs, and bake uncovered for 8 to 10 minutes more. Serves 8 as a side dish.

ALASKAN SOCKEYE SALMON STRUDEL

1 cup butter, melted
1 tablespoon fresh parsley, chopped
1 tablespoon fresh thyme, chopped
1 tablespoon fresh basil, chopped
2 pounds sockeye salmon
16 ounces sour cream
2 cloves garlic
½ cup oil-packed sun-dried tomatoes
1 tablespoon fresh oregano
salt and pepper to taste
1 package phyllo dough
1 cup pesto

In a small bowl, combine butter, parsley, thyme, and basil. Set aside. Cut salmon into thin strips. In a food processor, combine sour cream, garlic, tomatoes, and oregano. Season with salt and pepper and continue processing until smooth. Lay out 1 sheet phyllo dough on parchment paper. Brush with butter mixture. Place another layer of phyllo on top and brush with butter mixture. Continue until you have 7 layers. Spread evenly with sour cream mixture, leaving 1 inch on each side. Arrange salmon strips evenly over top and brush generously with pesto. Roll up dough and brush with butter mixture. Refrigerate for at least 1 hour. Bake for 20 to 25 minutes at 350 degrees until golden brown. Slice and serve immediately. Serves 8.

Note: Chef Todd Heslep serves Alaskan Sockeye Salmon Strudel with Lobster Cream Sauce.

SHAW'S

RESTAURANT & INN

123 NORTH BROAD STREET
LANCASTER, OH 43130
740-654-1842
WWW.HOCKINGHILLS.COM/SHAWS

Located in a National Register Historic District, Shaw's Restaurant & Inn practically rubs shoulders with history itself. Just down the road, visitors can find the Sherman House, birthplace of Civil War general William Tecumseh Sherman and his younger brother, United States senator John Sherman, the author of the Sherman Antitrust Act. No less popular with tourists is the Georgian Museum, located in the opposite direction. It's a strikingly beautiful restored 1832 mansion complete with furnishings from the period. It would be hard to find a finer collection of nineteenth-century mansions and homes in the Midwest. At the end of a long day of sightseeing, Shaw's is the perfect place to go to be sure of a warm welcome and a delicious meal.

Shaw's was erected at the location of the Pitcher Inn, a popular tavern of the very early 1800s. Rumor has it that the original owner, Rudolph Pitcher, lost the tavern in a poker game in 1806. Hungry travelers in need of a good meal have long made their way here. Indeed, Henry Clay and Daniel Webster could often be found dining on the premises. Current owners Nancy and Bruce Cork have been serving fine food and wine here for long enough to win not only local acclaim but also accolades galore from such publications as the *Mobile Guide* and *Zagat's Survey*.

The menu is short and changes every day, but it always includes a selection of meats, fresh fish, poultry, and pasta. Although we were there for lunch, we checked out the dinner menu and were delighted with the selection. From Ginger-Lime Baked Salmon to Char-Grilled Marinated Elk Chop with Poached Stuffed Pear, it all sounded delicious.

We sat in the lower dining room among the local businessmen and the bridge-club set. The richly paneled walls set with hunt-style sconces and the double valances with pull-back draperies at each of the large windows gave an opulent air to the room. Karen had no difficulty in choosing the Stir-Fried Coconut Curry Chicken with Bok Choy and Basil, an extremely creative favorite that came highly recommended by our server. Debbie selected a lighter dish that included a Chicken Salad Sandwich and a selection of fresh fruit. Both choices were extremely tasty.

The inn boasts twenty-two individually decorated suites and guest rooms, many with enormous whirlpools and thematic decorations. Shaw's Restaurant & Inn is definitely making history here in Lancaster, Ohio.

BUTTERMILK-ROASTED LEG OF LAMB

6-pound leg of lamb
3 cloves garlic
1 tablespoon Dijon mustard
½ teaspoon soy sauce
¼ teaspoon pepper
3 tablespoons olive oil
¼ cup buttermilk
½ cup dry white wine
1½ cups beef broth, divided
2 sprigs fresh rosemary
1 tablespoon butter
salt and pepper to taste

Using a knife, pierce holes in top of lamb. Cut 1 clove of garlic into slivers. Insert a sliver of garlic in each hole. Chop remaining 2 cloves of garlic. In a small bowl, combine chopped garlic, mustard, soy sauce, and ¼ teaspoon pepper. Slowly beat in oil and buttermilk. Pour mixture over lamb. Let stand in refrigerator for at least 6 hours, basting often.

Preheat oven to 400 degrees. Place lamb on a rack in a roasting pan, reserving buttermilk mixture. Roast lamb for 15 minutes. Combine buttermilk mixture, wine, and ½ cup of the beef broth. Pour around lamb. Add rosemary. Reduce temperature to 300 degrees and continue roasting 15 minutes per pound for medium-rare. Add remaining broth as juices dry up. Remove lamb from pan and set aside. Remove excess fat from sauce. Add butter to finish. Season with salt and pepper. Serve sauce with lamb. Serves 12.

FRENCH BREAD PUDDING

5 eggs
2 cups heavy whipping cream
1 cup sugar
dash of cinnamon
1 tablespoon vanilla
¼ cup raisins
¼ cup butter
12 1-inch slices French bread
Whiskey Sauce (see below)

Preheat oven to 350 degrees. In a large bowl, combine eggs, cream, sugar, cinnamon, vanilla, and raisins. Mix well. Grease bottom of a 9-by-12-inch pan. Pour mixture into pan. Lay slices of bread in mixture and let stand for 5 minutes. Turn bread over and let stand another 10 minutes. Dot with butter. Put pan into a larger pan filled halfway with water. Cover with foil and bake for 40 to 45 minutes, uncovering for the last 10 minutes so top lightly browns. Serve with Whiskey Sauce. Serves 12.

WHISKEY SAUCE

1½ cups sugar
½ cup bourbon
¾ cup butter
1/3 cup water
1 teaspoon cornstarch

Combine all ingredients in a saucepan. Simmer, stirring constantly, until sauce thickens. Serve warm over French Bread Pudding. Yields 1½ cups.

Hotel Millersburg

est. 1847

35 WEST JACKSON STREET
MILLERSBURG, OH 44654
330-674-1457

We arrived at Hotel Millersburg ahead of the normal lunch crowd and took advantage of being the only guests by looking around. The pictures hung on the peach-papered walls depicted scenes from around town. Among those displayed were a picture of the stately courthouse from 1884, one of workmen and horse-drawn wagons, and one from the mid-1920s showing a prosperous downtown. Other photos showed the homes of prominent citizens, including the William T. Hull residence. According to the placard beneath it, William McKinley was an overnight guest there in 1895 before making a campaign speech on the courthouse steps the following morning.

Hotel Millersburg was built in 1847. By 1864, the inn was expanded. It soon became the hub of social activity in the town. Over the years, the strain of maintenance began to tell, and the hotel fell into disrepair and ultimately closed. In 1980, Millersburg businessman R. Gene Smith began the slow, tedious process of renovation. Ten years later, local natives Thomas and Cheryl Bird purchased and reopened the hotel, with its handmade bricks and its woodwork painted sage green, burgundy, and gold-toned cream. Other buildings in this section of downtown are also quite interesting. The structure to the left, now a law office, has attractive purple stained-glass transoms. Maxwell's, the building to the right, has lettering on the second-story windows stating, "Trunks and Bags Since 1866." Just down the street is a well-kept emporium.

The Birds have maintained the original tin ceiling and oak trim in the hotel's lobby area. The formal dining room, located just to the left, is available by reservation for up to fifty people. We lunched in the hotel's tavern, a casual room with booths and butcher-block tables. Shortly after we seated ourselves, the restaurant began to fill with business people and local residents. Debbie chose the special of the day, the Open-Faced Roast Beef Sandwich, served with Mashed Potatoes and Applesauce. Karen opted for the Maurice Salad, which contained mixed greens and diced chicken and was served over toasted Sourdough Bread. The tavern offers traditional fare for lunch. Among the nine appetizer choices are Beer-Battered Mushrooms and Potato Skins. There are twelve sandwich options, three of which are highly regarded burger selections. For dinner, five different cuts of beef are advertised. We thought the Pork Tenderloin Medallions with Apricot Sauce sounded like something one of us might choose.

Holmes County, Ohio, is touted as having the largest Amish settlement in the world. If you're in the area for a bit of sightseeing, Hotel Millersburg will fill you up and allow you to save your pocketbook for some of the crafts that can be found along the country roads.

CHICKEN IN MUSHROOM CREAM SAUCE

½ cup flour
¼ teaspoon salt
¼ teaspoon pepper
¼ teaspoon herb of your choice
4 8-ounce chicken breasts
¼ cup clarified butter
½ cup cream sherry
4 ounces mushrooms, sliced
1 green pepper, julienned
2 cups heavy cream

In a shallow dish, combine flour and seasonings. Pound chicken breasts to ½-inch thickness and dredge in seasoned flour. Heat butter in a large, heavy skillet. Brown breasts on 1 side, turn, then place in a 350-degree oven for 15 minutes to finish cooking. Remove skillet from oven and set chicken aside. Drain butter and deglaze pan with sherry. Add mushrooms and peppers and cook about 3 minutes until tender. Add cream, bring to a boil, and reduce sauce to desired thickness. Replace chicken in skillet and warm through. Serves 4.

BEER CHEESE SOUP

20 ounces bacon
1 medium onion, chopped
8 cups milk
8 cups chicken stock
1 teaspoon Tabasco sauce
1½ teaspoons Worcestershire sauce
½ cup dry cheese sauce mix
1 12-ounce bottle beer

Brown bacon in a skillet. Add onions. Cook until onions are translucent. Pour off fat and discard. Process bacon and onions through a food mill or food processor until smooth. Place bacon mixture in a large stockpot and add milk and chicken stock. Heat until steaming but do not boil. Add Tabasco and Worcestershire. In a bowl, whisk cheese sauce mix into beer until there are no lumps. Add beer mixture to stockpot. Turn off heat and allow to sit for a few minutes before serving. Serves 10 to 12.

27 BROADWAY STREET
TOLEDO, OH 43602
419-241-1253

During the War of 1812, Major William Oliver served as a scout. He was stationed at Fort Meigs in nearby Perrysburg, under the command of William Henry Harrison. After the war, he and Cincinnati partners bought as much land as possible in the Port Lawrence area.

Although Oliver built Toledo's first warehouse, he was not immediately successful in his business speculations. He suffered many financial setbacks as he lobbied to have the Lucas County seat moved from Maumee to Toledo.

By 1853, his business ventures had finally succeeded to the point that he commissioned a palace-like hotel to be situated on the highest point of his landholdings. The hotel was to have the finest modern conveniences, including gas lights, running water, and a central courtyard. The courtyard was planned to maximize air circulation and natural sunlight for the 171 rooms.

Eventually, because of its location, the hotel was sold for industrial purposes and gutted. Riddle Lighting occupied the building from 1919 to 1947, followed by Toledo Wheel and Rim until 1967. Successful Sales next used the structure for display and storage of its novelty items.

Today, what remains of the former luxury hotel are its brick exterior, two ornamental marble mantels, wallpaper, and the black walnut and white ash floor in the lobby. The spacious upstairs dining room of Maumee Bay Brewing Co. occupies what was once the hotel's ballroom. It provides views of the Maumee River and area landmarks. Behind a glass enclosure, the fermenting tanks give diners a glimpse of the brewing process.

I sat in a comfortable booth and enjoyed the simplicity of the dining room's atmosphere. The house brews have been given names that evoke the area. The Buckeye Beer is the lightest on tap. The brewery also creates Glass City Pale Ale and Fallen Timbers Red Ale, among others. I made my dinner choice accordingly, choosing from the list of appetizers the Wings glazed in a dark stout. The serving size was ample enough that I needed to make no other selection. However, the Polynesian Salmon, the Almond-Crusted Pork Medallions, and the Steak and Mushroom Pie were all options that I'll consider on another visit. The desserts were equally appealing, among them Boston Cream Pie, Chocolate Truffle Tart, and Mud Hen Pie, named for the city's minor-league baseball team. It contains Coffee Ice Cream with toffee pieces in a Mint Cookie Crust, all drizzled with Chocolate and Caramel Sauces. I'll have to try it on my next visit, because it contains an interesting combination of flavors but more calories than I could in good conscience expend on that particular day. Perhaps Karen will be free to come with me next time to share the delicious burden.

STEAMED MUSSELS

2 pounds mussels, rinsed
½ cup coconut milk
¹⁄₈ cup red pepper, diced fine
¹⁄₈ cup cilantro, chopped

Place all ingredients in a medium sauté pan. Cover and let steam for 5 minutes. Divide equally between 2 large soup bowls. Serves 2.

ALMOND-CRUSTED PORK MEDALLIONS

16-ounce pork loin
3 tablespoons oil
2 tablespoons dark oyster sauce
¼ cup almonds, crushed

Slice pork loin into eight 2-ounce medallions. Heat oil in a large sauté pan. Place medallions in oil and brown on both sides for approximately 4 minutes. When cooked to desired doneness, divide equally between 2 plates. Drizzle with oyster sauce, then sprinkle with almonds. Serves 2.

CHEDDAR BEER SOUP

¼ cup oil
¼ cup carrots, diced
¼ cup celery, diced
¼ cup onion, diced
¾ cup beer
8 cups milk
½ teaspoon thyme
½ teaspoon white pepper
½ tablespoon granulated garlic
½ tablespoon salt
1 small bay leaf
1¼ pounds cheddar cheese, shredded
½ pound provolone cheese, cut into ½-inch cubes
¼ pound American cheese, shredded

Heat oil in a large pan and sauté carrots, celery, and onions. Whisk in beer, milk, spices, and cheeses. Continue whisking until cheese melts and mixture is creamy. Serves 10 to 12.

CHAPTER 12
Welcome Home

The Candlelight on Center Street

Home is a concept that each of us has, yet home is completely unique even for members of the same family. Typically, the word evokes feelings of warmth and contentment. At the restaurants in this chapter, all former homes, these same feelings are bestowed upon guests through the service, the ambiance, and the delicious meals served. Even if you're many miles away from your roots, let yourself be welcomed home.

The HOWARD HOUSE Restaurant

507 EAST MAIN STREET
MCCONNELSVILLE, OH 43756
740-962-5861

Just a few blocks from the Muskingum River in the town of McConnelsville sits a lovely gray and white antebellum mansion. It began in the 1850s as a small brick home built by the Honorable Cydnor Thompkins, an attorney and senator. In 1865, the property was purchased and the house enlarged by James Kelly Jones, a Morgan County native who became the director of First National Bank. Mr. Jones's daughter, Hattie, married into the Howard family and had a son named J. K. Howard. A respected, prominent woman in the community, Hattie eventually inherited her father's estate, known at the time as Rolling Acres. Like Hattie's father, her son became the director of First National Bank and raised his children at Rolling Acres.

Darl and Steve Hann purchased the mansion in October 1989 with an eye toward recreating its original grandeur. As soon as we entered through the enormous wooden doors, we could verify that they accomplished their mission. The intricate stained-gingerbread woodwork throughout the entry was marvel-ous. A grand piano sat beside the staircase, adding another touch of elegance. We dined in the ballroom, located to the left of the main hall. The walls were papered in a mauve magnolia pattern, and the window treatments of green moiré softened the large windows. The adjacent dining room was decorated in the same fashion but had an interesting stained-glass window in the back wall. Across the hall, a ladies' bridge club had already partaken of lunch and was enjoying an afternoon of cards. That room had a publike atmosphere, with deep, plush chairs, and darker, paisley-inspired wallpaper. It also had a fireplace with a painted mantel similar to that in the dining room. We hankered to sit in and play a hand, but we didn't interrupt and instead enjoyed the view over the parklike grounds. Carriage lights were festooned with red bows, bright reminders of the holiday season.

Our server was pleasant, helpful, and very prompt. Debbie, in the mood for something light, chose the Chicken Salad Sandwich on Sourdough Bread. Not too chunky and not too creamy, with a tasty overtone of chives, it hit the spot. It was served with a pickle slice and a choice of Pasta Salad, Potato Salad, French Fries, Chips, or Coleslaw. Without hesitation, Karen decided on the Tuesday special, aptly named Mile-High Meat Loaf. We asked our server just how tall it really was—but that is a mystery that has yet to be revealed. The stack starts with homemade Mashed Potatoes, followed by a slice of Meat Loaf. The recipe has a barbecue flavor that is just wonderful. The crowning layer is a nest of lacy Onion Rings, delicately fried and very delicious.

Had we been there for dinner, we may have chosen the Fettuccine Gardeniera, a combination of jumbo shrimp, scallops, and garden vegetables in Cream Sauce over fettuccine, or the Tenderloin Russo, a beef tenderloin sautéed with onions, mushrooms, and tomatoes in Cognac Sauce. Whether it's for lunch, dinner, or a hand of bridge, you can bet we'll be back.

HONEY CRACKED-WHEAT BREAD

3 cups flour, divided
2 tablespoons yeast
1 cup warm water
1 cup cracked wheat
¼ cup brown sugar, scant
¼ cup white sugar, scant
2 tablespoons salt
1 egg
2 tablespoons vegetable oil
2 tablespoons honey

In a large bowl, combine 1½ cups of the flour, yeast, and water. Add cracked wheat and mix. Add brown sugar, white sugar, and salt. Mix. Add egg, oil, and honey and combine thoroughly. Add additional flour to make a dough consistency. Cover dough with a cloth and place on a floured surface until it doubles in size. Knock down dough and divide into 4 equal balls. Place on baking sheets and let rise in a warm place until doubled in size. Bake at 350 degrees for 45 minutes until golden brown. Yields 4 loaves.

 THOUSAND ISLAND DRESSING

½ green onion, diced
½ small onion, diced
½ small green pepper, diced
½ tablespoon fresh parsley, chopped
2½ cups plus 2 tablespoons mayonnaise
4 tablespoons chili sauce
$1/8$ teaspoon Worcestershire sauce
dash of Tabasco sauce
½ teaspoon garlic, minced
8 tablespoons half-and-half
½ teaspoon salt

Put green onions, onions, green peppers, and parsley in a food processor. Mix until smooth. Add remaining ingredients and blend until well mixed. Store in a sealed container in the refrigerator until needed. Yields 4 cups.

 RASPBERRY VINAIGRETTE

½ cup raspberry vinegar
2 tablespoons Dijon mustard
2 teaspoons fresh garlic, minced
1 teaspoon anchovy paste
$2/3$ cup olive oil

In a medium bowl, whisk together all ingredients until thoroughly blended. Store in a sealed container until needed. Yields 1½ cups.

English Ivy

ENGLISH IVY RESTAURANT
104 PARK AVENUE
COSHOCTON, OH 43812
740-622-9201

Just a few blocks from downtown, tucked away in a quiet area of Coshocton, sits the English Ivy Restaurant. It's housed in a Victorian brick home built in 1895 for the Gray family, owners of the Gray Hardware Company in town. In 1906, the home came into the hands of another prominent citizen, Hippolyt Liewor, president of the Coshocton Glass Company. After passing through several other owners during the next ninety-two years, the home was purchased in 1998 by David and Jeanette Hamerdinger and fashioned into the English Ivy Restaurant.

This enjoyable eatery is open for lunch during the week. Guests can grab a simple breakfast here as well. There are just a few selections, such as muffins, but a more delicious and pleasant way to start your morning we cannot imagine. Dinner is served on Friday and Saturday evenings, giving area residents further opportunities to experience the English Ivy.

We lunched with Catherine Howard, an enthusiastic individual from the Coshocton Chamber of Commerce. She and Debbie swapped home-economics stories, since both of them have experience teaching that subject. We discovered that Catherine has had many interesting jobs in her life but is thoroughly enjoying her present task of promoting Coshocton County.

The restaurant was bustling, so we waited briefly in the entryway while our table was being readied. The lovely main staircase has stained handrails and painted spindles. An effect not seen too frequently, it coordinates beautifully with the lush wallpaper. The original pocket doors—one of Debbie's favorite features in houses of this era—divide the downstairs dining rooms from the entry. The room to the right of the waiting area has a painted mantelpiece and a burgundy swag border encircling its white walls. The delicate lace curtains repeat the lines of the border.

We were seated in the rear dining room just to the left of the tiled fireplace, which added warmth to both the nippy December day and the ambiance of the room. A crystal chandelier hung overhead from the tray ceiling. Again, this room was done in shades of burgundy and hunter.

All the offerings here are made from scratch. Although the menu is short, it was difficult to decide what to pick. Catherine ordered the Broccoli-Cheese Soup, which is always on the menu. She graciously offered us a taste, and it was delicious. Debbie's choice was the Raspberry Salad, a combination of mixed greens tossed with dried cranberries, mandarin oranges, and pecans and served with Raspberry Vinaigrette. Karen opted for the soup-and-sandwich combination of Mexican Cheddar Vegetable Soup and a Smoked Ham Sandwich topped with Havarti cheese. Full, and fearing a snowstorm, we asked for some of Jeanette's homemade cookies for the road. Both the Chocolate Chip Cookies and the Peanut Butter Cookies were delicious and let us enjoy the English Ivy Restaurant awhile longer.

RASPBERRY ALMOND SCONES

2 cups unbleached flour
½ cup sugar
2 teaspoons cream of tartar
1 teaspoon baking soda
¾ teaspoon salt
½ cup shortening
2 eggs, slightly beaten
¼ cup buttermilk or sour milk
3 teaspoons red raspberry jam or jelly
2 tablespoons almonds, sliced

Preheat oven to 400 degrees. Stir dry ingredients together in a medium bowl. Blend in shortening with a pastry blender until mixture resembles fine breadcrumbs. Add eggs and milk, mixing with a fork. Divide into 2 parts. Turn each part out on a floured surface and

form into a ball. Fold 1½ teaspoons of jam into each ball. Top with almonds. Flatten each ball with a rolling pin into a circle about ½ inch thick. Cut into triangles and place on a greased and floured cookie sheet. Bake for 15 minutes until golden brown. Serve warm and lightly buttered. Yields approximately 16 scones.

SAVORY POTATO-CHEESE SOUP

4 cups potatoes, peeled and diced
2 cups onion, chopped
1 cup celery, diced
5 cups water
15-ounce can cream of celery soup
1 teaspoon dry mustard
1 tablespoon steak sauce
4 cups milk
1 pound Velveeta cheese
2 teaspoons dried parsley
2 cups stewed tomatoes
2 pinches dill

Put first 4 ingredients in a heavy pan. Bring to a boil, cover, and simmer for about 15 minutes. Add remaining ingredients. Cook and stir until cheese is melted and soup is heated through. Serves 8 to 10.

179 SOUTH MARKET STREET
LOGAN, OH 43138
740-380-9177
WWW.HOCKINGHILLS.COM/
GREATEXPECTATIONS

When we checked into our hotel, we immediately had one of those "it's a small world" experiences. The manager, Valery Junge, asked what brought us to town. We explained our mission and told her our first stop was to be Great Expectations. "That house was in my husband's family! His great-great-grandfather built it," she proclaimed.

The home was constructed in 1892 and was occupied by a member of the Holl family until Irma Powell Holl passed away in 1986. In her nineties at the time of her death, she left an unfinished painting of the house that current owners Melissa Brown and Melinda Holland have hung in the upstairs hallway. In the painting, the exterior of the house is green, but at the time of our visit, it was painted a pleasant yellow. The front porch was whimsically tinted in large squares of lavender and white. Just inside the front door, tones of mauve and rose provided the basis for the décor. White lace curtains softened the large windows, allowing plenty of natural light. The

overhead light fixtures are original, as are the wooden floors and the mantelpieces.

Customers coming to eat are seated in two rooms. We chose to sit in the front, near the main desk, so we could easily chat with Melissa as we snacked. Debbie chose the Beef Noodle Soup, which was piping hot and full of flavor. While Debbie warmed up, Karen cooled down with her Tortellini Salad and Citrus Chiller Fruit Smoothie. The orange-pineapple combination of the smoothie was particularly refreshing. Other items on the menu included Espressos and Cappuccinos, salads, and Great Expectations' popular sandwiches, which are frequently served on Focaccia Bread. The Grilled Chicken with roasted red peppers, cheese, and onions sounded appealing, as did the Farmers Market Sandwich with tomatoes, onions, lettuce, portabello mushrooms, cheese, and cucumber.

In the summer, local residents enjoy eating in the grape arbor just outside the kitchen. The vines have been there as long as anyone can remember. The arbor produces enough Concord grapes that approximately fifteen families come and pick the fruit. On a recent visit, one sixty-year-old customer told Melissa that she'd played in that arbor as a child.

This old home offers much more than just a casual café. Three separate rooms house a bookstore—one room is for children's books, one for general literature, and the third for used books. Displayed throughout is the work of local craftspeople, including hand-woven sweaters, handmade jewelry, framed photographs, and oil paintings.

As we shopped (we can never go in a place like this and just look), Melissa told us one of the sad stories tied to the house. It seems that Andrew Holl, the man for whom the house was built, had three sons—George, Barton, and Andrew Jr., who died in 1892 at the early age of twenty-nine. Andrew Jr.'s wife, Josephine, a talented musician, was a passenger on the *Titanic*, which sank on its maiden voyage in 1912 after hitting an iceberg in the Atlantic Ocean.

RED-SKIN POTATO SALAD

2 pounds red-skin potatoes
3 medium scallions
4 slices bacon, cooked, drained, and crumbled
½ cup fat-free plain yogurt
½ cup mayonnaise
salt and pepper to taste

Cut potatoes into quarters. Place in a pot of water, bring to a boil, and cook until soft but not mushy. Drain, rinse, and cool. Cut into cubes. Place potatoes in a large mixing bowl. Thinly slice scallions and add to potatoes. Add bacon. Combine yogurt and mayonnaise in a small bowl. Gradually add to potato mixture

until coated to desired consistency. Add salt and pepper. Serves 8.

TORTELLINI SALAD

8-ounce package tricolored cheese tortellini
¼ cup strawberries, sliced
¼ cup mandarin oranges
½ cup grapes, halved
⅓ to ½ cup poppy seed dressing

Prepare tortellini according to package directions. Rinse, drain, and cool. Place tortellini in a large mixing bowl. Gently fold in fruit until well mixed. Add dressing to taste. Chill thoroughly before serving. Serves 4.

The
CANDLELIGHT
on Center Street

346 CENTER STREET
BRYAN, OH 43506
419-636-0343
WWW.THE-CANDLELIGHT.COM

Saturday, October 24, 1925, saw the auction of what was described as "the most beautiful lot in Bryan." On that lot was the lovely home of Mr. J. M. Yarnell, who had moved to Toledo. The three-thousand-square-foot, one-and-a-half-story house was built around 1850 in the Italianate style, which was quite popular at the time. The property was first owned by Isaac Wilson, who purchased the lot, along with several hundred acres, from the government in 1837. Sixteen years later, the lot came under the ownership of Walter Caldwell, who sold it in 1856 to Jacob and Emily Youse. It was sometime during Caldwell's tenure that the house was built.

The home's exterior has changed little since its construction. Its double brick walls over twelve inches thick have been a significant factor in the structure's longevity. The interior holds twelve rooms, plus maids' quarters. It was here during restoration that owner Carol Marquiss discovered signatures of old servants dating back to the 1890s. The first floor has twelve-foot ceilings, crown molding, a mahogany pocket door, stained glass, and etched glass. Originally, this area of the house had no fireplaces and was heated by wood stoves. In the summer, ventilation was achieved by opening the transoms above each door; those transoms are still in place. The dining room contains one of the home's most unusual features. Its parquet floor, created from one-inch pieces of walnut, white maple, and mahogany, with ebony in the corner designs, is nothing short of magnificent.

Karen was unable to join me that day. Carol and I chatted over a cup of tea as we sat in the lovely surroundings. She had graciously prepared a sampling of tea items. I thoroughly enjoyed the Banana Bread garnished with molded butter, the Cucumber Sandwiches, and the Lemon Tea Bread. Lunch and dinner are also served, but reservations are a must.

The Marquiss family has been busy since purchasing the home in January 2000. Restoration had been begun by the Steichen family but was by no means completed. The Steichens had purchased the home from the Plassmans in 1993. Herb Plassman, an illustrator and artist with *Ohio Art*, had spent many hours in the large bay-windowed room practicing his craft. The Plassmans had taken ownership from Cass Cullis, a former editor and publisher of the *Bryan Times* newspaper. It was Mr. Cullis who was fortunate enough to secure the highest bid at the 1925 auction.

History shows that this beautiful home has always been a family residence. It is with a strong sense of family that Carol Marquiss operates the dining room and guest rooms today. Her husband and children were actively involved in the restoration. Her son Nicholas designed The Candlelight's logo. During summer break, Nicholas and Kristen occasionally assist in serving guests. The sugar and creamer used during my visit belonged to a paternal grandparent. Likewise, the linen tablecloths and napkins have been handed down. The dishes that Carol is most fond of belonged to her great-aunt Anne. Carol, who has enjoyed many special dinners served on these plates, likes creating memories for her guests using memories of her own.

ASPARAGUS ROLL-UPS

1 pound asparagus spears
1 loaf white sandwich bread, crusts removed
8-ounce package cream cheese
½ cup Parmesan, grated
1 cup butter, melted
¼ to ½ cup sesame seeds

Blanch asparagus spears for 2 to 3 minutes. Immerse in cold water. Drain. Roll each slice of bread flat with a rolling pin. In a small bowl, combine cream cheese and Parmesan with an electric mixer. Spread cheese mixture on one side of each piece of bread. Place an asparagus spear diagonally on each slice of bread and roll up. Roll in butter and sprinkle with sesame seeds. Place on a cookie sheet and bake for 40 minutes at 325 degrees until puffy and golden. Serves 20 as an appetizer.

SOUR CREAM POUND CAKE

1 cup margarine or butter
3 cups powdered sugar
6 large eggs
3 cups all-purpose flour
¼ teaspoon baking soda
8-ounce carton sour cream
1 teaspoon vanilla
1 teaspoon almond extract
fresh berries

Beat butter at medium speed about 2 minutes until soft and creamy. Gradually add sugar. Add eggs 2 at a time, beating until the yellow disappears. Combine flour and baking soda. Add to creamed mixture, alternating with sour cream. Mix at low speed after each addition. Stir in flavorings. Pour batter into a greased and floured 10-inch tube pan. Bake at 325 degrees for 1 hour and 15 minutes until lightly browned on top and until toothpick comes out clean. Cool in pan on a wire rack for about 15 minutes, then remove from pan. Finish cooling on wire rack. Serve with fresh berries. Serves 16.

THE DAVENPORT HOUSE

136 WEST BUCKEYE STREET
CLYDE, OH 34310
419-547-4444
WWW.NWONLINE.NET/DAVENPORTHOUSE

Winesburg, Ohio is a very famous novel by Sherwood Anderson. It was one of the first tell-all books ever written, and it caused quite a stir in the small community of Winesburg, where many of the locals recognized the characters, even though the names had been changed. Today, Winesburg is known as Clyde.

Locals still wonder about Miss Irene Davenport, the original owner of The Davenport House, and whether she was a character in that scandalous book. Miss Davenport was a society lady, and as such, she was well taken care of by her wealthy relatives. She never married but did adopt a son, Harkness, whom she named after her wealthy uncle, a colonel in the Union army. The favorite niece of Colonel Harkness, she also had connections with John D. Rockefeller, one of the original seven stockholders who created Standard Oil. Throughout her life, Miss Davenport cashed Standard Oil stipend checks to support herself and her household. There exists some correspondence between Rockefeller and Irene that suggests that she often visited him and acted as his hostess at his home in Florida.

A family home for most of its one hundred years, The Davenport House now belongs to Claudia Laurendeau. Claudia explained to us that although she had to extensively renovate the building, she tried very hard to retain its charm and elegance. The high-ceilinged rooms with magnificent crystal chandeliers and Victorian-style globed sconces give the dining rooms a light, fresh feel. Everything is elegant, from the white linens to the tall vases of flowers. We wandered around trying to take in the richness of all the original furnishings that have been retained.

A peek upstairs showed us even more delights. Debbie was extremely fond of the vivid pink, beige, and teal bathroom tiles in one of the luxury bedrooms. On vacation in Italy, the Davenports were so taken with these tiles that they brought them back to Clyde, together with Italian craftsmen to install them. Karen was enamored with the hand-tooled leather wainscoting wrapped around the walls of the stairwell, having never seen such a fine example before.

The lunch menu was interesting. There were a significant number of salad, sandwich, and burger choices besides the main entrées. On the day we visited, the specials were a Barbecued Ham Sandwich and Chicken Pasta Alfredo. We opted for the Hawaiian Chicken with Raspberry Vinaigrette and the Chicken Marsala with Snow Peas and Potato Casserole. Both were delicious, as were the freshly baked Poppy Seed Rolls. Stuffed to the gills, we reluctantly passed on dessert, knowing we'd be back another day. Claudia was proud to tell us that all the food here is homemade using only the finest ingredients. The Davenport House guarantees that you will not eat fresher or more delicious food anywhere.

WARMED BLACKENED SALMON SALAD WITH TORTELLINI

2-pound package tricolored cheese tortellini
1¼ cups Italian Dressing
6 6-ounce salmon steaks
cooking spray
3 tablespoons olive oil
Jamaican Jerk seasoning to taste
2 heads romaine lettuce, washed
6 Roma tomatoes, quartered
1 medium red onion, sliced thin
freshly ground black pepper

Cook tortellini according to package directions. Drain. While still warm, toss tortellini with enough Italian Dressing to coat liberally. Set aside and keep warm.

Preheat oven to 400 degrees. Place salmon on a foil-covered pan liberally coated with cooking spray. Brush tops of steaks with oil and sprinkle heavily with Jamaican Jerk seasoning. Spray a little olive oil over top of seasoning and place salmon in oven for 8 to 10 minutes.

While steaks are cooking, arrange romaine leaves in spoke fashion on each of 6 plates. Place tomato quarters between leaves. Be sure to leave room in the center for tortellini and salmon.

Remove salmon from oven and place un-der broiler briefly to crisp tops. Spoon warm tortellini onto lettuce beds, place salmon in center of plates, top with red onions, and sprinkle with remaining Italian Dressing and pepper. Serves 6.

BAKED FUDGE

2 cups sugar
½ cup flour
¾ cup cocoa
5 eggs, beaten
1 cup plus 2 tablespoons butter, melted
2 teaspoons vanilla
½ cup pecans, chopped
Kahlua Cream (see below)

Preheat oven to 300 degrees. In a large bowl, combine sugar, flour, and cocoa. Add eggs. Beat in butter and vanilla. Stir in pecans. Pour into 8 custard cups. Set cups in a 13-by-9-by-2-inch pan and add water halfway up. Place in oven and bake for 40 to 45 minutes. Remove from oven and serve immediately with Kahlua Cream on top. Serves 8.

KAHLUA CREAM

1 cup whipping cream
½ cup powdered sugar
3 tablespoons kahlua

In a medium bowl, whip cream until it starts to thicken. Add sugar and kahlua and continue to beat until mixture reaches desired consistency. Yields 2 cups.

Lenhardt's

151 WEST MCMILLAN AVENUE
CINCINNATI, OH 45219
513-281-3600

In 1836, some 5 percent of Cincinnati was German. By 1850, Germans made up more than 77 percent of the population. One such immigrant was Christian Moerlein, who arrived in America from Bavaria in 1841 and headed for Pittsburgh. Not finding work and down to his last fifty cents, he went to Wheeling, West Virginia. Unsuccessful there, he continued to Cincinnati, doing odd jobs along the way. Eventually, he saved enough money to open a blacksmith shop, ultimately employing as many as ten men.

He left that business in 1853 to pursue brewing beer. He and partner Adam Dillman produced a thousand barrels of beer during their first year. The Moerlein Brewery prospered, increasing production to twenty thousand barrels per year in 1860, just seven years after its inception. By 1895, the operation turned out half a million barrels! This growth came in part because Christian Moerlein was one of the first to use pasteurization in making beer, allowing him to export.

Moerlein married in the late 1840s. He and his wife had three children, only one of whom survived to adulthood. He later remarried. That union produced nine children, one of whom was named Elizabeth. Upon her marriage to John Goetz, Jr., in the 1890s, Moerlein commissioned a lovely home as his wedding gift to the couple. That home subsequently was used by a pediatrician. During World War II, the army housed soldiers there. A paddle dated 1953 found on the premises documents the use of the home as a clubhouse for the American Commons Club.

About that time, Anton and Emmi Lenhardt arrived from Yugoslavia. In 1955, Anton and his brother, Kristoff, and their wives opened Lenhardt's Restaurant, a small establishment located at 201½ McMillan Road. They quickly expanded. In 1963, Anton bought the Moerlein estate to house Lenhardt's, which offered Schnitzels, Sauerbraten, and Goulash, alongside American foods. In 1977, Anton and Emmi retired and Erika Lenhardt Windholtz and her husband, Joe, took over.

We chatted with Christy Windholtz, the third generation of the Lenhardt family to run the restaurant, as we enjoyed our dinners of Hungarian Goulash with Spatzle and Sauerbraten served with a wonderful Potato Pancake. Seated in what once was the music room, we enjoyed the lovely painting of cherubs (purported to be holding hops) on the ceiling. The artwork was uncovered just after the Lenhardts took over the building. A radiator burst, damaging the ceiling. When repairs began, this lovely painting was uncovered. Much of the home's original opulence is still evident, including the ceramic tiles surrounding the fireplaces, said to have been made by the craftsman who taught the Rookwood Pottery people their trade.

When it came time to choose dessert, we had difficulty. How can one select among several varieties of Strudels, Tortes, and other delights? We let Rainy, our server, choose for us. She and Wilma, the gracious hostess, have been with Lenhardt's for more than thirty years. Rainy knew perfectly what we'd enjoy. The Hungarian Cheesecake proved as delicious as it was unusual, and the Linzer Torte was the best we'd ever sampled!

HUNGARIAN GOULASH

3 large onions, diced
1 green pepper, diced
1 tablespoon shortening
2 pounds stew beef
2 tablespoons paprika
1 cup water
1½ teaspoons salt

In a large skillet, sauté onions and green peppers in shortening. Add beef and cook until brown. In a small bowl, combine paprika, water, and salt. Add to meat. Pour into an ovenproof container and bake at 350 degrees for 2 hours. Serves 6. Lenhardt's serves this dish over spatzle.

APPLE STRUDEL

6 Granny Smith apples, peeled and sliced
1 cup sugar
¼ cup flour
1½ tablespoons cinnamon
1 sheet puff pastry
1 egg
1 tablespoon water

Combine first 4 ingredients in a large bowl to make filling. Prepare puff pastry according to package directions. Visually divide puff pastry in half lengthwise and place filling in the center of one of those halves. Fold remaining pastry over and seal edges. In a small bowl, whisk egg and water together. Brush over pastry. Bake at 350 degrees for 1 hour. Cut into 1½-inch slices to serve. Serves 6 to 8.

LIVER DUMPLINGS

1 pound chicken livers
1 onion
6 cloves garlic
1 large egg
4 tablespoons flour
3 tablespoons breadcrumbs
½ teaspoon salt
½ teaspoon pepper

Grind livers, onion, and garlic through a meat grinder into a large bowl. Add egg, flour, breadcrumbs, salt, and pepper. Combine well. Drop dumpling mixture by the teaspoonful into boiling water. Reduce heat and continue to boil for 15 minutes until done. Yields approximately 2 dozen dumplings.

·JAVA SUPREME·

134 EAST COURT STREET
BOWLING GREEN, OH 43402
419-354-3188

It was quiet the morning I stopped in for a Banana Chocolate Chip Muffin and a cup of Toffee Mocha Latte. Of course, this is a college town, and it was before nine in the morning. The menu isn't limited to coffees and baked goods. The restaurant also serves up four salads and a daily soup special ranging from Cream of Potato to Chicken Noodle to Tomato Tortellini. The hot grilled sandwiches include American Buffalo Chicken, Tuscan Turkey, and Four Cheese Pesto, among others. Java Supreme also offers deli sandwiches made to order with five choices of bread, six condiments, five cheeses, and meats.

Located near the courthouse just off Bowling Green's main drag, this was once a private home built around the turn of the twentieth century. It later became a sorority house. Karen was elsewhere that day. As I sat in the morning solitude, it was easy to imagine the laughter and chatter of coeds as they came and went from class, dealt with the ups and downs of relationships, or anxiously got dressed for a fraternity dance.

The restaurant is peaceful. Its simple wooden floors are unadorned except in the sitting room, where an area rug adds coziness to the space. In that room, a sofa and chairs offer comfortable seating for patrons to relax. Games and magazines encourage people to stay awhile. The other two rooms have stark white walls with woodwork painted a subtle shade of taupe, a perfect backdrop for the photography hung throughout. Wood-topped tables in a rich cherry and wrought-iron chairs padded in black and white stripes tastefully complete the gallery effect of one of the dining rooms. The other, where I was seated, had simple round tables and attractive metal-tubing chairs. Small, decorative stained-glass squares accented the perimeter of each window.

After I arrived, several people came and went across the old home's welcoming front porch. Many were greeted by name. Amid the corporate giants against which it must compete, Java Supreme has managed to find a niche in this popular college town. As the campus woke up that day, I had no doubt that many students would find Java Supreme the perfect place to get a cup of joe.

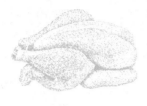

AMERICAN BUFFALO CHICKEN

6-ounce chicken breast
1 piece focaccia, approximately 4 inches X 4 inches
1½ teaspoons commercial spicy buffalo-wing sauce
1½ teaspoons blue cheese dressing
2 slices American cheese

Grill breast for approximately 12 to 15 minutes until done, turning halfway through. Cut breast in half on the bias. Cut focaccia in half horizontally. Spread with buffalo sauce and blue cheese dressing. Place a chicken breast half on each half of focaccia. Top each half with a slice of cheese. Heat slightly before serving. Serve open-faced. Serves 1.

CHICKEN CAESAR

6-ounce chicken breast
1 piece focaccia
1½ teaspoons Caesar dressing
2 slices tomato
1 slice provolone cheese
2 teaspoons Parmesan, shredded

Grill breast for approximately 12 to 15 minutes until done, turning halfway through. Cut breast in half on the bias. Cut focaccia in

half horizontally and spread with Caesar dressing. Place a chicken breast half on each focaccia half and top with a tomato slice. Cut provolone in half and place a half-slice on each focaccia half. Sprinkle with Parmesan. Warm slightly. Serve open-faced. Serves 1.

FOUR CHEESE PESTO SANDWICH

1 piece focaccia
1½ teaspoons pesto
2 slices tomato
1 slice provolone cheese
1 slice cheddar cheese
1 slice American cheese
2 teaspoons Parmesan

Cut focaccia in half horizontally. Spread with pesto. Top each half of focaccia with a tomato slice. Put provolone and cheddar on one half and American and Parmesan on the other. Place under broiler or on grill until cheese is melted. Put halves together. Serves 1.

THE GARDEN RESTAURANT

226 EAST PERRY STREET
PORT CLINTON, OH 43452
419-732-2151
WWW.GARDENRESTAURANT.COM

The Garden Restaurant was fashioned out of the dwelling that was once the home of Port Clinton's lighthouse keeper. Following the Battle of Lake Erie in 1813, maritime trade flourished in northern Ohio. This encouraged the government to purchase Lot I, Square 3, from Mr. and Mrs. Ezekial Haines of Cincinnati. Four granite monuments etched with *USLHE* (United States Light House Engineer) were buried at the corners of that property. It is believed that the entire city of Port Clinton was then platted using those markers.

The United States Lighthouse Service was very specific in its instructions for construction of the lighthouse. It was to be a round, rough-split stone tower forty feet in height. It was to be twenty-two feet in diameter at the base, slimming to ten and a half feet at the lantern deck. Six oil lamps, each with a fourteen-inch silver reflector, made the Port Clinton Lighthouse visible as far as ten miles out on Lake Erie. Austin Smith seems to have had the longest tenure as light keeper. Robert Waterfield

and Daniel Finn were also keepers here. Although the United States Lighthouse Service made recommendations to discontinue operations at Port Clinton as early as 1843, service was not officially stopped until 1870.

I was seated in a bright dining room that had the feel of a summer porch. I situated myself so that I could gaze out across Lake Erie. In the park across the street, a small hut caught my eye. That hut was the light keeper's boat-house when the Portage River flowed toward Catawba. At that time, the river cut Catawba off from the mainland, making it an island. After service at the lighthouse was discontinued, local officials decided to change the river's course. It now makes a ninety-degree turn to Lake Erie just across the street from The Garden Restaurant. At the time of the change, two jetties were built and a new lighthouse was constructed. That lighthouse is now in the keeping of a local marina.

With all this maritime history, I chose my meal accordingly, settling on the house specialty, Fish Market Salad. A delicious mixture of greens, fresh fruit, and baby shrimp tossed in Poppy Seed Dressing, it was as refreshing as it was unusual. When it came time to choose dessert, I deferred to the recommendation of my server, having been equally tempted by the Crème de Menthe Parfait, the Almond Cheesecake, the Chocolate Crème Brûlée, and the Upside-Down German Chocolate Cake. The latter is what arrived. Of the two of us, Karen is fonder of chocolate desserts, and after just one bite, I was sorry that she wasn't with me to enjoy The Garden Restaurant's unusual version of a longstanding favorite.

The restaurant has a popular dinner theater organized by owner J. Bou-Sliman's wife, Brenda. The couple seated next to me had so enjoyed their dinner here the previous evening that they were back to try the Cajun-Seasoned Salmon and the Chicken Frisco. As their entrées were served, I heard them remark that they'd be back again for dinner and a show.

SEAFOOD PASTA SALAD

1 6-ounce package penne pasta
1 cup artificial crabmeat, chopped
½ cup salad shrimp
¼ cup black olives, sliced
1 cup ranch dressing
¼ cup mild salsa
¼ cup mayonnaise

Cook pasta according to package directions. Let cool. Mix pasta with crabmeat, shrimp, and olives. In a separate bowl, combine ranch dressing, salsa, and mayonnaise. Toss pasta mixture with mayonnaise mixture. Refrigerate for 2 hours to marinate before serving. Serves 4 as a side dish.

THE GARDEN'S TARTAR SAUCE

1 cup mayonnaise
¼ small red onion, diced fine
½ cup pickle relish
2 scant tablespoons Dijon mustard
salt and pepper to taste

In a small mixing bowl, combine all ingredients until well mixed. Chill until served. Yields approximately 1½ cups.

ALLISTEN
MANOR

1307 GARBRY ROAD
PIQUA, OH 45356
937-778-0848

We were seated in a small dining room at a table beside a crackling fire. Over the mantel was an oil painting of the property, looking out from the house across the side porch to the gardens beyond. Our table was covered with an antique tablecloth embroidered with morning glories. The floral motif continued in the wallpaper, printed with hyacinths and roses, and in the floral needlepoint chair seats.

Allisten Manor was named for the first granddaughter of owners Sue and Don Smith. She was born about the time the Smiths acquired the property back in 1982. This was once an eight-room farmhouse built on land granted by President James Madison. Over the years, several prominent Piqua families lived in the house and added a bit here and there. These gradual changes resulted in an evolution in appearance from an 1800s farmhouse to the colonial mansion of today. Around the turn of the twentieth century, the property became more of a gentleman's farm than a working farm. It had an orchard, and some truck farming was done. During the 1940s, the estate was known as Jalna, after a series of books by Frenchman Mazo de la Roche. Although quite an avid reader, Debbie had never heard of the books. However, Karen had loved them as a young teen. Jalna is the name of the house in the books, which take readers through stories about the family that builds and lives in the house across several generations.

Allisten Manor serves lunch and dinner by reservation. The Smiths also have a very successful catering business, so the reservations are a must in order for the restaurant to be appropriately staffed. The menu offers a selection of five meals for lunch and four for dinner. Each of the dinner options includes soup or salad, an entrée, and a dessert. The items change seasonally. The evening menu from mid-January to early May includes choices such as Winter Pear Salad and Tomato Dill Soup. Entrées like Chicken Saltimbocca, Grilled Pork Brochette with Zesty Southwestern Salsa, and Tenderloin of Beef Wesley are offered.

Of the five lunches, Karen chose the Cajun Chicken Breast, served with Mixed Vegetables and homemade muffins. That was preceded by a salad, which she chose to dress with Caesar Vinaigrette. It was an unsual twist to a popular flavor combination. Debbie chose the Raspberry Vinaigrette, also very good, to top her salad, which was followed by Broiled Ocean Whitefish and Steamed Vegetables. Having been so very calorie conscious in our entrée selections, we promptly lost our will power and finished our meal with a creamy piece of Cheesecake topped with chopped pecans and Caramel Sauce. It was good to the last bite!

ORANGE CHEESECAKE WITH GRAPES

Crust

¾ cup fine graham cracker crumbs
½ cup all-purpose flour
½ cup pecans, chopped fine
¼ cup sugar
½ cup unsalted butter, melted

Combine all ingredients well. Press mixture into a standard-sized, ungreased springform pan. Bake at 350 degrees for 8 minutes.

Filling

3 8-ounce packages cream cheese, softened
²/₃ cup sugar
3 eggs
1½ teaspoons orange peel, shredded fine
¹/₃ cup orange juice

Beat cream cheese and sugar in a mixing bowl until combined. Add eggs, orange peel, and orange juice; mix well. Pour into baked crust. Bake at 350 degrees for about 30 minutes until set. Cool.

Glaze

½ cup orange marmalade
¹/₃ cup white grape juice
3 tablespoons Grand Marnier
2 teaspoons cornstarch
2½ cups seedless grapes, halved

Combine marmalade, grape juice, Grand Marnier, and cornstarch. Cook until bubbling, stirring constantly; cook for an additional minute. Cool. Arrange grapes on top of cheesecake; cover grapes with glaze.

Chill cheesecake for a minimum of 6 hours before serving. Serves 12 to 15.

FLAMBÉED SPINACH SALAD

¼ cup brandy
1 cup malt vinegar
1 tablespoon lemon juice
1 tablespoon Worcestershire sauce
½ cup white sugar
¹/₃ cup raw or light brown sugar
¼ pound bacon, cooked crisp and crumbled
6 cups fresh spinach, washed, stems removed
1 hard-cooked egg, chopped

Heat brandy in a saucepan until warm, then flambé. Add next 6 ingredients and heat until warm. Pour over spinach and toss until spinach begins to wilt. Do not overdo or spinach will cook. Arrange spinach on plates and garnish with egg. Serves 4.

5878 LONGACRE LANE
CHIPPEWA LAKE, OH 44215
800-922-5736; 330-769-2601

The Oaks Lodge derives its name from the trees around its doorway. At one point, there were five, but time and weather have taken their toll. Only three remain today. These hardy trees, which sit facing the lake, have witnessed the history of this property for quite some time. Some experts have dated them to the days of the Native American mound builders of the area.

During the late 1800s, the Townsend families were closely associated with the railroad. They would come to vacation at Chippewa Lake, transported by their own private railroad cars. Ultimately, they purchased the Robb Farm, as well as additional acreage along the east and south shores. Mr. J. F. Townsend remodeled the farmhouse and named it Five Oaks to commemorate the trees standing in a semicircle in front of the home. Townsend added a barn, a carriage house, a boathouse, and formal gardens. A sporting man, he even built a pheasant run. During our visit, we marveled at the portico he added, constructed of a concrete lattice roof supported by thirty-six

Doric columns. Lined with hostas in the summer, it is a popular spot for local weddings. The renovations and additions were finally completed in 1914.

The home and family were well known for their hospitality and gracious living. Mr. Townsend entertained friends from all over, including influential men of the time, such as J. Pierpont Morgan. In his travels, Townsend collected stones from around the world, which have been incorporated into the fireplace in today's lounge. The one in the old barroom is interesting, too. We enjoyed looking at its unique design while we filtered through the buffet line.

Sunday buffet is quite a tradition here. Many local families consider this *the* place to come for celebrations and special events. The salad table, situated in front of what was once the home's picture window, included four choices—an attractive Tossed Salad, Coleslaw, Fruit Salad, and Pasta Salad. In addition to the lunch choices, there were quite a few breakfast items, including omelets made to order. Karen's favorites were the Pasta Primavera and the Sweet and Sour Chicken, while Debbie enjoyed the Oriental Beef. Faced with indecision at so many dessert selections, we took bite-sized samples of several. The Grand Marnier Chocolate Mousse was tasty, as was the German Chocolate Cake. The Coconut Cake was quite good, and so was the Strawberry Swirl Pound Cake. We have no doubt that the other selections—which included Peach Cobbler, Banana Pudding, and Lemon

Pound Cake—were every bit as yummy. Had we been there for dinner, Debbie would have chosen the Chicken Bartolucci, lightly battered, sautéed, and then topped with Ricotta, Spinach, and Mushroom Stuffing. Karen most certainly would have had the Poached Salmon, served in creamy Dill Cucumber Sauce, one of her favorite flavor combinations.

WILD MUSHROOM AND ASIAGO CHEESE POLENTA

3 tablespoons butter
2 cups shiitake mushrooms, diced fine
1½ teaspoons shallots, diced fine
2¼ cups chicken stock
1½ cups polenta
2¼ cups cold water
1 cup Asiago cheese, shredded
1 tablespoon fresh parsley, chopped

Melt butter in a medium sauté pan. Sauté mushrooms and shallots until tender. Set aside. In a large saucepan, heat chicken stock to boiling. Meanwhile, combine polenta and cold water in a medium bowl, mixing well. Add polenta to chicken stock, then stir in mushrooms and shallots. Cook 6 to 8 minutes, stirring constantly. Remove from heat. Add Asiago and parsley. Lightly grease a loaf pan. Pour mixture into pan, cover with plastic wrap, and let cool. Serves 8.

SWEET AND SOUR DRESSING

¾ tablespoon dry mustard
1½ teaspoons celery seed
1½ teaspoons salt
½ cup sugar
1½ tablespoons onion, grated
1¹⁄₈ cups salad oil
½ cup ketchup
1 tablespoon water
½ cup red wine vinegar

Place all ingredients into a blender. Combine at high speed until creamy. Yields 2½ cups.

Restaurant Index

Recipe Index